LIFE APPLICATION® BIBLE COMMENTARY

GALATIANS

Bruce B. Barton, D.Min.
Linda K. Taylor
David R. Veerman, M.Div.
Neil Wilson, M.A.R.

Series Editor: Grant Osborne, Ph.D.
Editor: Philip Comfort, Ph.D.

Tyndale House Publishers, Inc.
WHEATON, ILLINOIS

Editor: Philip Comfort, Ph.D.
Contributing Editors: James C. Galvin, Ed.D. and Ronald A. Beers

Life Application is a registered trademark of Tyndale House Publishers, Inc.

Scripture quotations marked NIV are from the *Holy Bible,* New International Version®. Copyright © 1973, 1978, 1984 by International Bible Society. Used by permission of Zondervan Publishing House. All rights reserved. The "NIV" and "New International Version" trademarks are registered in the United States Patent and Trademark Office by International Bible Society. Use of either trademark requires the permission of International Bible Society.

Scripture quotations marked NKJV are from The New King James Version. Copyright © 1979, 1980, 1982, Thomas Nelson Inc., Publishers.

Scripture quotations marked NRSV are from the New Revised Standard Version of the Bible, copyrighted, 1989 by the Division of Christian Education of the National Council of the Churches of Christ in the United States of America, and are used by permission. All rights reserved.

(No citation is given for Scripture text that is exactly the same wording in all three versions—NIV, NKJV, and NRSV.)

Scripture quotations marked NASB are taken from the *New American Standard Bible,* © 1960, 1962, 1963, 1968, 1971, 1972, 1973, 1975, 1977 by The Lockman Foundation. Used by permission.

Scripture verses marked NEB are taken from *The New English Bible,* copyright © 1970, Oxford University Press, Cambridge University Press.

Scripture verses marked Phillips are taken from *The New Testament in Modern English* by J. B. Phillips, copyright © J. B. Phillips, 1958, 1959, 1960, 1972. All rights reserved.

Scripture quotations marked RSV are from the *Holy Bible,* Revised Standard Version, copyright © 1946, 1952, 1971 by the Division of Christian Education of the National Council of the Churches of Christ in the United States of America, and are used by permission. All rights reserved.

Scripture verses marked TJB are from *The Jerusalem Bible,* copyright © 1966, 1967 and 1968 by Darton, Longman, & Todd, Ltd., and Doubleday & Company, Inc.

Scripture verses marked TLB are taken from *The Living Bible,* copyright © 1971 owned by assignment by KNT Charitable Trust. All rights reserved.

Library of Congress Cataloging-in-Publication Data

Galatians / Bruce B. Barton . . . [et al.].

     p.   cm. — (Life application Bible commentary)

    Includes bibliographical references and index.

    ISBN 0-8423-3026-7

    1. Bible. N.T. Galatians—Commentaries.   I. Barton, Bruce B.

II. Series.

BS2685.3.G35   1994

227'.407—dc20   94-2246

Printed in the United States of America

00 99 98 97 96 95 94
7   6   5   4   3   2   1

CONTENTS

Gospels MATTHEW
MARK: between
LUKE

ACTS
Paul's Epistles ROMANS: about 5?
1 CORINTHIANS: about 55
2 CORINTHIANS: about 56–5?
GALATIANS: about 49

EPHESIANS
PHILIPPIANS
COLOSSIANS
1 THESSALONIANS: about 51
2 THESSALONIANS: about 51–5?
1 TIMOTHY
2 TIMOTHY
TITUS
PHILEMON

General Epistles JAMES: about 49

1 PETER
2 PETER

JUDE

NEW TESTAMENT

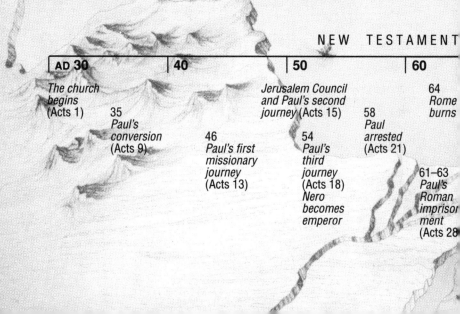

| AD 30 | 40 | 50 | 60 |

The church begins (Acts 1)

35 Paul's conversion (Acts 9)

46 Paul's first missionary journey (Acts 13)

Jerusalem Council and Paul's second journey (Acts 15)

54 Paul's third journey (Acts 18) Nero becomes emperor

58 Paul arrested (Acts 21)

64 Rome burns

61–63 Paul's Roman imprisonment (Acts 28

between 60–65

55–65

about 60

about 63–65

JOHN: probably 80–85

about 61

about 62

about 61

about 64

about 66–67

about 64

about 61

HEBREWS: probably before 70

about 62–64

about 67

1 JOHN: between 85–90

2 JOHN: about 90

3 JOHN: about 90

about 65

REVELATION: about 95

TIMELINE

| 70 | 80 | 90 | 100 |

67–68
Paul and
Peter
executed

Jerusalem
destroyed

79 Mt. Vesuvius
erupts in Italy

About 98
John's
death
at Ephesus

68
Essenes hide
their library
of Bible
manuscripts
in a cave
in Qumran
by the
Dead Sea

About 75
John begins
ministry in
Ephesus

75
Rome begins
construction
of Colosseum

FOREWORD

The Life Application Bible Commentary series provides verse-by-verse explanation, background, and application for every verse in the New Testament. In addition, it gives personal help, teaching notes, and sermon ideas that will address needs, answer questions, and provide insight for applying God's Word to life today. The content is highlighted so that particular verses and phrases are easy to find.

Each volume contains three sections: introduction, commentary, and reference. The introduction includes an overview of the book, the book's historical context, a timeline, cultural background information, major themes, an overview map, and an explanation about the author and audience.

The commentary section includes running commentary on the Bible text with reference to several modern versions, especially the New International Version and the New Revised Standard Version, accompanied by life applications interspersed throughout. Additional elements include charts, diagrams, maps, and illustrations. There are also insightful quotes from church leaders and theologians such as John Calvin, Martin Luther, John Wesley, A. W. Tozer, and C. S. Lewis. These features are designed to help you quickly grasp the biblical information and be prepared to communicate it to others.

The reference section includes a bibliography of other resources and an index.

INTRODUCTION

Slavery comes in many forms. Historically, slaves were men and women forced to serve their conquerors or captors. But there are other ways to become enslaved. Some men and women, trapped by destructive habits, struggle under the control of drugs or alcohol. Others, trapped in destructive relationships, struggle to live with an abusive spouse or parent. Still others, trapped in dead-end jobs or systems, struggle to extricate themselves from financial and emotional strangleholds. And all who do not live in Christ are slaves to sin.

Yet all slaves share a common dream—to be free!

As a highly educated world traveler, Paul had seen and known many slaves—men and women subjugated by powerful governments, powerful leaders, and powerful personalities. In fact, Paul himself had been a slave to religious zealotry and legalism. But Paul also knew what it meant to be free, to know true liberty in Christ. And since meeting his Liberator on the road to Damascus, Paul had spent his life spreading the news of that freedom.

Having seen both sides, nothing bothered Paul more than seeing people return to bondage. That's what he learned about his friends in Galatia: Men and women, who had found freedom in Christ, were being pressured and persuaded to return to the slavery of religious rules and regulations. Paul's response was quick and strong—don't desert Christ (1:6), don't be foolish (3:1), don't be cursed (3:10), don't be a prisoner (3:23), and don't be a slave (4:8); instead, be free (4:7), be free (4:31), be free (5:1), BE FREE (5:13)!

Paul's letter to the Galatians is called the charter of Christian freedom. In it Paul proclaims the reality of believers' liberty in Christ—freedom from the law and the power of sin, and freedom to serve the living Lord.

Are you trapped in sin? You can be a child of God through faith in Christ Jesus, an heir to the promise, and free (3:26-29). Are you trapped in legalism, trying to earn favor with God by doing good and being good? Don't be burdened again by a yoke of slavery—stand firm and free in Christ (5:1). Are you unsure how to channel the energy from your newfound liberty? Use your freedom to serve others with love (5:13).

AUTHOR

Paul (Saul of Tarsus): Pharisee, apostle, teacher, church planter, evangelist.

The very first line of this letter names Paul as the author (1:1). He is also mentioned in 5:2, "Mark my words! I, Paul, tell you that if you let yourselves be circumcised, Christ will be of no value to you at all" (NIV). In addition to this internal evidence, Paul's authorship of Galatians is affirmed by many early church fathers, including Clement of Rome, Irenaeus, and Tertullian. Paul's authorship of Galatians has been widely accepted by virtually all biblical scholars, including Bible critics, from the heretic Marcion (mid-second century) to those of the Tübingen school of higher criticism in the last century. And Galatians traditionally has been recognized as the standard for measuring other documents' claims to Pauline authorship.

To fully understand this profound letter, we need to understand Paul, because it flows out of his past personal experience with Judaism and his newfound relationship with his risen Lord.

Paul was a Jew, culturally and religiously, by birth and by choice. Little is known of Paul's birth and childhood except that he was from Tarsus in Cilicia, far north and west of Jerusalem. Trained by Gamaliel, the most respected rabbi of the day (Acts 22:3), Paul became a Pharisee (Philippians 3:5). As with most serious Pharisees, Paul focused his attention and energy on keeping the law and guarding the purity of the faith. Wanting more than anything to please God and believing that the Jews alone were God's chosen people, Paul threw himself into the practice of his religion.

As a young Pharisee, Paul was zealous for orthodoxy as defined by that group of religious leaders. Pharisees saw themselves as the divinely appointed guardians of the faith, and they strongly opposed anyone who would not submit to their authority and rules.

Jesus often had conflicted with Pharisees and other leaders of the Jewish religious establishment. In fact, the Pharisees had worked tirelessly to rid the nation of this self-proclaimed Messiah. Seeing through their works-oriented and self-serving religion, Jesus had blasted the Pharisees as hypocrites (Matthew 23:15, 23, 25, 27, 29), blind guides (Matthew 23:16, 24), blind fools (Matthew 23:17), whitewashed tombs (Matthew 23:27), and snakes (Matthew 23:33). Thinking that they had heard the last of Jesus at the Crucifixion, the Pharisees were outraged that

men like Peter, John, and Stephen would continue to promote
Jesus as the Messiah and claim that he had risen from the dead. In
Acts 6:8–7:60 we read of their intense anger, culminating in the
stoning of Stephen. Paul was part of that group of Pharisees; in
fact, he held the coats of those throwing the stones and gave his
approval to Stephen's execution (7:58–8:1).

Immediately following Stephen's death, Paul became obsessed
with eliminating Christianity because he viewed it as a heretical
sect (Acts 8:1-3; 9:1-2; 22:4-5). With the authority of the high
priest, Paul went from house to house capturing and imprisoning
believers in Christ. Eventually, he obtained permission to root out
Christians from Damascus and bring them back to "justice" in
Jerusalem.

On the way to Damascus, however, he had a personal encounter with Jesus Christ through a miraculous event (Acts 9:3-6;
22:6-10); so Paul, too, became a believer. After this dramatic conversion, Paul spent three years in Damascus with Ananias and the
believers in that city (Galatians 1:18). There his Christian ministry began (Acts 9:20-23). Then Paul returned to Jerusalem, spon-
sored by Barnabas, who encouraged him and presented him to
the apostles. After attempts on Paul's life by his former associ-
ates—zealous Jews—the apostles sent him to Tarsus, where he
remained for about eight years, becoming established in the faith
and teaching in the churches, especially in Antioch (Acts 11:25-
26). Always strong and energetic, Paul channeled his energy into
spreading the gospel. Because he had found the truth, personal
forgiveness, and spiritual freedom, he wanted everyone in the
world to know Christ, too.

Paul's intense desire to tell others about Christ led him to make
three extensive missionary journeys. The first began in A.D. 46,
when he and Barnabas were commissioned by the church at Antioch and sent to Cyprus, Pamphylia, and Galatia (Acts 13:4–
14:28). At each town, they first would try to reach Jews with the
gospel; then they would reach beyond the synagogue to the Gentiles, who responded in great numbers. During this time, they
established several churches in Galatian cities, including Lystra,
Derbe, Iconium, and Antioch of Pisidia.

The great response by Gentiles further enraged the Jews and
even caused the apostles and other Jewish believers to question
Paul's ministry. This issue of taking the gospel to non-Jews was
somewhat resolved at the council of Jerusalem in A.D. 50.

Paul took two other missionary trips, establishing churches in
Ephesus, Philippi, Thessalonica, Corinth, and other cities along

the Mediterranean coast and inland. These trips occurred in A.D. 50–52 and 53–57.

Evidently, upon returning from the first missionary journey, Paul heard of the influence of Judaizers on the Galatian converts. Judaizers were Jewish Christians who believed strongly that converts to Christ must keep Jewish laws and follow Jewish rites and rituals, especially circumcision and dietary laws. In other words, they were teaching that Gentiles had to become "Jewish" in order to become Christian. Judaizers acknowledged Jesus as Messiah but still looked for salvation through the works of the law. These teachers were undermining Paul's authority and the message he preached. So Paul wrote to vindicate his apostleship, to refute the Judaizers, and to build the Galatian believers in their faith. The date and occasion for writing Galatians will be discussed in detail later.

Significant events in Paul's life:
- 4 B.C. Birth (about the same time as Jesus)
- A.D. 32 or 33 Conversion on the road to Damascus
- 46–48 First missionary journey
- 50 Council at Jerusalem
- 50–52 Second missionary journey
- 54–57 Third missionary journey
- 57 Arrest in Jerusalem
- 61 First imprisonment in Rome
- 62 Release from prison
- 62–66 Traveling and writing
- 67 Second imprisonment in Rome
- 68 Execution under Nero

SETTING

Written from Antioch in A.D. 49.

Dating Paul's letter to the Galatians depends for the most part on the question of its destination. Galatia covered a large area that extended almost from the coast of the Black Sea to the coast of the Mediterranean, through the mountains and plains of central Turkey. In Paul's day, the word *Galatia* could be understood in two different ways. Geographically, it could refer to the northern territory inhabited by Celtic tribes. If Paul had visited this area, it would have been on his second or third missionary journeys. Thus, the letter to the Galatians would have been written around A.D. 57–58.

This theory gained credence among some biblical scholars

because of Paul's reference in 4:13 to ministering among the
Galatians because of illness. Although there is no mention in Acts
of illness on any of the missionary journeys, Acts 16:6 states that
on the second journey, Paul and his companions traveled throughout Galatia, kept by the Holy Spirit from going elsewhere. Perhaps the Holy Spirit used Paul's illness to keep him in Galatia.
That area is also mentioned (Acts 18:23) as a stop on the third
missionary journey. During these journeys, Paul encountered
heavy opposition from Jews (Acts 17:5-9; 18:6; 20:3). Their influence may have led to some of the problems that he addressed in
this letter. In addition, the last phrase of 4:13, translated "first
time" or "first" seems to imply that a second visit had been made
to these believers. Multiple visits to Galatia are more easily reconciled with a later date.

But "Galatia" could also be interpreted politically, referring to
the Roman province in the south, which included Lycaonia, Isau-
ria, and parts of Phrygia and Pisidia. Thus Paul's Galatian letter
would have been addressed to churches in Derbe, Lystra, Iconium, and Antioch in the southern part of Galatia. These churches
were founded on the first missionary journey (Acts 13:3–14:26).

Today, many scholars (including Ramsey, Burton, Bruce, and
Longenecker) hold to the south Galatian view and the earlier dating of Paul's letter. The reasons for this view are as follows:

1. Barnabas is mentioned in 2:1 and 13. Barnabas accompanied Paul only on the first missionary journey. Paul's traveling
companions on journeys two and three were Silas and others. It is
unlikely that Paul would mention Barnabas to the Galatians
unless they knew him.

2. There is no account of specific churches being founded in
North Galatia, even on Paul's second missionary journey, and
there is no certainty that churches existed there at the time of
Paul's writing. For example, no representatives from North Galatia accompanied the gift collected by Paul for the Jerusalem poor
as did those from South Galatia.

3. The cities in South Galatia would have been more accessible
to the Judaizers than those in the north. Thus the problems
addressed by Paul could have arisen quickly after his departure
from that area.

4. As a Roman citizen, Paul always used the provincial names
of the areas under Roman control. Paul used the term *Galatia*
only three times (1 Corinthians 16:1; Galatians 1:2; 2 Timothy
4:10), and all seem to refer to the Roman province.

5. There is no mention of the council at Jerusalem, which
occurred in A.D. 50. The express purpose of this council was to

confront the same issues addressed by Paul in his letter to the Galatians. The decision of the council favored Paul and his ministry among the Gentiles (Acts 15:1-35), so Paul certainly would have referred to the council's decision, to bolster his case; after all, he did not hesitate, in his letter, to review a brief history of the controversy, even naming specific individuals involved (2:1-21).

Evidently, after Paul and Barnabas had returned to Antioch at the end of the first missionary journey (Acts 14:26-28), they learned that some men "were teaching the brothers, 'Unless you are circumcised according to the custom of Moses, you cannot be saved'" (Acts 15:1 NRSV). Paul had to move quickly to counter these Judaizers, who had already influenced many in the new churches in South Galatia. So he wrote his letter to the churches in Galatia.

AUDIENCE

The churches in southern Galatia founded on Paul's first missionary journey.

The Galatian people were Gauls who had migrated to that area from western Europe. In fact, the term *Galatia* is derived from *Gaul* ("Gaul-atia").

Paul first visited South Galatia, the Roman province, during his first missionary journey. In Antioch of Pisidia, Paul and Barnabas went to the synagogue where they presented Jesus as the Christ (Acts 13:13-41). At first they were warmly received, but then many jealous Jews began to speak against them. So Paul and Barnabas announced that they would take God's Word to the Gentiles (Acts 13:42-47). "When the Gentiles heard this, they were glad and praised the word of the Lord; and as many as had been destined for eternal life became believers" (Acts 13:48 NRSV). The gospel spread rapidly throughout the area, but the Jews were able to have Paul and Barnabas expelled from the city (Acts 13:49-52).

Next, they traveled to Iconium, where they again spoke in the Jewish synagogue and had a very positive response. Soon opposition arose again, but this time Paul and Barnabas were able to stay in the city for a while, speaking boldly for the Lord (Acts 14:1-3). Their message divided Iconium, however, and upon learning about a plot to stone them, they left the city and traveled to Lystra (Acts 14:4-7).

In Lystra they encountered a man who had been crippled from birth. When God healed the man through Paul, the crowd thought that Paul and Barnabas were gods and began to honor them as such (Acts 14:8-13). Paul and Barnabas tried to convince the people that they were only human, but many still tried to worship them (Acts 14:14-18). Eventually some Jews from Antioch and Iconium turned the crowd against Paul and Barnabas. In fact, they stoned Paul and left him for dead outside the city (Acts 14:19). "But after the disciples had gathered around him, he got up and went back into the city. The next day he and Barnabas left for Derbe" (Acts 14:20 NIV). The mention of "disciples" implies that many in that area had responded to the gospel message and had trusted Christ as Savior.

In Derbe, Paul and Barnabas had a very good response and encountered little opposition to their message. After ministering there, they retraced their steps through Lystra, Iconium, and Antioch, strengthening and encouraging the new believers in those cities and appointing elders in each church (Acts 14:21-23).

From the way the Galatians responded to Paul and Barnabas, it is clear that they were easily swayed. On one hand, they were warmhearted and generous (Acts 13:42-43, 48; 14:11-18; Galatians 4:15); on the other, they were fickle and quickly misled (Acts 13:50; 14:4-5, 19; Galatians 1:6). On the positive side, the Galatians were ready to listen and respond, able and willing to work hard for their religion, and very sincere. But they were easily impressed and influenced because they were not rooted in faith and grace. No wonder Paul could call them "foolish Galatians" (3:1, 3).

It's easy to judge the Galatians for their fickle ways, wanting to worship Paul and Barnabas as gods and then suddenly turning and trying to kill them, committing themselves to Christ but then being deceived by the Judaizers. Yet many in churches today act similarly. Eager, at first, to learn about Christ and God's Word, they soon tire of Bible study and personal application and are swept along by the latest religious fad. Instead of becoming rooted in the faith, they remain shallow and are easy victims of modern false teachers. Don't be fooled by those who claim to be authorities or by new ideas that sound good; stay true to God's Word, focus on Christ, and deepen and strengthen your faith.

OCCASION

Judaizers had influenced the Galatian believers, pulling them into Judaized Christianity.

After finishing their very successful missionary journey on which they had seen hundreds come to faith in Christ and had established several new churches in Asia and in the Roman province of Galatia, Paul and Barnabas returned to Antioch (in Syria). Upon their return, however, they found that some men had come "from Judea and were teaching the brothers, 'Unless you are circumcised according to the custom of Moses, you cannot be saved'" (Acts 15:1 NRSV). These false teachers, called Judaizers, claimed to have come from James, taught that the legalistic commands in Scripture were linked to salvation, and made the covenant restrictions more important than the Cross. They were promoting, not legalized Judaism, but more of a nomistic or labelized form of Christianity. They were pushing circumcision and food laws, not Isaiah's or Abraham's faithful response to God. In short, these Judaizers were teaching that in order for Gentiles to be saved, they first had to become Jews.

Evidently, Paul also learned that Judaizers had been spreading their false teachings in Galatia and that many of the believers there had been influenced. In fact, these doctrinal debates were splitting the churches apart (5:25; 6:1, 3) and causing believers to lose heart (6:9). To enhance their own authority as Bible teachers and spiritual leaders, these Judaizers had undermined and minimized the authority of Paul, representing him as an inferior teacher and apostle.

When Paul heard this news, he wrote immediately to the Galatian believers, denouncing the Judaizers and their false teachings and emphasizing his credentials as an apostle (1:1, 11-24), teaching and ministering with the blessing of the apostles in Jerusalem (2:1-10).

PURPOSE

To refute the Judaizers, reestablish Paul's authority, and call believers to faith and freedom in Christ.

In order to refute those who were leading the Galatian believers astray, Paul had to reassert his authority. So Paul began his urgent letter by establishing the fact that he was an apostle of Jesus Christ (1:1), sent and called by God (1:1, 15), and approved and commissioned by James, Peter, and John, who were "pillars" in the church (2:8-9). Next, he had to show that both Jews and Gentiles come into a right relationship with God the same way—through faith, not works (3:1-14, 26-29). In fact, all legalistic versions of the gospel are perversions of it (5:2-6, 11-12); salvation is by grace through faith in Christ alone. Nothing needs to be added; in fact, nothing can be added. Believers are free, not bound to the law.

In addition to refuting the Judaizers and emphasizing the truth of salvation by faith alone, Paul also sought to show that with Christian freedom comes responsibility. In other words, believers should use their freedom in Christ to love and serve each other and to obey Christ by living under the control of the Holy Spirit and not giving way to the sinful nature (5:13-14; 6:22-23).

Even today, many Christians swing to either of those extremes: legalism or libertinism. That is, some, like the Judaizers of the first century, seek to find God's approval through doing good works—church attendance, Bible reading, "full-time" Christian service, tithes—and refraining from bad activities. They judge others who fail to meet their behavioral standards or their particular interpretation of devotion or dedication. In so doing, they become slaves to the law. Others, however, go to the other extreme, emphasizing their freedom and easily rationalizing self-indulgence and lack of commitment to the church. But Paul's message to us is the same as to the Galatians: "You are free from the law; salvation is by faith alone. But that means you are free to serve Christ. Don't leave the slavery of the law only to become slaves of sin!"

MESSAGE

Law, faith, freedom, flesh, Holy Spirit.

Law (1:6-8; 2:15-21; 3:1-25; 5:2-6; 6:12-16). A group of Judaizing teachers had traveled from Jerusalem to Galatia and were insisting that non-Jewish believers must obey Jewish law and traditional rules. They taught that a person was saved by following the law of Moses (with emphasis on circumcision for males, the sign of the covenant), in addition to faith in Christ. In other words, Gentiles had to first become Jews in order to become Christians. Some Galatians had been convinced by these teachings, and many had become confused. Paul opposed the false teachers (Judaizers) by showing that the law is powerless to save anyone. Only God's grace through personal faith in Christ makes people right with God.

Importance for Today. No one can be saved by keeping the Old Testament laws, even all the Ten Commandments. The law served as a guide to point out people's need to be forgiven, as a straightedge to show people how crooked they are. Even the most loving, generous, kind, and moral person falls short of God's standard. But Christ fulfilled all of the obligations of the law for us. We must turn to him, and him alone, to be saved.

Don't be fooled by those who suggest that performance of certain works or religious rituals are necessary to obtain eternal life. Only Christ can make a person right with God!

Faith (2:15-21; 3:6-18, 23-29). If people cannot be saved by keeping the Jewish laws or by living good, moral lives, how can they be saved? Paul answered this question by reminding the Galatians of Abraham's faith and pointing them again to Christ. Salvation is a gift from God, made available to human beings through Christ's death on the cross. Individuals receive God's salvation by faith—trusting in Christ—not by anything else. Becoming a Christian is in no way based on a person's initiative, wise choice, or good character. A person can become right with God only by believing in Christ. This common faith in Christ unites all believers, everywhere—Jews, Gentiles, men, women, slaves, and those who are free; all are true descendants of Abraham and children of God.

Importance for Today. A person's acceptance with God comes only by believing in Christ. We must never add to or twist this truth. We are saved by faith, not by the good that we do. And we must never exclude anyone because of sex, race, or social standing from the Good News of Christ. All can come through faith.

What or whom are you trusting for salvation? Have you placed your whole trust and confidence in Christ? He alone can forgive you and bring you into a relationship with God.

Freedom (4:1-31; 5:1, 13-15). In answering the Judaizers, Paul emphasized the believers' freedom in Christ. Christians were neither under the authority of Jerusalem nor under the jurisdiction of Jewish laws and traditions. Faith in Christ brings true freedom from sin and from legalism—the futile attempt to be right with God by keeping the law.

Paul also emphasized that the freedom in Christ must not be abused or flaunted. Believers' freedom must be used to serve one another in love and to submit to the Holy Spirit's control. So we have this paradox: Believers are freed from sin in order to be slaves of Christ.

Importance for Today. When a person trusts Christ as Savior, he or she becomes a new person, forgiven, empowered, free from the bondage of sin. Yet this freedom is a privilege, with responsibility. Christians are not free to disobey Christ or practice immorality; they are free to serve the risen Christ.

Before trusting Christ you were a slave to sin, but now you are forgiven and free from sin's power and penalty. Use your freedom to love and serve, not to do wrong.

Flesh—sinful human nature (5:13, 16-21; 6:7-8). The tendency of human beings to sin is inherited from Adam. This sinful nature continues to trouble believers and cooperates with the world and Satan to stifle their effectiveness. The "flesh" is not the physical body but selfish desire, the continued attraction to sin. The sinful nature affects the body and also the mind.

Importance for Today. Our sinful nature opposes the Spirit and becomes more active when we try to live by the Spirit, hindering our relationship with God. The flesh is not limited to sensual desires and often is more dangerous as pride or apathy. There is a constant battle between our sinful nature and the Holy Spirit in us. But we can overcome the flesh by recognizing its presence and yielding our lives to God's Spirit.

Don't be surprised or discouraged by how easily you are influenced by the flesh. Then yield to the control of the Holy Spirit daily, moment by moment.

Holy Spirit (5:16-26; 6:1-10). People become children of God, regenerated, through the work of the Holy Spirit. He brings new life, and even the faith to believe in Christ is his gift. Then, after conversion, the Holy Spirit continues to live in believers, instructing, guiding, leading, and giving power. Paul told the Galatians that if they would submit to the Holy Spirit's direction, he would produce love, joy, peace, and many other wonderful changes in them.

Importance for Today. When a Christian allows the Holy Spirit to work, the Spirit produces his fruit in him or her. Just as becoming a Christian was a work of God in us through faith, so too is living the Christian life and the process of spiritual growth. The secret is in submitting to his leadership, trusting him to guide us, and then, by faith, following his guidance.

Do you live by the Spirit? Instead of submitting again to the desires of your sinful nature, daily submit to the Holy Spirit. He will produce heavenly by-products in your life, transforming you into the person God wants you to be.

VITAL STATISTICS

Purpose: To refute the Judaizers (who taught that Gentile believers must obey the Jewish law in order to be saved) and to call Christians to faith and freedom in Christ

Author: Paul

To whom written: The churches in Galatia (including those in Iconium, Lystra, and Derbe—founded by Paul on his first missionary journey), and all Christians everywhere

Date written: About A.D. 49, from Antioch

Setting: The most pressing controversy in the early church was the relationship of new believers, particularly Gentiles, to the Jewish laws. This was especially a problem for the converts and for the young churches that Paul had founded on his first missionary journey. Paul wrote to correct this problem.

Key verse: "It is for freedom that Christ has set us free. Stand firm, then, and do not let yourselves be burdened again by a yoke of slavery" (5:1 NIV).

OUTLINE

1. Authenticity of the gospel (1:1–2:21)
2. Superiority of the gospel (3:1–5:1)
3. Freedom of the gospel (5:2–6:18)

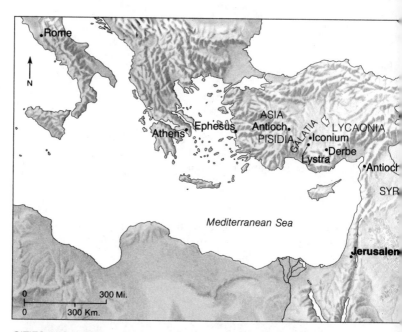

CITIES IN GALATIA

Paul visited several cities in Galatia on each of his three missionary
journeys. As widely as he traveled, Paul may well have considered the
Galatian churches to have been his hometown neighbors. Raised in
Tarsus, just southeast of the Galatian province, the apostle probably
knew the area well. Tarsus had a well-known port and was situated on a
main east/west overland route through Asia Minor. A heavily used pass
through the Taurus mountains was located just north of the city.

On his first journey, Paul went through Antioch in Pisidia, Iconium,
Lystra, and Derbe, and then retraced his steps. On his second journey,
he went by land from Antioch in Syria through the four cities in Galatia.
On his third journey, he also went through those cities on the main route
to Ephesus.

Galatians 1

The year was probably A.D. 49. Paul and Barnabas had just completed their first missionary journey (Acts 13:2–14:28). By their standards, it must have been a whirlwind adventure. Following a brief stay on the island of Cyprus, they had visited Iconium, Lystra, and Derbe, cities in the Roman province of Galatia (present-day Turkey). In their travels they had met with both wholehearted response and deep-seated resistance.

Usually Paul and Barnabas would introduce the gospel in a new area by starting in the local Jewish synagogue, demonstrating from the Scriptures that Jesus was the long-awaited Messiah. But they would venture beyond the Jewish community to offer the promise of forgiveness and eternal life to the Gentiles. And that would get them in trouble. Declaring that God wanted to save Gentiles placed Paul and Barnabas under a cloud of suspicion by Jews and Jewish Christians. As a result of their preaching, however, many Jews and Gentiles converted to Christ. The success of Christianity also created deep resentment in those holding positions of leadership in society and in religious circles. The work of Paul and Barnabas threatened their standing.

Thrilled by the number of persons who accepted their message, upon arriving back in Antioch, Paul and Barnabas "gathered the church together and reported all that God had done through them and how he had opened the door of faith to the Gentiles" (Acts 14:27 NIV).

Shortly after their return to Antioch, some Jewish Christians arrived from Judea. These Judeans claimed that the Antioch church and its missionaries were diluting Christianity to make it more appealing to Gentiles, and they challenged Paul's authority as an apostle. They disagreed with Paul's teaching that Gentiles did not have to follow many of the religious laws that the Jews had obeyed for centuries. The resultant heated debate touched almost every church in the first century. The issue: how to maintain a proper place for the Jewish root from which the vine of Christianity was flourishing.

LEGALISM AND LABELISM

Paul encountered two forms of Jewish attitudes toward the law. Modern forms of these same attitudes can be found in Christianity today.

Legalism

"Legalism" is attempting to win God's favor by our own determined efforts of dedication and obedience.

Then In Paul's time, Jews and many Jewish Christians believed that by faithful adherence to the law they could win God's approval. By strict and rigid adherence to the Mosaic code, they could earn righteous standing with God.

Now Often without realizing it, we try to live up to God's and other people's expectations of how Christians should be—all this as a means of winning God's approval. We do this by our efforts at obedience, dedication, full-time Christian service, academic study, and volunteer work. Some people try to be saved by working their way into heaven; more often, however, Christians find themselves trying to win God's love or approval through perfectionistic duty.

Result Frustration, bitterness, or resentment over our failure to live up to the standards.

Lesson We must obey and serve freely out of love and gratitude to Christ. The Holy Spirit must empower us. Our dedicated service cannot remove sin or obtain saving grace.

Labelism

"Labelism" is pride of ownership for having the "right" religion.

Then Jews saw their commitment to the law (primarily the Jewish food laws and circumcision) as a badge of ownership, a symbol of their performance of the historic covenant between them and God. They felt superior for their religious correctness and for upholding the "right" religion. Too often this adherence to the law was in name only.

Now Some Christians display this same love for having the "right" label, identifying with the right church, pastor, denomination, or religious viewpoint. Often their only identity as believers is a stance taken quite proudly over a single issue. By comparing themselves spiritually, they demean others who don't hold their view.

Result Pride, smugness, self-righteousness.

Lesson Only Christ's faithful work on the cross, that enables us to respond in faith, can save us.

Some of Paul's accusers went to the Galatian churches and insisted that the Gentile converts had to be circumcised and follow all the Jewish laws and customs in order to be saved. According to these people (called *Judaizers*), Gentiles had to first become Jews in order to become Christians. This caused much confusion in the churches that Paul and Barnabas had planted in Galatia.

In response to this threat, Paul wrote this letter to the Galatian churches. In it, he explained that following the Old Testament laws or the Jewish laws would not bring salvation. A person is saved only by grace through faith. Most likely, Paul wrote this letter about A.D. 49, shortly before the meeting of the Jerusalem council, which settled the law-versus-grace controversy (Acts 15). By this time, Paul himself had been a Christian for about fifteen years.

STAKING HIS CLAIMS
The Galatian Christians were in danger of being led astray by false teachers. Paul wrote to protect them from this danger. To combat the false teachers, Paul made three primary claims:

1. Paul claimed divine authority for his appointment as an apostle. He contrasted his mandate with those who were sent by human institutions or presumed to be God's messengers (1:12).
2. Paul claimed his spoken and written message embodied the directly revealed will of God (1:11). Therefore, if he himself contradicted the message, he would be subject to judgment (1:8).
3. Paul claimed that opposition and distortion of his message were evidences of the present evil age. The fact that the gospel offered hope to persons lost in sin made the message as much a threat to the evil age as Christ himself had been when he died on the cross (1:4).

1:1 Paul, an apostle.^{NKJV} First-century letters often began by introducing the writer, although this "writer" often dictated his letters to a scribe. Paul used a secretary for most, if not all, of his letters (see Romans 16:22), usually writing the last few lines in his own hand to authenticate his message (6:11). Tertius served Paul in this way (Romans 16:22).

Saul (*Paul* was probably his Roman surname) was born into a Jewish family from the tribe of Benjamin. He was raised as a strict Pharisee (Philippians 3:5), grew up in Tarsus, and was educated under a well-known teacher, Gamaliel (Acts 22:3). However, he was also a Roman citizen, a privilege he used to great advantage at times (Acts 22:27-29). Out of this diverse background, God formed and called a valuable servant, using every aspect of Paul's upbringing to further the spread of the gospel.

The Jewish name *Saul,* given to a man born in the tribe of Benjamin, evoked memories of the tribe's days of glory—the first king of Israel was named Saul and came from this tribe (1 Samuel 10:20, 24-26). The Roman name Paul *(Paulus)* was a common surname (see, for example, Sergius Paulus in Acts 13:7). We know nothing of the origins of Paul's Roman citizenship; the name may have been a family name, or Paul may have chosen the name simply because of how close it sounded to his Jewish name. In Acts, Luke wrote, "Then Saul, who also is called Paul" (Acts 13:9 NKJV), then used only the name *Paul* throughout the rest of the book. When Paul accepted the Christian faith and began his mission to the Gentiles, part of his effort to identify with his listeners included using his Roman name. In all of his letters, Paul used his Roman name, linking himself with the Gentile believers to whom he had been sent with the gospel of Christ.

Paul was called to be an *apostle* by Jesus Christ and God the Father. Paul was not one of the original twelve disciples (later called apostles), but Jesus had especially called him on the road to Damascus to preach the gospel to Jews and Gentiles (Acts 9:3-19). The apostles' mission was to be God's representatives; they were envoys, messengers, and delegates who were directly under the authority of Jesus Christ. They had authority to set up and supervise churches and discipline them if necessary. Paul presented his credentials as an apostle at the beginning of this letter because his authority was being undermined in the churches in Galatia.

COURSE REVERSED
What a change had occurred in Paul's life! At first he had been a fierce "apostle" of the Sanhedrin, persecuting the first Christians in the name of Judaism. But that calling was replaced by God's call to follow Christ and to offer God's grace to Jews and Gentiles alike. Paul's apostleship was transformed. His intensity and zeal remained, but his purpose had been reversed. Paul had begun as the apostle of death to those who dared to be Christians, but he ended as the apostle for Christ who offered life to anyone willing to believe.

Whatever our past, God is able to call us out by his grace, transform us by his power, and give us a new purpose for life. Has God given you a new purpose for serving him?

Sent neither by human commission nor from human authorities, but through Jesus Christ and God the Father, who raised him from the dead.NRSV The title *apostle* means "one sent on a mission." Paul had gone on a mission while he was still a committed Jew. Acts 9:1-2 records his mission, authorized by the high priest, to imprison Christians in Damascus. However, Paul's mission here was of an entirely different character from an entirely different authority. Paul was *sent* with the gospel not by any person but by *Jesus Christ and God the Father.* Jesus' name side-by-side with "God the Father" reveals Paul's understanding of the oneness of God and Jesus Christ.

No human had commissioned him; no human authority had called him; instead, Jesus Christ himself had spoken to Paul (Acts 9:4-5). Thus Paul added, *who raised him from the dead,* further clarifying that it was the living, risen Christ who had met him on the road to Damascus. Paul was not called during Jesus' ministry on earth; rather, he was called after Jesus' resurrection and ascension. Paul wrote that Jesus appeared "last of all . . . to me also, as to one abnormally born. For I am the least of the apostles and do not even deserve to be called an apostle, because I persecuted the church of God. But by the grace of God I am what I am, . . ." (1 Corinthians 15:8-10 NIV).

Paul explained his apostleship in these words, not to separate himself from the original Twelve, but to show that his apostleship rested on the same basis as theirs. If the believers in Galatia questioned Paul's apostleship, then they also should question the apostleship of Peter, John, James, and all the others—and such questioning would be absurd. All the apostles were called by Jesus Christ and God the Father, and they answered to God as their final authority.

ON WHOSE AUTHORITY?
When challenged, Paul based the credibility of his teaching on the authority of Jesus Christ. In other words, he claimed to be consistent with what Jesus said and did. Those who questioned his message or methods were in danger of questioning Christ's. But if they could find a discrepancy between Paul's words and Christ's, then they had a right to be suspicious.

We do not ignore the wisdom of humans, but we must base our theology, teaching, and ministry on Jesus Christ and his Word. As Peter said, "Lord, to whom shall we go? You have the words of eternal life" (John 6:68 NIV). Christian teachers are not to be evaluated on their personal charisma, the size of their following, or the boldness of their claims of truthfulness. Rather, what they say and do must be measured against the standard of Jesus Christ. Cult leaders are notorious for trying to dodge the standards of Jesus by claiming to be Christ. What sad results come when followers fail to question why someone who claims to be Jesus acts so unlike the original.

Paul was also challenging those who were calling his teaching into question. Paul used *neither by human commission* as part of his defense against the Judaizers, who challenged his apostolic commission and rejected his credentials. From whom did they take *their* authority? The Galatians needed to develop a more discerning approach to those who claimed to speak for God.

1:2 And all the brothers with me.NIV Paul's fellow workers in Antioch joined him in sending greetings to the Galatian believers, for all of them together were *brothers* or "members of God's family." These coworkers in Antioch, a sizable group, included Barnabas, Titus, Timothy, and some of the men listed in Acts 13:1 (see also Acts 19:29; 20:4).

In most of his letters, Paul sent greetings at the outset from himself and one or two traveling companions whom he named, reserving the greetings from others who were with him for the end of the letters (see, for example, 1 Corinthians 1:1 and 16:19-20; 2 Corinthians 1:1 and 13:13; Philippians 1:1 and 4:21; Colossians 1:1 and 4:7-14). In this letter, however, he sent greetings from "all the brothers with me" immediately after his salutation. Paul may have wanted to reinforce the solidarity of the Christian church to show that he was not alone in opposing the false teachings of the Judaizers and in confirming the truth of the gospel. Others, many of whom the Galatians may have known, were "with Paul" in being concerned for their faith.

On one hand, in verse 1 Paul declared that he was not sent from men or by men, meaning that he did not need or seek their endorsement. On the other hand, the unity of his fellow workers added force to his argument. Those with Paul in the Asian ministry were single-minded about the gospel content, Paul's authority, and the role of the law in salvation.

To the churches in Galatia.NIV This letter is an example of Paul writing to a region or group of churches. Another such epistle is Ephesians, which was probably a circular letter to the whole region. The words "to the Ephesians" are missing in several early manuscripts and were probably added because that city's copy was used to produce later copies. Each of Paul's other epistles is addressed to an individual church (such as Philippians) or person (such as Titus). In Paul's time, *Galatia* was the Roman province located in the center section of present-day Turkey. Much of the region was on a large and fertile plateau; many people had moved to the region because of its favorable agriculture. During his missionary journeys, Paul planned to visit regions with large population centers in order to reach as many people as possible and to plant churches in those centers. This letter was to be circulated among the *churches in Galatia* planted by Paul and Barnabas during the first missionary journey—in Derbe, Lystra, and Iconium (see the map in the Introduction).

While much has been written about the possibility of two distinct "Galatian areas," one north and one south, the weight of scholarship and tradition still affirms the southern Galatian cities as the correct addressees for this letter. In either case, the addressees are not as crucial to identify as the message itself. After all, we study this letter as if written to us.

Either Paul expected each church to read the letter, perhaps make a copy, and then pass it along; or Paul's scribe made several copies on which Paul wrote the authenticating final lines (6:11) and then had a copy delivered to each church. The first explanation is most likely correct, if Paul usually implemented the procedure explained at the end of his letter to the Colossians: "After this letter has been read to you, see that it is also read in the church of the Laodiceans and that you in turn read the letter from Laodicea" (Colossians 4:16 NIV).

PRECIOUS WORDS

We can hardly appreciate the impact and value of Paul's letters to the early church. To English speakers, the abundant availability of the Bible has resulted in our treating God's Word as common. In a world without books, people were probably better listeners. Their minds were expected to retain more. Writing was a valued ability and a treasured product.

As you study Galatians, read the sentences again, aloud. Imagine hearing them for the first time. Treasure these important words revealed from God to us through Paul.

1:3 Grace to you and peace from God our Father and the Lord Jesus Christ.NRSV Paul used *grace* and *peace* in all his salutations, wishing his readers the benefits of both. "Grace" was the Greek greeting, as "peace" was the Jewish greeting. The two expressions were common greetings; jointly used in the context of the gospel, they gained unfathomable depth. The word "grace" *(charis)* reminded Paul's readers of God's kindness in offering salvation to undeserving people. It refers to the multifaceted gift that God makes available to us despite our unworthiness. Not only does God mercifully withhold the judgment and punishment that we so clearly deserve, he grants, instead, the almost unbelievable gift of forgiveness, salvation, and eternal life. God's grace requires faith because the moral and legal case against us leads to an inevitable verdict—guilty. Grace means the forgiveness of our sins. It cannot be earned by works or by any goodness in us. It is free and undeserved favor on us by Christ's faithful act of redemption. As long as we insist on finding or making our own way we remain lost. We who have shown a marked proficiency at sin find ourselves relentlessly pursued by God's grace. We do not discover God's grace; it finds us (see Romans 5:1-11)!

"Peace" *(eirene)* was a familiar word often used in salutations of letters even by unbelievers. Paul used it to remind the readers of Christ's offer of peace to his disciples as they lived out their faith in an evil world (John 14:27). Christian letters not only expressed the wish for peace, but identified the source of peace. If "grace" summarizes God's gift to us, then "peace" summarizes the personal results

> Grace releases sin, and peace makes the conscience quiet. The two fiends that torment us are sin and conscience. But Christ has vanquished these two monsters, and trodden them under foot, both in this world, and in the world to come.
> *Martin Luther*

of that gift (see John 14:27; 16:33). Peace describes felt grace. Peace combines a quiet conscience, cleansed by forgiveness, with a growing sense of joy in the unlimited possibilities of freedom in Christ.

True peace comes only from a right relationship with God because peace comes *from God our Father and the Lord Jesus Christ.* As in verse 1, the connecting of "God" and "Jesus" reveals their oneness (John 10:30). God is called "Father," a name Jesus taught his disciples to use in the Lord's Prayer (Matthew 6:9). In contrast with verse 1, Paul here personalized the divine name by adding "our" to Father. The earlier titles emphasized the authority of the Father and Jesus, while this expression pointed to God as the provider of grace and peace. Also, Jesus Christ is identified as "Lord," a title given to him after his resurrection and ascension that reveals him as worthy of worship (see John 20:28; Acts 2:36; Philippians 2:9).

1:4 Who gave himself for our sins to rescue us from the present evil age.[NIV] Our Lord Jesus Christ (1:3) *gave himself for our sins.* "Giving" refers to Christ's ultimate sacrifice for sin offered by his death on the cross. Jesus said of himself, "For even the Son of Man did not come to be served, but to serve, and to give His life a ransom for many" (Mark 10:45 NKJV). Jesus died for "our sins," not his own, for he was sinless. Jesus' sacrifice was ultimate, voluntary, and substitutionary. This refers to Christ's substitutionary atonement. Christ died for *our* sins, in *our* place, so we would not have to suffer the punishment we deserve (see 1 Peter 2:24). In 1 Corinthians 15:3 Paul regards this truth as a key element of the early Christian confession of faith.

> This is probably the earliest written statement in the New Testament about the significance of the death of Christ.
> *F. F. Bruce*

Paul wasted no time in laying the groundwork for his message to the Galatians. If they were to accept as valid any other "gospel" as an answer to sin, including the one offered by the Judaizers, they would be denying the value and effectiveness of Christ's sacrifice. So, having claimed his authority to speak, Paul briefly summarized the gospel that he had given them in person.

> Our most active participation in God's work of saving us is simply allowing ourselves to be saved.
> *Neil Wilson*

ACCEPTABLE
God does not have to go against his own nature or be inconsistent in order to accept us. We cannot solve our sin problem that separates us from God, but God solved the problem for us by sending Christ to die for us. God's demand for justice is satisfied by the ultimate sacrifice of Christ. Christ's giving himself for us is the essence of love. Spiritual rebirth and all of our Christian experience begin as a gift.

- "He who did not spare his own Son, but gave him up for us all—how will he not also, along with him, graciously give us all things?" (Romans 8:32)
- "All this is from God, who reconciled us to himself through Christ and gave us the ministry of reconciliation." (2 Corinthians 5:18)
- "I have been crucified with Christ and I no longer live, but Christ lives in me. The life I live in the body, I live by faith in the Son of God, who loved me and gave himself for me." (Galatians 2:20)
- "For if the inheritance depends on the law, then it no longer depends on a promise; but God in his grace gave it to Abraham through a promise. . . . But the Scripture declares that the whole world is a prisoner of sin, so that what was promised, being given through faith in Jesus Christ, might be given to those who believe." (Galatians 3:18, 22)
- "And live a life of love, just as Christ loved us and gave himself up for us as a fragrant offering and sacrifice to God." (Ephesians 5:2)
- "Husbands, love your wives, just as Christ loved the church and gave himself up for her." (Ephesians 5:25)
- "[Christ] gave himself as a ransom for all men—the testimony given in its proper time." (1 Timothy 2:6)
- "[Christ] gave himself for us to redeem us from all wickedness and to purify for himself a people that are his very own, eager to do what is good." (Titus 2:14)

(The above verses are quoted from the NIV.)

The benefits cannot be fully appreciated until they are personally appropriated. Have you received Jesus, who gave himself for you?

The result of Jesus' gift of himself was *to rescue us from the present evil age.* The Greek word for "rescue" *(exeletai)* could also be translated "deliver." The NRSV used "to set us free" to emphasize the result of Jesus' action; the rescue and deliverance had a purpose—to set us free. Christ not only gave himself for our sins; he also delivers us from the helpless condition where we cannot resist sin (present evil age) to his kingdom where he is Lord. Paul wanted his brothers and sisters in Galatia to be alarmed that they had exchanged their freedom in Christ for slavery under a system based on human effort.

RESCUE MISSION
Every rescue operation begins with an awareness of a problem. God's rescue plan for us can be broken down into four specific components:

1. We recognize that we live in an evil age. Sin has created a world hostile to God's love and toward the church, or body of Christ, those who have been transformed by that love.
2. We admit that without Christ our sins have enslaved us and keep us trapped in the evil age. Therefore, we acknowledge that Christ's giving himself for us was necessary. Our helplessness required his personal intervention.
3. We confess our willing participation in sin and our inability to rescue ourselves from it. Help and hope must come from outside our resources.
4. We accept the loving Father's concern for us and his provision of escape by faith in Jesus Christ. We acknowledge and submit to Jesus as our deliverer.

This rescue or deliverance does not remove believers from the world (at least not yet); instead, it gives us the blessings of our future eternity with Christ and offers us his guidance and presence as we serve him in "the present evil age." Indeed, if all the early believers had been rescued out of the evil age in which they lived, there would have been no hope for us. To use Jesus' expression, though we are still "in" the world, we are no longer "of" the world (see John 17:15-18). In his letter to the Colossians, Paul enlarged his picture of Christ's deliverance: "For he has rescued us from the dominion of darkness and brought us into the kingdom of the Son he loves" (Colossians 1:13 NIV). From outward appearances we are still living in the same world, but our allegiance and "nationality" have been changed! (This is similar to Paul's message to the Romans in Romans 12:1-2.)

Paul's "present age" was "evil"; our present age could also be characterized as evil because Satan rules the world (1 John 5:19). The present evil age of Paul's time was the Greco-Roman world.

It was known for its intrigues, murders, adulteries, and military oppression. Has our age gone farther into decadence? Each newspaper contains stories of great wickedness. A man kills a woman because she won't have sex with him. Several people kill another for twenty dollars so they can buy drugs. A neighbor systematically abuses young children. Millions of unborn children are destroyed with little if any remorse. Satan acts in every age, but we must see the tragedy of sin and the necessity for rescuing people in our own present evil age. The early believers committed themselves to their mission to carry the gospel down through the ages to us. Are we as committed to passing the gospel on to future generations?

DELIVER ME
God's plan all along was to save us through Jesus' death. We have been delivered from the power of this present evil age—a world ruled by Satan and full of cruelty, tragedy, temptation, and deception. Being delivered from this evil age means, not that we are taken out of it, but that we are no longer enslaved to it. You were saved to live for God. Does your life reflect your gratitude for being rescued? In what specific ways have you transferred your loyalty from this world to Christ?

According to the will of our God and Father. God's will is to bring people to himself (1 Timothy 2:4). But sin separates sinful people from a holy God. Thus, God made a way of salvation—the ultimate sacrifice of sending his only Son to die on the cross, taking the penalty for humanity's sins. People can only be saved through Christ. Jesus said, "I am the way, the truth, and the life. No one comes to the Father except through Me" (John 14:6 NKJV). Salvation lies in Christ's work, not in any works we do. Our role is to be glad receivers of what we neither deserve nor earn.

God is the Father, he is also *our* God and Father. All who believe are adopted into God's family, becoming heirs with Christ of all God's promises. Paul expands this theme in chapter 4 of this letter to the Galatians.

1:5 To whom be glory forever and ever. Amen.NKJV Paul's spiritual depth broke through as he uttered an expression of love and awe upon speaking the holy names "our God and Father" (1:4). Thoughts of God's love, mercy, and guidance, and Christ's ultimate sacrifice on our behalf evoke words of praise and thanks. Does the glory of God mean that much to us? *Glory* belongs to God alone. Even if

> All I know about Jesus Christ lies in His name.
> *Martin Luther*

God had not done so much for us, he would still be the only one deserving glory from his creation. As believers, we will be able to glorify our God *forever and ever* because of the promise of eternal life with him.

NAMING NAMES
The third commandment (Exodus 20) may bear the distinction of being the most frequently broken of the Decalogue. God's name is used in vain regularly. But using God's name this way by unbelievers should not be surprising—those people are being consistent with their attitude toward God.

We believers, on the other hand, ought to reflect on our familiar use of God's name and the ways in which we refer to Christ. Do we convey reverence and awe? Can those who overhear us give examples of our respect and honor for the Lord's name? How can we demonstrate for them what the name *Jesus* really means to us?

With a decisive *Amen* ("Let it be so," "Let it come to pass"), Paul closed his introduction to this letter. In these first five verses, Paul touched on what would be the intent of his letter: his authority as an apostle, and the fact that salvation is not by works but by grace through faith in Christ alone.

CARING CONFRONTATION / 1:6-10

Paul was amazed at how easily the believers in the Galatian churches had given up the good news of the gospel of Christ for the bad news that they had been taught.

Paul's concern was not over alternative viewpoints of interpretation; he was warning Galatian Christians about turning from the truth to lies, from what was right to what was wrong.

The apostle made it clear that he was not concerned about competing in popularity with other messengers. He wanted it understood that once the truth of the gospel had been declared, all amendments were false. Paul also predicted dire consequences to those who propagate any false gospel.

> One of the great difficulties is to keep before the audience's mind the question of Truth. They always think you are recommending Christianity not because it is *true* but because it is *good*.
>
> C. S. Lewis

1:6 I am astonished that you are so quickly deserting the one who called you in the grace of Christ and are turning to a different gospel.[NRSV] The news that the apostle had received about the

Galatians left him stunned. In most of his letters, Paul would follow his greeting with a prayer of thanks for his readers based on what he had recently heard about them. Paul thanked God for the Romans and commended them for their well-known faith (Romans 1:8); he thanked God for the Corinthians (despite the moral lapses that he denounced in his letter, 1 Corinthians 1:4-9); he thanked God for the Ephesians (Ephesians 1:15-16), the Philippians (Philippians 1:3-10), the Colossians (Colossians 1:3), and the Thessalonians (1 Thessalonians 1:2-3).

However, no words of thanks occur in this letter; instead, Paul immediately expressed astonishment at the Galatians' behavior. The expression "I am astonished" *(thaumazo)* conveys a rebuke similar to our expression, "I can hardly believe what I am hearing about you!" Paul found it difficult to comprehend that the believers could desert *the one who called* them. The believers were turning away from God (or Christ) himself—the Gcd who loved them and called them because of his great *grace* in *Christ.* These believers were throwing aside that grace in order to try to earn their salvation. Paul was amazed that someone would insist on attempting to pay for a free (and priceless) gift!

The verb is in the present tense, "are . . . deserting" *(metatithesthe),* and was used in military circles to indicate that a soldier was AWOL (absent without leave). The process of desertion, of turning away from the faith, was happening as Paul wrote. This desertion connoted apostasy. Those who turned to this *different gospel* would no longer be Christians. Because it was in process, Paul was warning them against apostasy. Paul hoped to stop it immediately because desertion from the faith held dire consequences. Part of Paul's astonishment focused on how *quickly* the believers were deserting—that is, so soon after Paul's last visit and/or so soon after the false teachers had begun their destructive work. Apparently, it wasn't taking much for the Galatians to be led away from the faith and to become enthusiastic about this different gospel.

What was the "different gospel"? If the original gospel involved God calling the Galatians by the grace of Christ, then this alternative "gospel" must invite a different trust and response. The Galatians were being invited to desert the kingdom of Christ for service in a kingdom without grace and, therefore, without hope.

The false teachers, Judaizers, taught that to be saved, Gentile believers had to follow Jewish laws and customs, especially the rite of circumcision. Faith in Christ was not enough. Note that they may have included in their teachings the need for faith in

Christ for salvation, but they taught that additional requirements had to be met before true salvation could occur. Their message was "faith plus." This infuriated Paul because the Judaizers' message undermined the truth of the good news that salvation is a gift, not a reward for certain works.

Jesus Christ has made the gift of salvation available to all people, not just to Jews. And faith in Christ is the only requirement for salvation. Beware of people who say that we need more than simple faith in Christ to be saved. When people set up additional requirements for salvation, they deny the power of Christ's death on the cross (see 3:1-5).

THE FATAL FLAW

The gospel of Jesus Christ is good news because it gives us the true life-changing message of hope from God. The world today is flooded with different "gospels," each claiming to offer an easier, better, more meaningful, more effective plan than God's original version. Not only do these "gospels" abound in the world; sadly, they even invade the church.

The fatal flaw in every different gospel lies in ignoring or trying to bypass grace. These gospels develop their "hope" from the wisdom of humans (technology, education, science). They assign divine value to ideas and principles limited to this present physical world (humanism, materialism, determinism, scientism), and they glorify self-effort (design-your-own-spirituality, moral progress, self-perfection through some program, or even reincarnation).

We must analyze ourselves and our faith in light of biblical truth. Helpful questions include: Is my life squarely founded on Christ's gospel? Have I been taking grace for granted? Have I allowed other "requirements" to take their place alongside faith in Christ in my understanding of salvation? Am I living by "another gospel"?

1:7 Not that there is another gospel.^{NRSV} Paul's sarcastic words in verse 6, "a different gospel," were still too positive for the error he was resisting; so Paul pointed out that the Judaizers' teaching was no gospel at all. There is only one way given to us by God to be forgiven of sin—through believing in Jesus Christ as Savior and Lord. No other person, method, or ritual can give eternal life. Attempting to be open-minded and tolerant, some people assert that all religions are equally valid paths to God. In a free society, people have the right to their religious opinions, but this doesn't guarantee that their ideas are right. God does not accept human-made religion as a substitute for faith in Jesus Christ. He has provided just one way—Jesus Christ (John 14:6). That message alone constitutes the true *gospel*.

**But there are some who are confusing you and want to per-
vert the gospel of Christ.**[NRSV] The people who were confusing
the Galatian believers were zealous Jewish Christians who
believed that the Old Testament practices, such as circumcision
and dietary restrictions, were required of all believers (see 5:10).
As long as Jewish believers made up the majority of the church,
their emphasis made little difference. But the influx of Gentile
believers with no Jewish background caused problems. Because
these teachers wanted to turn the Gentile Christians into Jews,
they were called "Judaizers." This teaching confused the Galatians because they hadn't heard from Paul about all these acts
that they were being told were requirements.

In any event, the Judaizers had perverted *the gospel of Christ.*
This term can be understood as a subjective genitive (Christ's
gospel—the gospel given to us by Christ) and an objective genitive (the gospel about Christ—Christ is the content of the gospel).

IT'S SIMPLE, BUT NOT CHEAP!
Make no mistake, people still find the bold simplicity of the gospel scandalous. "There must be more to it," they say, "than
merely realizing we are sinners, repenting of our sins, and
accepting God's absolutely free gift of forgiveness."
    But we wouldn't think of asking a baby to pay for the costs of
being brought into the world. So how could we imagine any
way of meeting the cost for our spiritual birth? Confusion
among Christians usually results from forgetting about God's
amazing grace in Jesus Christ. His grace keeps us from confusion.

Many of the newer Galatian Christians were Greeks who were
unfamiliar with Jewish laws and customs. The Judaizers were an
extreme faction of Jewish Christians. Both groups believed in
Christ, but their lifestyles differed considerably. We do not know
why the Judaizers traveled so far to teach their mistaken notions
to the new Gentile converts in Galatia. They may have been motivated by (1) a sincere wish to integrate Judaism with the new
Christian faith, (2) a sincere love for their Jewish heritage, or
(3) a jealous desire to destroy Paul's authority. Whether or not the
Judaizers were sincere, their teaching threatened these new
churches and had to be countered. Based on Acts 15:24, the
elders in Jerusalem denied giving any sanction to the teaching of
the Judaizers, so any claim for their authority was false. But more
to the point, the effect these "teachers" had on young Christians
bears chilling similarities with Jesus' description of the missionary efforts of the Pharisees: "Woe to you, teachers of the law and

Pharisees, you hypocrites! You travel over land and sea to win a single convert, and when he becomes one, you make him twice as much a son of hell as you are" (Matthew 23:15 NIV). Whatever the Judaizers' intentions, their efforts led to confusion. They were loading down people with the requirements of the "law" instead of encouraging them to live by grace in joyful obedience to Christ.

THE TWIST
A twisting of the truth is more difficult to spot than an outright lie. The Judaizers were twisting the truth about Christ. They claimed to follow him, but they denied that Jesus' work on the cross was sufficient for salvation. There will always be people who pervert the Good News. Either they do not understand what the Bible teaches, or they are uncomfortable with the truth as it stands. How can we tell when people are twisting the truth? Before accepting the teachings of any group, find out what the group teaches about Jesus Christ. If their teaching does not match the truth in God's Word, then it is not true.

When Paul said others wanted *to pervert the gospel of Christ,* he was not rejecting everything Jewish. Paul was a Jew who worshiped in the temple and attended the religious festivals. But he was concerned that nothing get in the way of the simple truth of his message: salvation, for Jews and Gentiles alike, is through faith in Jesus Christ alone. Any other teaching is a perversion of that truth. The term "pervert" *(metastrepsai)* goes beyond the idea of confusion or complication; it implies reversal, or making something the opposite of what it was originally. Those who were trying to "improve" on Paul's message to the Galatians were in danger of destroying their faith.

Paul's concern invites the question: What is the gospel of Christ to which he was referring? At this time, the Galatians would not have had much more than eyewitness accounts of the life and ministry of Jesus. The application of that history and the invitation to believe had been given to them through Paul. We who have the Gospels in hand are perhaps able to answer the question: Was Paul himself consistent to the message and claims of Jesus as they are recorded in the Gospels? How did Jesus define the gospel?

The book of Mark introduces itself as "the gospel about Jesus Christ, the Son of God" (Mark 1:1). Mark's record of Jesus' first public message indicates that Jesus was the source of the term *good news,* or *gospel* in referring to himself and his message: "Jesus came to Galilee, proclaiming the good news of God, and

saying, 'The time is fulfilled, and the kingdom of God has come
near; repent, and believe in the good news'"(Mark 1:14-15
NRSV). Twice in this Gospel (Mark 8:35; 10:29) Jesus placed
equal and supreme value on the gospel and himself, claiming that
he and the gospel were worthy of the most devoted followers.
Jesus also prophesied that the gospel would be carried worldwide
(Mark 13:10). Jesus and the gospel cannot be separated; to understand either one properly you must understand both. Jesus presents in person the invitation described in the gospel: Repent and
believe. Paul was rightly amazed that the Galatian believers were
swallowing the pseudomedicine of those who offered a works
religion when they already knew they could be healed by God's
grace.

ON GUARD!
People pervert the gospel of Jesus Christ in many ways. Some
are blatant; some are more subtle. Be on guard against the following strategies of those who pervert:

- *Weakening:* those who undermine or deny the foundation of
  Jesus Christ and faith in him. They say, for example, that the
  Bible isn't true and that the Resurrection is a myth.
- *Diluting:* those who allow half measures to stand instead of
  absolute moral claims. They say, for example, that sex outside of marriage is all right for consenting adults.
- *Distorting:* those who misrepresent what the Bible says in
  order to make it either "more palatable" or to make it appear
  to say what it does not. They say, for example, that the Bible
  only applied to people at the time it was written.
- *Blending:* those who readily admit as authoritative the teachings of sources other than the Bible. For example, the Mormons regard the Book of Mormon as authoritative in addition
  to the Bible.
- *Poisoning:* those who deliberately mix dangerous error and
  lies in with their teaching. They say, for example, that you
  should leave your spouse if you're not being fulfilled in your
  marriage.
- *Deflecting:* those who ricochet off of key words to promote
  their own ideas. They use the "church of Christ" to promote
  their own empire.

**1:8 But even if we or an angel from heaven should preach a gos-
pel other than the one we preached to you, let him be eternally condemned!**NIV Paul denounced the Judaizers' perversion
of the gospel of Christ. Using strong language to deal with this
life-or-death issue, Paul said that even if an *angel from heaven*
were to come preaching another message, that angel should be
eternally condemned (other versions say "accursed," meaning

doomed to destruction). If an angel came preaching another message, he would not be from heaven, no matter how he looked. (This passage, for instance, strongly refutes the claim by Mormons regarding the source of Joseph Smith's teaching, that the angel Moroni appeared to him.) Some think that Paul was referring ironically to the leaders of the Jerusalem church. Others think he was springboarding off the Jewish belief that angels had delivered the Law to Moses at Mount Sinai (3:19; Hebrews 2:2). Most likely, Paul was referring to the emissaries of Satan.

> The outward person of the messenger does not validate his message; rather, the nature of the message validates the messenger.
>
> *Alan Cole*

SLIPS AND FALLS
Paul included himself among those who ought to be held suspect if they preach a different message. Once right does not necessarily mean always right. Recent times have been filled with stories of ministers who have fallen into sin. Their failures have done great harm to those who trusted in Christ under their ministries.

Is it possible that God allows some very successful ministers to fall in order to remind all of us who we are supposed to be trusting? Charisma or past effectiveness does not exempt anyone from remaining true to God's Word. None of us become spiritual enough to make our own rules as we go along!

In 2 Corinthians 11:14-15, Paul warned that Satan masquerades as an angel of light. Here he invoked a curse (*anathema,* see note below at 1:9) on any angel who spreads a false gospel—a fitting response to an emissary of hell. Paul extended that curse to include himself and any of the apostles *(we)* if they should pervert the gospel. For in the case of both apostles or angels, faithfulness in communicating the unchanging truth from God was the ultimate test of their rightful authority.

If the truth is changed, the teacher is false, regardless of his or her qualifications, accomplishments, or experience. Paul has already noted that there is no other gospel (1:7), thus *a gospel other than the one we preached to you* would be false. The gospel teaching must not be changed, for the truth of the gospel never changes.

1:9 As we have already said, so now I say again: If anybody is preaching to you a gospel other than what you accepted, let him be eternally condemned![NIV] Paul's words *As we have already said* could refer to a warning Paul gave the Galatian

THE MARKS OF THE TRUE GOSPEL
AND OF FALSE GOSPELS

Marks of a false gospel

2:21 Treats Christ's death as meaningless.

3:12 Says people must obey the law in order to be saved.

4:10 Tries to find favor with God by observing certain rituals.

5:4 Counts on keeping laws to erase sin.

Marks of the true gospel

1:11-12 Teaches that the source of the gospel is God.

2:20 Knows that life is obtained through death; we trust in the God who loved us and died for us so that we might die to sin and live for him.

3:14 Explains that all believers have the Holy Spirit through faith.

3:21-22 Declares that we cannot be saved by keeping laws; the only way of salvation is through faith in Christ, which is available to all.

3:26-28 Says that all believers are one in Christ, so there is no basis for discrimination of any kind.

5:24-25 Proclaims that we are free from the grip of sin and that the Holy Spirit's power fills and guides us.

Christians at the time he and Barnabas preached the gospel to them, or simply to his words in verse 8. In either case, Paul knew that some would come to distort the gospel, and so he had warned the new converts. Indeed Jesus himself had warned his disciples that false teachers would come, attempting to lead people away from the truth (Matthew 24:11; Mark 13:22-23).

In verse 8, Paul condemned anyone who preached a gospel "other than the one we preached to you"; here, he condemned anyone who preached a gospel *other than what you accepted.* In both cases, the *gospel* is the same—the apostles taught and the Galatians had believed the truth of the gospel of Jesus Christ. The tense of the verb "accepted" *(parelabete)* signifies once-for-all action. Paul and Barnabas preached; the Galatians accepted. That decisive experience did not need to be added to by certain actions required by the false teachers. The acceptance of the message alone accomplished their salvation.

THE CURSE
Paul's repeated use of the condemnation "let that one be
accursed!" (1:8-9 NRSV) conveys the most severe penalties
imaginable for distorting the truth of the gospel. In the larger
biblical context, "accursed" *(anathema)* relates to the extreme
curses that were invoked and carried out against blatant sin in
the Old Testament (see Exodus 17:13-16; Numbers 21:2-3;
Joshua 6:17; 7:12). The deliberate repetition by Paul indicates
that the curse was no angry outburst. His intent was deadly serious. And he included himself as liable to the same judgment of
God if he were to be guilty of preaching an altered gospel. The
matter was of such importance that Paul was willing to endure
the same measure on himself that he invoked for others (Matthew 7:1-2).

**1:10 Am I now seeking human approval, or God's approval? Or
am I trying to please people? If I were still pleasing people, I
would not be a servant of Christ.**^{NRSV} Undoubtedly the Judaizers had accused Paul of compromise, saying that he taught freedom from the Jewish law to the Gentiles in order to meet their
approval and thus win as many converts as possible. The little
word *now* has great meaning, for Paul meant, in essence, "Reread
what I just said and tell me whose approval I'm seeking." Anyone seeking approval from either *human* camp—the Galatian
believers or the Judaizers—would not use such harsh language,
berating the believers and cursing the false teachers. No, Paul's
purpose was always to seek *God's approval.*

WAS PAUL TOO NARROW-MINDED?
No! Everything that we know about Paul shows him to have
been a man of keen intellect, eager to engage in debate and
reason about the truth of the gospel. This letter itself demonstrates that Paul could exercise authority without being auto-
cratic.
But here he was dealing with the gospel itself. He was not
discussing a theory, view, or concept about which there might
be several human perspectives. Rather, the subject was the
unchangeable truth of God's message. The gospel was
revealed by God (see 1:1, 11, 16). Paul did not own the message; he was owned by it! Christ had ordered him to pass on a
dynamic message of salvation (see Romans 1:16) that must be
kept pure and direct.
Some will always be offended by the truth of Christ. Both subtle and forceful pressure will come to change the message. But
our efforts to be tolerant of others must never bring us to the
point of betraying the gospel of Jesus Christ.

Much of church growth philosophy centers on a "market" approach, discovering what people want and need. For a culture that treats God and the Bible as irrelevant, this approach may be the only way to break through barriers. But we must have our motives clearly understood. If our desire is to please people, our packaging of the gospel may take priority over the content. If our purpose is evangelism, then reaching people through felt needs can be legitimate. We must not forget that our allegiance to Christ comes first. We must never water down his authority in the life of a believer in order to bring him or her into a church.

While it is noteworthy that in some instances Paul did attempt to reconcile disagreeing believers when no vital issue was at stake (see, for example, 1 Corinthians 8–9), he was completely unbending when the truth of the gospel was the issue. There could be no compromise—the truth stood on its own, unchanging. Paul's conversion itself displeased many people (especially his fellow Jewish zealots), so Paul knew from the beginning of his Christian life that his goal could never be to *please people.*

CONFLICT OF INTEREST
Pleasing people conflicts with being Christ's servant. True servants know the master and the master's priorities. They are not diverted from the main tasks by what other "servants" or would-be "masters" tell them to do.

Gaining the approval of others distracts us from pleasing God. As we do God's will, we must resist the desire to please people.

The clarifying question of the believer will always be, Who am I really serving? If the answer is "people," then we will be tossed back and forth by their conflicting demands and expectations. But if our answer is consistently "Christ," we will only have one person to please and not have to worry about how much or how little we are pleasing others. Seeking to serve Christ alone will settle many conflicts of interest!

Paul's use of the word *still* offers us a glimpse into his inner self and his past life as a Pharisee. Paul understood that by living a strict, law-abiding, judgmental, and appearance-focused life of a Pharisee, his goal had really been to please people. Religious and pious people may receive mountains of praise for their supposed character and good works. Christians are rarely accorded such praise. Thus if Paul were *still pleasing people,* he would not be *a servant of Christ.* As there is no compromise with the truth, there is no compromise for the Christian with the "present evil age" (1:4). The life of serving Christ does not put people in the limelight, offer great material rewards, or promise worldly security. Thus, if Paul wanted to please people, he could have chosen many other routes or stayed a Jewish Pharisee. Instead, Paul's conversion changed his life so completely that his only goal was to please God and serve Christ (see also 6:12-14; 1 Thessalonians 2:4). A servant can have only one master (Matthew 6:24).

PLEASE, PLEASE
Do you spend your life trying to please everybody? Paul had to speak harshly to the Christians in Galatia because they were in serious danger. He did not apologize for his straightforward words, knowing that he could not serve Christ faithfully if he allowed the Galatian Christians to remain on the wrong track. Whose approval are you seeking—others' or God's? Pray for the courage to seek God's approval above anyone else's.

PAUL RECEIVED THE GOSPEL FROM GOD / 1:11-24

Having pointed to the uniqueness of the gospel in the last paragraph, here Paul turned his attention to his authority as an apostle. Why should the Galatians have listened to Paul instead of the Judaizers? Paul answered this implicit question by furnishing his credentials: His message was received directly from Christ (1:12); he had been an exemplary Jew (1:13-14); he had had a special conversion experience (1:15-16; see also Acts 9:1-9); he had been confirmed and accepted in his ministry by the other apostles (1:18-19; 2:1-9). Paul also presented his credentials to the Corinthian and Philippian churches (2 Corinthians 11–12; Philippians 3:4-9).

1:11 For I want you to know, brothers and sisters, that the gospel that was proclaimed by me is not of human origin.NRSV In verse 1, Paul had introduced himself as "sent neither by human commission nor from human authorities, but through Jesus Christ and God the Father" (NRSV). As Paul launched into a repudiation of those who would refuse to recognize his authority as an apostle, he began at the beginning. Paul wanted the Galatian believers (the *brothers and sisters*) to *know* beyond any doubt that he was an apostle—called separately from the Twelve and received as an equal by the Twelve.

The *gospel* that Paul *proclaimed* was the true gospel, not any false gospel, as he had discussed in verses 6-9. The gospel Paul taught was *not of human origin*—that is, it was not a belief or doctrine handed down to him through tradition. The laws and

rites, which the Judaizers taught had to be followed, came from
that source. Again, Paul was not refuting tradition, but he was
making it known that following traditions did not give anyone salvation.

THEIR OWN DEVICES
Anthropologists who study cultures talk about the "anthropocen-
tric" (human-centered) origin of religion. The religious quest
begins with humans trying to find something ultimate in which
to believe. Without revelation and left to their own devices and
intellect, people have created gods who represent power, sometimes even evil power. Some gods are the deification of sexual
or romantic love. For these gods, humans are more or less the
inept captains of their own souls, whose task it is to find,
please, or sometimes control the supernatural.

Paul's gospel had to be from God, not of human origin,
because grace is totally opposite of humanity's religious quest.
God's free gift of unearned and undeserved favor on those who
trust in Christ to save them goes against intellectual and moral
self-effort. Grace cannot be a human invention because it goes
against our pride and love of power.

1:12 **For I did not receive it from a human source, nor was I
taught it, but I received it through a revelation of Jesus
Christ.**NRSV The gospel itself was not of "human origin" (1:11),
and Paul *did not receive it from a human source.* The Judaizers,
refusing to acknowledge Paul as an apostle, most likely claimed
that Paul owed his salvation and gospel knowledge to Peter and
James in Jerusalem, and that he had to turn to them for approval
and support of his teaching. But, as Paul would point out, he had
become a believer before he ever met these leaders in the Christian church. Paul had heard Stephen's defense (Acts 7:1–8:1), but
that did not constitute his entire knowledge of the gospel, for the
gospel is more than mere facts. Nor was Paul *taught* the gospel.
As a young man, Paul had sat at the feet of Gamaliel, learning by
rote and repetition the Hebrew Law and Scriptures. But that was
not the gospel, nor could it give salvation.

Instead, Paul *received it through a revelation of Jesus Christ.*
We do not know the extent or manner of this revelation. Paul
could be referring to his vision of Christ on the road to Damascus
(Acts 9:3-6), to the time after Ananias returned Paul's sight (Acts
9:17-19), to the three years spent in Arabia (Galatians 1:17-18),
or to his ongoing contact with Christ in his ministry (Acts 9:19-
22; 22:17-18). Paul was probably referring to something more
than his Damascus road experience. At that point, Paul was personally confronted by Jesus himself, and during that blinding

encounter he was instructed to continue into Damascus, where he would eventually be told what to do (see Acts 9:1-22). In one of Paul's accounts of his roadside conversion (Acts 26:15-17), he recalled Jesus' immediate statement of commissioning for special service. While Paul fasted during the three days after meeting Christ, he had at least one "enlightening" vision of someone who would be coming to restore his sight. After Ananias was sent to personally convey God's healing to Paul, we are told that the new convert was baptized and almost immediately began to proclaim his new conviction about Jesus: "He is the Son of God" (Acts 9:20 NRSV). The time between Jesus' appearance to Paul and his first public statements was very brief. The change in Paul was not only profound, it also affected every area of his life.

THE LAST WORD
Paul's background made him a perfect example of the benefits and liabilities of an extensive education. He realized that in the world of students, learning, and the pursuit of truth, someone new will always be stepping up with the claim to have the last word. Paul was deliberately denying the tendency to compare teachers' pedigrees: Where did they go to school? Who did they learn this from? How did they get their training? Paul claimed an incomparable source, Jesus himself. If Paul was telling the truth, his teaching carried an authority over which there could be no higher appeal. By handling Paul's letters as part of God's Word, we uphold Paul's claim for their divine origin.

There are two possible meanings consistent with the grammar of this phrase, "revelation of Jesus Christ": (1) This was a revelation by Christ to Paul "spelling out the gospel message"; or (2) it was the personal revelation by Christ of his true identity that suddenly confirmed the gospel message against which Paul had been in bitter conflict. The ambiguity is in the Greek as well. Although the second meaning seems more probable (given the fact that Paul did hear Stephen preach the gospel), the first remains possible. All true revelation comes from God; in this case, the content of the revelation was Jesus Christ in a way that delivered the gospel message to Paul. Paul's use of the word "revelation" *(apokalupseos)* probably did not have any hidden meaning beyond confirming Paul's claim of a divinely authorized mission and message. Christ's revelation did show Paul how all his Jewish learning was fulfilled and made sense in Jesus Christ, who was the Jews' promised Messiah, Suffering Servant, Lamb of God. This, in essence, *is* the true gospel.

Paul didn't say it, but he implied at this point: "How can any-

one doubt my authority? How can anyone doubt the divinely
revealed truth about Jesus Christ?"

UNDER LOCK AND KEY
If the gospel message is the lock that opens the door of forgiveness and eternal life, then Jesus is the key to making the lock
operate. Without Jesus, the possibility of heaven and the solution for sin remain a fascinating mechanism that inspires hope,
but lacks a key. Without Jesus, the gospel seems too good to
be true. Knowing the facts about the lock will not help us if we
doubt or are unwilling to turn the key. Let Jesus unlock the door.

**1:13 For you have heard of my previous way of life in Judaism,
how intensely I persecuted the church of God and tried to
destroy it.**^{NIV} To further support his apostolic claim, Paul showed
how radically Christ had transformed him from a persecutor of
the church to an apostle of the church. Paul's *previous way of life
in Judaism* included being one of the most religious Jews of his
day, scrupulously keeping the law and relentlessly persecuting
the church of God. The Greek word for *persecuted* here is the
same word used in Acts 9:4, when Jesus asked him, "Saul, Saul,
why do you persecute me?" (NIV). Not only did Paul persecute
the Christian church, he also sought to *destroy it.* So adamant was
he for upholding the traditions of his faith, so convinced was he
that Christianity was a false religion deviating from Judaism, that
he wanted to see it annihilated (see Acts 7:57–8:1; 9:1-2; 26:9-
11). Yet to persecute God's church was to persecute God himself—the God Paul claimed to love and serve.

How had the Galatians *heard* this? In the book of Acts, Paul often
told the details of his conversion as part of his testimony (see 22:1-
10; 26:2-18). The Galatians probably heard about his previous lifestyle from Paul himself. But Paul's reputation may have preceded
him on occasion. The news may have been passed along by Jews
through the Mediterranean grapevine; the conversion of a powerful
man who had set out to destroy believers certainly would have
spread quickly. Another source may have been the Judaizers who, in
their attempts to discount Paul's authority, might have mentioned
that Paul used to persecute Christians. They may have been hoping
the Galatians would come to the conclusion that Paul couldn't be a
true believer, and certainly not an apostle.

But militant Judaism was in Paul's past—it was his "previous"
way of life. When he met Jesus Christ, his life changed. He then
directed all his energies toward building up the Christian church.
As Paul would write in chapter 2: "I have been crucified with

Christ; it is no longer I who live, but Christ lives in me; and the life which I now live in the flesh I live by faith in the Son of God, who loved me and gave Himself for me" (2:20 NKJV).

SPEAKING UP
What Paul wrote in these verses constitutes a brief account of his spiritual life. Among many Christians, this would be called his "testimony" or perhaps his "witness for Christ." The apostle was naturally doing what Peter encouraged all believers to do: "Always be prepared to give an answer to everyone who asks you to give the reason for the hope that you have" (1 Peter 3:15 NIV).

An essential part of inviting others to believe in Christ involves telling them why and how we became Christians. Thinking deeply about how God has worked graciously in our lives can, in fact, be one of the best motivators for telling others about Christ. If someone gave you a three-minute opportunity, what exactly would you say about your faith and how you came to believe in Christ?

1:14 I was advancing in Judaism beyond many Jews of my own age and was extremely zealous for the traditions of my fathers.^{NIV} The word *Judaism* refers not only to nationality but also to religion. To be fully Jewish, a person must have descended from Abraham. In addition, a faithful Jew adhered to the Jewish laws. Before his conversion, Paul had been even more *zealous for the traditions* than the Judaizers themselves could ever claim to be! Paul used a fierce word, "zealous" *(zelotes),* to describe himself. It was a term reserved for those who ardently and often violently observed the Torah or what they perceived to be the laws of God. Paul's single-minded persecution of the Christians was consistent with his zealous life. He had advanced beyond *many Jews of [his] own age* (probably fellow students) in religious knowledge and practice. As a child, Paul probably went to Jerusalem to begin rabbinic training. In Acts 22:3 Paul says, "Under Gamaliel I was thoroughly trained in the law of our fathers and was just as zealous for God as any of you are today" (NIV). Rabbi Gamaliel was the son of Simon and grandson of Rabbi Hillel, founder of the more liberal of the two main schools of Phariseeism. Gamaliel believed the law to be divinely inspired, but he emphasized a more human application in its interpretation. For example, he stressed a less rigid, less burdensome observance of the Sabbath; he regulated divorce to protect women; he urged tolerance of the Gentiles. Paul's intense study under one of the most respected teachers of his day helped to establish his credentials. Paul wrote about himself, "Circumcised on the eighth day, of the people of Israel, of the tribe of Benjamin, a Hebrew of Hebrews; in regard to the law, a Pharisee; as for zeal, persecuting the church; as for legalistic righteousness, faultless" (Philippians 3:5-6 NIV, see also Acts 22:3-13; 26:4-18). Paul had been sincere in his zeal, but wrong.

GOING UP OR GIVING UP?
Like most religious systems, Judaism established certain benchmarks of progress or growth for its adherents. They were expected to demonstrate "advancement" through education and moral development. Paul proved to be a master. He was on the "fast track" of religious achievement, but was actually in total opposition to God. He was advancing in religion, but not in the Spirit. Religious accomplishments do not accurately measure genuine spiritual growth.

Does this mean we are to avoid spiritual change or growth? Or does it mean that we must be aware of the danger of religious effort that is merely pretense? Going through religious rituals without conscious reflection on their meaning can be a danger sign of a life without spiritual power (see 3:3). Those born into a Christian environment can develop a "Christian" way of living, not out of obedience to Christ or gratitude for salvation, but simply because "it's expected." Is there spiritual growth in your life, and how genuine is it?

The "traditions" *(paradoseoi)* on which Paul had previously based his zealous life could have referred to two parallel streams of teaching within Judaism at that time.

1. The first included the time-honored teachings and practices developed in the Pharisaic schools that grew in the shadow of the temple rebuilt under Nehemiah and Ezra. These teachings had been codified in several revered collections: the Mishnah, the Palestinian and Babylonian Gemaras, and the Midrashim. All of these were essentially commentaries on the Mosaic writings that had achieved an authoritative status of their own.

2. A second source of Paul's "traditions" may have been the popular interpretations of the law that were current in the synagogues of Paul's day. In their written forms they were referred to as the Targumim.

1:15-16 But when God, who set me apart from birth and called me by his grace, was pleased to reveal his Son in me so that I might preach him among the Gentiles.NIV What changed Paul's life from persecutor of the church to preacher of the faith? The little phrase *but . . . God* reveals what happened. God got hold of

Paul's life. Paul did not expect it, did not deserve it (in fact, he described himself as the *last* person worthy to deserve God's grace—see 1 Timothy 1:16), and did not seek it but rather fought against it. Paul's conversion happened only *by [God's] grace.* And God used every part of Paul's life, even prior to his conversion, to prepare Paul for the ministry.

TRADITIONS

All traditions are not bad. Our churches have many of them. Good traditions are practical attempts to fulfill or express a truth of Scripture. These applications achieve special recognition and become repeated patterns for worshiping, serving, or running a church.

Traditions may in fact keep us doing what we really ought to do. But mindless repetition of a tradition without attempting to understand its background can actually lead to wrongdoing. Paul admitted he was violently defending a tradition that was out of step with God's plan. He was actually persecuting God under the guise of preserving faith in God. Scripture provides an absolute source of truth, but our applications from it cannot claim absolute inerrancy. Our traditions are only as true as their faithfulness to what the Scriptures actually affirm.

God had *set [Paul] apart from birth.* The phrase literally says, "He, having separated me from my mother's womb." Paul realized that God's designs on his life clearly began before his birth. Similarly, Jeremiah was divinely informed that God had called him even before he was born to do special work (Jeremiah 1:5). Paul's expression recalls the profound awe described by the psalmist in Psalm 139 in recognizing the scope of God's awareness of us. The context indicates that Paul was humbled by God's grace in calling him to be an apostle rather than proud about any personal qualifications that made him noticeable to God. The fact that God would accomplish his work through any of us ought to inspire deep humility.

How God's foreknowledge of us actually determines what we do in life has always fascinated and sometimes perplexed believers. Does God's knowledge of our future mean that our choices are only an illusion? Or, in this context, was Paul teaching that his apostleship was inevitable? Could he have said no to God's separating him and calling him? In answering such legitimate questions, we must begin with humility. God does not think as we do (see Isaiah 55:8-9). Our ability to think and wonder is an expression of the image of God in us, but it is a limited gift. There are many aspects of God's dealing with us that he has chosen not to reveal to us. But all that God does clearly reveal to us never removes the necessity of faith. The truth of the Scriptures, the evidences in creation, and the confirmation by experience together do not rule out our need for faith. We are neither mindless robots acting out God's preprogrammed operation, nor are we completely independent beings capable of decisions and actions entirely outside of God's control. God allows us enough freedom to fail, to comprehend our responsibility for our failure, and to respond to his invitation.

The understanding that Paul and all believers are "set apart" before birth by God is referred to as the doctrine of election. This was a key part of Paul's theology (see, for example, Romans 8:29-30; 9:11-29; Ephesians 1:4-5). In the Bible, election refers to God's choice of an individual or group for a specific purpose or destiny. God's sovereignty, not people's works or character, is the basis for election.

Election, being chosen, being "set apart" before we're born, is like receiving an invitation for a wonderful banquet. But the invitation comes to us unearned and unmerited. No friendship, political pull, or effort makes it necessary that we be on the invitation list. The guest list is purely the host's choice. After all, it is his banquet. The invitation comes with the traditional RSVP. God's gracious invitation does require our response and attendance. Only those who respond to God's call receive the gift of salvation; it is "by invitation only." It comes to us completely undeserved so that we might have no basis for pride. When we understand God's sovereignty as well as his mercy, we respond with humility and gratitude that God would be merciful to even us.

Believers still may wonder why or how they could be chosen while others might be rejected. God is sovereign and, in reality, *no one* has any claim on his mercy. He prepared us in advance by his gift of salvation, and he will reveal his glory when we are finally with him for eternity. Instead of focusing on God choosing some and rejecting others, we should stand in awe at God's offer of grace to any of us. Thus, no one can demand that God explain why he does what he does. He makes all the rules, but he loves to show his mercy to us. What an amazing God he is! What may seem to us to be an inconsistency on God's part actually reveals our own inability to see as God sees.

When God *called* Paul on the road to Damascus, Paul accepted the gracious invitation of salvation. Part of that call was that God *was pleased to reveal his Son* to Paul. This revealing of God's Son included several aspects:

- *A new confirmation of the Resurrection:* Paul heard the voice of the resurrected and living Jesus Christ (Acts 9:4-6), confirming for him the fact of the Resurrection.
- *A new understanding of Jesus Christ:* In his appearance to Paul, God revealed who Jesus really was—the Jews' promised Messiah, the Savior.
- *A new strategy for mission:* The revelation of Jesus carried with it the command to go with the message to others. This included a law-free gospel to the Gentiles.

Some translations say that God revealed his Son "in" Paul, while the NRSV says "to" Paul. What began with Christ being revealed "to" Paul became a revelation of Christ "through" and "in" Paul because the Holy Spirit produced his fruit in Paul. And as Paul proclaimed Christ to the Gentiles, Christ revealed himself through Paul. Paul's phrase "in me" *(en emoi)* corresponds with 2:20 and 4:6, where Paul explained the inward reality of the Christian experience. Christ takes up residence "in us"; while we live "in him" (see 3:26-28). The outward revelation to Paul continued as an inward revelation in him which, in turn, became a revelation of Jesus to others through Paul's life, his message, and his letters. As we study Galatians, we are still receiving the revelation of Jesus through Paul.

NO MIRACLE REQUIRED
Many people claim that if only they could have an experience like Paul's, having Jesus Christ speak to them, then they would believe. Believers sometimes wish for an irresistible experience like Paul's for unsaved loved ones. *Who could refuse salvation after such a miracle?* you wonder. Paul's experience was unique, and God knew how Paul needed to be "called." He knows the required means to bring each person to the point of decision. In his parable about Lazarus and the rich man (Luke 16:19-31), Jesus made a crucial point for those who desire a startling supernatural confrontation: "If they do not listen to Moses and the Prophets, they will not be convinced even if someone rises from the dead" (Luke 16:31 NIV). God is sovereign; his methods, work, and timing are sovereign. His ways are loving and just. As you pray and witness to unbelievers, trust God's sovereignty.

The doctrine of election comes down to this: we do not just happen to exist; we are created for a purpose. The little phrase *so that* carries great weight. Paul was saved "so that" he could serve God.

Paul understood exactly what that service was to be: *I might preach him among the Gentiles.* God guided Paul's ministry, thus Paul wasn't doing anything that God hadn't already planned and given him power to do. At the time of Paul's conversion, God said, "This man is my chosen instrument to carry my name before the Gentiles and their kings and before the people of Israel," and then added, "I will show him how much he must suffer for my name" (Acts 9:15-16 NIV). Paul knew his mission, and he also knew that it would entail suffering. Yet he willingly accepted both, for he knew the ultimate value of the gift God had offered. A look at any map of Paul's travels and a reading of the book of Acts and Paul's letters will reveal how well Paul fulfilled his mission to proclaim the gospel among the Gentiles.

THE CHOSEN
As he did with Paul, God has a purpose and plan for your life. But his perspective is eternal, while we are rooted in time. We simply cannot know the scope of all God might accomplish in and through us. We are like the young person who gave his lunch of five loaves and two fish to Jesus. In the face of the hunger of so many, the gift seemed insignificant. But in Jesus' hands, the little became much.

We may not know as clearly as Paul knew what God had chosen him to do, but we can share the same confidence, based on our faith in Jesus Christ. God has chosen us also. Our purpose, then, must be to cooperate with what God has planned.

"Gentiles" *(ethnesin)* were non-Jews, whether in nationality or in religion. In Paul's day, Jews thought of all Gentiles as heathens. Jews avoided Gentiles, believing that contact with Gentiles brought spiritual corruption. Although Gentiles could become Jews in religion by undergoing circumcision and by following Jewish laws and customs (they were called "proselytes"), they were never fully accepted.

Many Jewish Christians had difficulty understanding that the gospel enabled both Jews and Gentiles to have equal standing before God. Some Jews thought that Gentiles had to become Jews before they could become Christians. But God planned to save both Jews and Gentiles. He had revealed this plan through Old Testament prophets (see, for example, Genesis 12:3; Isaiah 42:6; 66:19), and he had fulfilled it through Jesus Christ; he was proclaiming it to the Gentiles through Paul (see also Acts 13:46-47; 26:20; Romans 11:13; 15:16; Ephesians 3:8; 1 Timothy 2:7).

I did not confer with any human being.NRSV The word *confer (prosanethemen)* could also be translated "consult." His personal encounter with Jesus was so compelling that no further confirmation was required. Paul did not seek out anyone of authority in order to discuss doctrine, theology, the Old Testament Scriptures, or the specifics of the gospel message. His teaching did not result from consultations *with any human being.* Repeating the thought from verse 12, Paul emphasized that his authority did not come secondhand. The Judaizers were attacking Paul's authority by saying he could be no more than a student of the apostles. But Paul never even spoke to any of the apostles about the gospel until three years after his conversion. His understanding of the gospel message had come from God himself.

1:17 Nor did I go up to Jerusalem to those who were apostles before me.NKJV As if to answer any unspoken objections, Paul reiterated, "No, I did not go to Jerusalem to talk to the apostles, as the Judaizers are claiming." The twelve apostles *were apostles before* Paul became an apostle, but beyond that, there was no difference between them. When he finally did go to Jerusalem to meet with the church leaders, he went as an equal. The other apostles recognized him as such.

But I went to Arabia, and returned again to Damascus.NKJV Although the book of Acts doesn't seem to allow time for this retreat by Paul, here Paul explained that he went away from all human contact for several years in order to spend time alone with God. This was vital for the newly converted Jewish Pharisee and persecutor of Christianity. Paul was converted; he needed time to rethink his former position against Christianity in light of the truth of the gospel that had been revealed to him. During this interim, Paul probably studied the Scriptures, prayed, and thought about the meaning of Christ's crucifixion and resurrection in relation to the Old Testament that he knew so well. God revealed to Paul the meaning of the gospel, and from Paul's time of study, we today have the New Testament letters that focus on explaining God's plan (especially the doctrinal book of Romans). Paul's point in explaining this itinerary was to show that he formed his theology, not from consulting with any other believers, but alone, with God's guidance.

The region of *Arabia* probably means the vast desert area northeast and southeast of the city of *Damascus.* Some scholars, among them Luther, have suggested that Paul's time in Arabia was actually an initial preaching journey wherein he took the gospel to the Gentiles there. Others have wondered if Paul's Arabia was the Sinai Peninsula, where Paul would have taken in the atmosphere of Mount Sinai as he pondered the teachings of Moses

and Elijah in the light of Christ's revelation. The consensus of
opinion still holds that Paul took time away to consolidate the
changes God had brought into his life. Then Paul picked up his
life where it was interrupted, but his agenda was radically   '
revised. There were Christians in Damascus (Paul had been on
his way there to arrest them—Acts 9:1-2), but Paul did not form
his theology by discussion with them. After his time in Arabia,
Paul *returned again* to Damascus.

Although the sequence of events making up this part of Paul's
life appears clear, fitting it into the chronology of the book of
Acts presents some challenges. Luke did not mention a three-
year time period similar to Paul's account. The primary accounts
covering this time period are Acts 9:1-31 and Galatians 1:13-24.
The following presents a suggested chronology:

- On his way to Damascus to imprison Christians, Saul was confronted by Christ and converted.
- Journeying on into Damascus, Paul waited until he was con-
  tacted by Ananias, who prayed for his healing and arranged for
  his baptism.
- Two events are given description as "immediate:" (1) "Immediately he began to proclaim Jesus in the synagogues" (Acts 9:20
  NRSV), and (2) "I went immediately into Arabia" (1:17 NIV).
  The point of reference, however, for each immediate action is
  different. Luke described the prompt beginning of Paul's public ministry in relation to his conversion, while Paul was
  emphasizing to the Galatians how much time had elapsed between the beginning of his ministry and his first encounter with
  the other apostles in Jerusalem. Paul was saying, "Instead of
  immediately seeking confirmation from those in Jerusalem,
  what I did first was spend time alone in Arabia." The first "immediate" accents the overnight transformation of Paul's life.
  He left clear evidence of his conversion before he went into
  Arabia. The second "immediate" points to Paul's retreat into
  solitude in order to consolidate and integrate the central change
  in his life with the rest of his experience and training.
- Three years pass. During that time, Paul left Damascus twice:
  first to spend time alone in Arabia, second to avoid plotters
  against his life and visit Jerusalem. Paul's escape from Damascus fits better at the end of the three-year time period than
  shortly after his conversion. The Pharisees were probably upset
  by Paul's desertion from their ranks and the effect that he had
  on their numbers within the city after a while. As Luke
  described it, "After some time had passed" (Acts 9:23 NRSV).

By then, Paul had "disciples" (NRSV) or "followers" (see Acts 9:25 NIV).

1:18 Then, after three years, I went up to Jerusalem to get acquainted with Peter and stayed with him fifteen days.NIV Paul's visit to *Jerusalem* was his first as a Christian. This was where the church began, and this was where some of the apostles lived and worked, specifically Peter, whom Paul went to see. By referring to this actual event, the Judaizers may have felt that they had proved their point—Paul *did* go to Jerusalem. However, Paul further explained that his visit was *to get acquainted with Peter,* not to get instruction from Peter nor to be commissioned by him. While Paul does not mention the reason for the brevity of the visit, we are told by Luke that the opposition had plans in motion to kill Paul. Perhaps because of concerns for his life, as well as for the ongoing safety of believers in Jerusalem, Paul was given safe conduct by the believers to Caesarea, where he set out toward his home in Tarsus (see Acts 9:30).

1:19 I saw none of the other apostles except James, the Lord's brother.NKJV To further repudiate the Judaizers' claim that Paul needed the twelve apostles' instruction and approval, Paul pointed out that although he spent fifteen days getting acquainted with Peter, he *saw none of the other apostles.* Paul's intention to meet with Peter implies a self-perception of equality with the apostle who was acknowledged as the leader among Jesus' disciples. Paul planned an apostolic summit with Peter. But there was no general apostolic meeting to confirm Paul, no official gathering to approve this new convert and missionary. Instead, Paul talked only with Peter and *James, the Lord's brother.* This was not James the apostle (one of the Twelve) whom Herod put to death (see Acts 12:2); it was James, Jesus' younger half brother. During Jesus' ministry on earth, James did not believe that Jesus was the Messiah. But after the Resurrection, Jesus appeared personally to James (1 Corinthians 15:7), and James believed. He became the leader of the Jerusalem church. However, the structure of the Greek here does not make clear whether James was considered to be an apostle.

The fact that Paul had seen none of the other apostles might at first seem rather odd. Why didn't he? Most of the apostles made their homes in Jerusalem. Acts 8:1 explains that although many Christians had fled the city after Stephen's murder, the apostles had not. Perhaps they feared Paul, as Acts 9:26 suggests: "When [Paul] came to Jerusalem, he tried to join the disciples, but they were all afraid of him, not believing that he really was a

disciple" (NIV). But Barnabas stepped in to become the link between the new apostle and the church in Jerusalem. He presented
Paul to the believers and spoke out in behalf of Paul's conversion
and the ministry he had already accomplished in Damascus. Luke
implies (Acts 9:26-27) that while Paul was unable on his own to
make contact with the outer edges of the church in Jerusalem,
Barnabas was able to bring him before the leadership. We are not
told who exactly was present at that encounter, but of the twelve
apostles, only Peter and James (who Paul may have considered
an apostle) were. Perhaps the other apostles were away on mission trips of their own.

**1:20 I assure you before God that what I am writing you is no
lie.**NIV Assuring his readers *before God* of the truth of his words,
Paul made clear that any assumption on anyone's part that he was
taught and/or commissioned by the twelve apostles was absurd.

Some readers feel compelled to resolve every apparent contradiction between parallel accounts of events in the Scriptures. In
this case, the "difficulty" comes from the overlap between Luke's
and Paul's accounts of events. Does Luke's use of the word *apostles* (Acts 9:27) create a damaging contradiction with Paul's
forceful claim that he only met with Peter and James during his
first visit to Jerusalem? The solution is not clear. Perhaps the best
explanation is that Barnabas used it as a generalizing plural, as
we might say someone "met with the deacons." But perhaps there
is a good reason the apparent contradiction cannot be easily
unraveled. Students often find that ambiguities in the Bible have
a greater purpose than creating troubling inconsistencies. Those
who are eager to condemn the Gospels for their apparent differences of detail regarding the life of Jesus would probably be the
loudest in denouncing the writings as "copies" if they were identical. In Paul's case, his explanation to the Galatians needed to
accomplish two purposes: (1) to establish the independence of his
apostleship from human authority, and (2) to preserve the solidarity and mutual respect that existed between those commissioned
by God to begin the task of delivering the gospel to the world.
His version of his first trip to Jerusalem accomplished a balance
between those purposes. Luke's concerns were historical; Paul's
were apologetic. Because of that difference, they did not emphasize the same events or details in their accounts. But those differences need not be called contradictions.

1:21 Afterward I went into the regions of Syria and Cilicia.NKJV
The same Paul who has been accused of hyperbole (2 Corinthians 11:23-28) proved here he was also capable of under-

statement. Paul's arrival in Jerusalem caused real problems. His preaching stirred up a hornet's nest of opposition. Paul's life was in danger. Many of the believers were hesitant to accept his roadside conversion. His presence may have also caused added persecution for other believers. Those who did accept Paul were committed to keeping him alive. So Paul was urged to leave after only fifteen days. His departure eventually took him to his hometown of Tarsus in Cilicia (see Acts 9:30; 22:3). On his way, while in *the regions of Syria and Cilicia,* Paul most likely continued preaching the gospel. These small details serve to emphasize Paul's claim of direct authority from Jesus apart from the equal authority of those in Jerusalem. In the remote areas Paul mentioned, he had no opportunity to receive instruction from the apostles or have his ministry overseen by them. Thus, he was not part of the Judean authority structure.

1:22 I was personally unknown to the churches of Judea that are in Christ.[NIV] Although Paul was known to the Christians in Jerusalem at this time, because of both his personal visit and his brief ministry there, he was *personally unknown* outside the city limits. *Judea* was the name of the Roman district, as was "Galatia" (see the parallel phrase in 1:2).

CHECK IT OUT!
One of the recent trends among churches has been the loss of denominational hold on members. Believers are moving from one church to another, considering the spiritual health of local churches to be at least as important as the Christian denomination they might represent. These individualized choices can be made wisely or foolishly—all the more reason to know the marks that distinguish a church that is in Christ.

Three questions provide a good foundation for evaluating a local church:

1. Does the doctrine and teaching of the church flow from, emphasize, and remain accountable to God's Word?
2. Are the person, teaching, resurrection, and gospel of Jesus Christ central in the life of the church?
3. Is the fellowship genuine and consistent with the gospel?

The last question is unfortunately given too much priority in most people's decisions about a local church. How well does your present church meet the criteria? In what ways might God use you to move your church toward being more clearly "in Christ"?

There were identifiable groups of believers meeting in towns throughout Judea. Paul referred to them with a phrase of honor, *the churches . . . that are in Christ.* He used the same expression

in 1 Thessalonians 2:14, referring to the same group of churches.
Perhaps this was simply a way Paul showed his respect for those
earliest Christian fellowships. But it also served to emphasize
that the church in Christ was more than the church in Jerusalem.
It was one, but not the only church in Christ in Judea. Believers
everywhere needed and still need to see the connection between
their own local expression of the body of Christ and Jesus himself. The spiritual connection is direct.

**1:23 They only heard the report: "The man who formerly perse-
cuted us is now preaching the faith he once tried to
destroy."**NIV Paul was unknown to the churches in Judea, yet they
recognized the message he preached and glorified God because
of it (1:24). Paul was making the point that his authority and ministry were recognized by people who had never even seen him;
yet the Galatians had met him, listened to him, and believed his
message, only to turn around and doubt him! The Judean Christians *heard the report* (perhaps as the Galatians had, 1:13) that
Paul had *persecuted* believers but now was *preaching the faith he
once tried to destroy.* Instead of doubting Paul's credibility, these
churches believed and glorified God.

1:24 And they glorified God because of me.NRSV This was Paul's
final blow to the Judaizers: The *Jewish* Christians in Judea were
rejoicing and glorifying God *because of* Paul—his conversion,
his message, his ministry. How ironic that the Judean Christians
had given Paul full status and recognition without ever seeing or
hearing him, but the Galatian Christians, who had no reason to
doubt Paul or his message, were beginning to join the Judaizers
and thus to undermine Paul. They needed to cast aside their
doubts, get back to the truth, and get on with what God wanted
them to do.

WHAT DO THEY SEE IN YOU?
Paul's changed life brought joy to the believers who saw him or
heard about him. His new life had astonished them. They
praised God because only God could have turned this zealous
persecutor of Christians into a Christian. We may not have had
as dramatic a change as Paul, but our new lives should still
honor God in every way. When people look at you, do they recognize that God has made changes in you? If not, perhaps you
are not living as you should.

Galatians 2

Paul had not finished establishing his authority, which he would use to call the Galatians back to the freedom of the gospel. He was alarmed at how easily the new believers had allowed themselves to be led into a different form of the slavery from which they had so recently been released. Patiently, Paul built a case to prove that the doubts the Galatians had about him had been planted by those Judaizers who had less claim to authority than Paul did.

To defend himself against the Judaizers' charges, the apostle pointed to his fourteen years of independent ministry between his first two visits to Jerusalem following his conversion. He functioned directly under Jesus' authority during that time, not under the official body at Jerusalem. He helped the Galatians understand the complex relationship existing between himself and the apostles in Jerusalem. So when Paul wrote about his visit to the mother church, he showed both his independence from the other apostles' authority and his respect for them. Paul gave four significant aspects of his visit that established his credentials: (1) the companions on his journey; (2) the content of his message; (3) the confirmation of his ministry; and (4) his commission to come to Jerusalem.

First, his companions: Paul was escorted by a recognized leader (Barnabas) among the Christians in Jerusalem and accompanied by a living product of his ministry (Titus). Paul brought living credentials to endorse his ministry. Second, his content: Paul spelled out the content of his message, inviting correction by the other apostles. He interacted with them as apostolic peers, exercising the same divine authority to preach the same unique message. Third, his confirmation: Having heard the gospel Paul was preaching, the apostolic band recognized it as true and identical to theirs. They recognized his mission to Gentiles as valid and parallel to their mission to Jews. And fourth, his commission: Paul went to Jerusalem in response to divine revelation and at the request of the Jerusalem authorities.

Centuries later, the settings have changed, but the issues

remain the same. How do we sail between the rocks of crushing legalism that leave people without joy and the reefs of antinomianism that do away with all standards and encourage an individualized, make-it-up-yourself form of faith? To the same issues comes the same answer: the gospel of Jesus Christ. (See the chart on "Legalism and Labelism" in the Introduction, page 2.)

HAVING IT HIS WAY
Few can miss Paul's intensity, but many overlook the organized way he pursued his service for God. Examining his relationships shows us how Paul included others in his ministry. He never worked or traveled alone. He worked with people and through people. Paul coordinated with other ministries. He interacted on important issues. His confidence about God's call never developed into arrogance. Paul compromised on nonessentials and demonstrated that strong convictions on the essentials open doors of opportunity for ministry. Many doors will remain shut if we have to have our way in every issue.

2:1 Then after fourteen years I went up again to Jerusalem with Barnabas, taking Titus along with me.NRSV Paul continued the itinerary from 1:21 and explained that he "went to the regions of Syria and Cilicia"; afterward he *went up again to Jerusalem.* Although Jerusalem lay far to the south of the regions of Syria and Cilicia, Paul used the term "up" most likely describing land elevation. Jerusalem sat high above the surrounding countryside, and travelers usually spoke of going "up to Jerusalem."

The book of Acts records five visits to Jerusalem by Paul: (1) the visit to get acquainted with Peter (around A.D. 35, Acts 9:26-30; Galatians 1:18-20); (2) the visit to deliver a gift to the Jerusalem church for famine relief (around A.D. 44, Acts 11:27-30); (3) the visit to attend the Jerusalem council (around A.D. 49/50, Acts 15:1-30); (4) the visit at the end of the second missionary journey (around A.D. 52, Acts 18:22); and (5) the visit that resulted in his being imprisoned and sent to Rome (around A.D. 57, Acts 21:15–23:35).

The visit to Jerusalem mentioned here in Galatians 2:1 is most likely the second visit, when he delivered the famine relief gift to the Jerusalem church. Some scholars have suggested that it was the Jerusalem council visit; however, Paul spends time in this letter dealing with questions that the Jerusalem council ultimately settled, so the council could not yet have taken place. Those who opt for this visit coinciding with the Jerusalem council explain Paul's silence about that event by attributing to him a reluctance to appeal to the authority of the council in settling the issue of his own authority with the Galatians. However, the council could be more fairly characterized

A WHOLE PART, AND PART OF THE WHOLE

In the early chapters of Galatians, Paul conveyed both his *independence* as an apostle, called and commissioned by God, as well as his *solidarity* as he ministered with the other apostles. Paul's problems were not with the other apostles, but with those false teachers who sought to drive a wedge between Paul and the apostles.

Evidence of Independence:

Paul was not sent from men (1:1).

Paul claimed that his accountability was to God (1:10).

Paul's aim was to please God (1:10).

Paul's message was not derived from human sources or reason, but by divine revelation (1:11).

Paul's conversion and subsequent ministry did not come as a result of consultations with anyone (1:16).

Paul took the initiative in contacting Peter (1:18).

Evidence of Solidarity:

By traveling with Barnabas and Titus, Paul demonstrated that he was unified with the Christian community. The fact that Barnabas was a Jew and Titus was a Greek showed that Paul could work with others and had support from key leaders in Asia (2:1).

Paul "placed his message on the table" for the other apostles to examine (2:2).

The rest of the apostles affirmed Paul's message to be the true gospel and his ministry to be directed to the Gentiles (2:7).

Jesus was clearly working through both Peter and Paul (2:8).

The apostolic band demonstrated their unity with Paul and Barnabas by publicly giving them "the right hand of fellowship." They were adding their endorsement to Christ's commission (2:9).

Later, Paul lovingly confronted Peter as an equal about an inconsistency in Peter's behavior (2:14).

as a time when the apostolic leaders publicly agreed with Paul rather than the reverse. If the council had occurred already, Paul would have had a direct contradiction to the accusations of the Judaizers in Galatia. Since they were claiming to speak for the mother church in saying that Paul was in error, what better refutation could there have been than the apostolic letter endorsing Paul? One of the main arguments settled by the council was the issue of circumcision. This issue was particularly troublesome to the church in Galatia and was one of the main reasons that Paul wrote this letter. Silence here is best explained by the fact that the council and its letter had not yet occurred.

Though, in fact, neither the famine nor the council are specifically mentioned, Paul's reference to his visit being motivated by a revelation (2:2) may well refer to Agabus's vision (Acts 11:28) of the famine.

The phrase *fourteen years* most likely is dated, not from the last mention in his itinerary (that is, from his time in Syria and Cilicia), but rather from his conversion. The first and fourteenth years were partial years. Like history itself, Paul tended to divide and orient his life around "before Christ" and "after Christ." Paul was converted around A.D. 32, dating this visit at A.D. 44/45. Paul was pointing out that he had been preaching to the Gentiles for a long time, and thus had a specific message that could be discussed with the church leaders in Jerusalem. Following this relief visit, Paul then took the first missionary journey (Acts 13:1–14:28), wrote this letter to the Galatians in response to the troubling news of spiritual desertion by the new believers, and later attended the Jerusalem council that settled many of the issues discussed in this letter to the Galatians.

A FRIEND LIKE YOU
Barnabas was a friend and a fellow worker. Friendships are an important part of evangelism. Most people discover that their relationships with friends change following conversion. Sometimes old friendships simply vanish in the light of a new commitment to Christ. Entering the fellowship of the church with other believers also creates new friendships. Much of this comes naturally with change.

But preconversion friends should not be dropped lightly. Destructive friendships should be forgiven and left behind, but others may present us with opportunities to share the gospel. Besides, who other than our friends will be the first to notice a change in us? The Bible tells us (1 Peter 3:15) we should be ready to explain to them what has happened.

Barnabas and Titus were two of Paul's close friends. According to the book of Acts, *Barnabas* recognized Paul's sincerity as a truly converted former persecutor and introduced Paul to the apostles. Many believers, even the apostles themselves, may have feared that Paul simply was acting in some extravagant ruse in order to find out and capture more Christians. But Barnabas was not afraid (Acts 9:27). His name means "Son of Encouragement," and Paul knew firsthand about Barnabas's kind encouragement. Barnabas accompanied Paul on the so-called famine relief visit to Jerusalem (Acts 11:27-30) and traveled with him on the first missionary journey during which Galatia was evangelized (Acts 13:2-

3). Thus, Barnabas was well known to the Galatian Christians to whom Paul was writing.

GROWING UP
Titus gives us a living example of God's pattern of spiritual maturity in a person's life. We first meet him as a young convert, traveling with Paul. Already he had taken strides in demonstrating himself to be a faithful disciple. Eventually, he became a disciple maker himself, sent by Paul to oversee the churches in Crete.

To what degree has your life followed this pattern? At what stage do you presently find yourself? What action or decision would move you toward greater maturity in Christ?

Titus, a Greek, was one of Paul's most trusted and dependable coworkers. Paul called him "a true son" (Titus 1:4 NKJV), so he was probably one of Paul's converts. This trip to Jerusalem with Paul became the first of many journeys for Titus, who would later become a true right-hand man to Paul. Although Acts does not mention Titus, other epistles point out that he later fulfilled several missions on Paul's behalf. Paul sent Titus to Corinth on several special missions to help the church in its troubles. Titus brought back positive reports to Paul and then was sent back to Corinth with news of Paul and to gather an offering for the Jerusalem church (2 Corinthians 7:6-7, 13-15; 8:6, 16-17, 23). Titus showed that he could be trusted with money. Paul and Titus also traveled together to Jerusalem (2:3) and Crete (Titus 1:5). Paul eventually left Titus in Crete to lead the new churches springing up on the island. Titus is mentioned the last time by Paul in 2 Timothy 4:10, Paul's last recorded letter. As Titus exhibited leadership abilities, Paul assigned him leadership responsibilities, urging him to use those opportunities well.

DON'T RUSH!
After his conversion, Paul spent many years preparing for the ministry that God had given him. This preparation period included time alone with God (1:16-17), as well as time conferring with other Christians.

Often new Christians, in their zeal, want to begin a full-time ministry without investing the necessary time studying the Bible and learning from qualified teachers. We shouldn't wait to share Christ with our friends, but we may need more preparation before embarking on a special ministry, whether volunteer or paid. While we wait for God's timing, we should continue to study, learn, and grow.

Exactly why Paul brought Titus along to Jerusalem is unclear. Possibly because Titus was a pure Gentile convert, he was presented as a "test case" to the church leaders (2:3-5). We should not assume that Barnabas and Titus were Paul's only fellow travelers; Paul mentioned them by name because their presence was significant to the purpose of his letter.

2:2 I went in response to a revelation and set before them the gospel that I preach among the Gentiles.NIV God told Paul, through a revelation, to confer with the church leaders in Jerusalem about the message he was preaching to the Gentiles so they would understand and approve of what he was doing. Paul's point here was that his visit to Jerusalem was not because the apostles had summoned him or because he had felt a need to talk to the apostles about his ministry among the Gentiles. Rather, he had gone *in response to a revelation* from God, telling him to go.

This revelation may have been to Paul personally, or it may have come through someone else. It is probable that Paul was referring to the prophecy made by Agabus, who had "predicted that a severe famine would spread over the entire Roman world" (Acts 11:28 NIV), for we are told that this prophecy led to Paul and Barnabas being sent to Jerusalem, and Paul using that God-given opportunity to then talk to the church leaders.

WHO'S IN CHARGE HERE?
We must insist on the authority of Christ and his Word over the rule of human teaching. By Christ's authority we are bound to cooperate with human leaders as long as their requirements do not deviate from the commands of Christ. We are free to obey all as long as in so doing we are not disobeying Jesus Christ. And we must not reject the leadership of others who are actually directing our obedience to Christ. In our relationships with human leaders, our goal must always be to obey Christ.

If this refers to the famine relief visit, then the *them* mentioned are the apostles and the church leaders, notably James (Jesus' half brother), Peter, and John (2:9). If this refers to the Jerusalem council visit, the *them* is the entire council. In either case, before these men Paul *set . . . the gospel that [he was preaching] among the Gentiles.* Note the conscious word usage. Remember that one reason Paul wrote this letter was to combat the false teaching of the Judaizers who were trying to undermine Paul's authority as an apostle. Paul did not go to Jerusalem at the call of the apostles, and he did not go to discuss the gospel he preached or to get it approved. Instead, Paul went to "set" it before them for their acceptance (which was really the only response they could have). In 1:16, Paul had written that he did not "confer" or "consult" *(pro-sanethemen)* with any human being in order to be approved before beginning to preach. Here, he uses the word *anethemen* to say he "displayed," "communicated," "set" that gospel before the

> If there is only one gospel in the New Testament, there is only one gospel for the church. The gospel has not changed with the changing centuries.
>
> *John R. W. Stott*

church leaders. Paul knew he didn't need approval because the gospel had been revealed to him by God himself. The essence of the "gospel" Paul preached to both Jews and Gentiles was that God's salvation is offered to all people regardless of race, sex, nationality, wealth, social standing, educational level, or anything else. All types of people can be forgiven by trusting in Christ (see Romans 10:8-13; Galatians 3:28).

LET'S TALK
How well God understands human beings! Even though God had specifically sent Paul to the Gentiles (Acts 9:15), he wanted Paul (who at this point may have been considered the "leader" of the Gentile churches) to explain the gospel message to the leaders of the Jerusalem church. God brought his chosen people together to talk and make some important decisions. This meeting protected the young Christian faith by revealing that Gentiles were part of God's plan (Peter received the same message—see Acts 10; 15:7-11), prevented a split in the church, and formally acknowledged the apostles' approval of Paul's message and ministry to the Gentiles. We, like Paul, should "set our ideas" before mature Christian leaders for guidance and feedback. No one, not even Paul, should regard himself/herself as a rugged individualist, accountable to no one.

The language Paul used here may seem harsh or even boastful, but it preserves an important distinction. Paul believed and taught the principle of mutual submission among believers (Ephesians 5:21). But the truth does not submit. Paul voluntarily came before the leaders in Jerusalem and calmly presented to them the message he was preaching. He was maintaining accountability and solidarity with other Christian leaders, without for a moment assuming that what Christ had given him was open to their approval. The submission that he specifically mentioned that he withheld in verse 5 refers to the unbelievers (false brothers) who somehow got into the meeting.

TALK IT OUT
Sometimes we avoid conferring with others because we fear
that problems or arguments may develop. Instead, we should
openly discuss our plans and actions with friends, counselors,
and advisers. Good communication helps everyone understand
the situation better; furthermore, it reduces gossip and builds
unity in the church.

**But I did this privately to those who seemed to be leaders, for
fear that I was running or had run my race in vain.**[NIV] Paul
discussed the gospel he was preaching among the Gentiles in a
private meeting with *those who seemed to be leaders.* The term
for "leaders" *(tois dokousin)* refers to reputation and may indicate
that at this point Paul was not able to identify each of them as
leaders but had to take the word of those in Jerusalem. This may
account for the fact that some who were clearly not leaders (the
false brothers) were able to disrupt this meeting. Among the leaders who did meet with Paul were probably James, Peter, and John
(2:9).

Peter, John, and James seem to have emerged as the central
leadership team in the church. James was Jesus' half brother who
became a believer after the Resurrection (1 Corinthians 15:7) and
then headed the Jerusalem church. Peter and John had been
Jesus' disciples and were recognized apostles. The phrases
"seemed to be leaders," "supposed to be acknowledged leaders"
(2:6 NRSV), and "reputed to be pillars" (2:9 NIV) display a slight
note of disparagement from Paul (for more on this, see 2:9). This
does not mean that Paul rejected their authority; rather, these
expressions show that Paul was probably ridiculing other people
(especially the Judaizers) for esteeming Peter, John, and James
too highly. Note that Paul deliberately refused to use the term
"apostles" in all three cases, for to do so would be to open himself to more attacks by the Judaizers. This wording implies his
own tongue-in-cheek attack on the attitudes of the Judaizers who
made much of the church leaders in Jerusalem in order to assail
Paul's claims to authority. Yet, as noted below, these leaders and
pillars accepted Paul as an equal, extending to Paul and Barnabas
"the right hand of fellowship" (2:9).

Next, Paul explained why this meeting was necessary. His purpose in meeting *privately* can be understood in several ways. By
meeting alone with the leaders, Paul was seeking to avoid public
confrontation in case there were disagreements. Apparently this
tactic was effective, because even though the "false brothers"
tried to create problems, neither Paul nor his companions were

inconvenienced in any way. The private meeting also points away from identifying this visit with the Jerusalem council visit, since the accounts in Acts explain that those deliberations were carried out among the community of believers at large.

The meeting in privacy was not, as the Judaizers hoped to claim, for the purpose of correcting Paul's message. Instead, Paul met privately *for fear that [he] was running or had run [his] race in vain.* Paul was not afraid that he had been mistaken about the gospel message; instead, he was afraid that the apostles would incorrectly disagree with him and agree with the Judaizers (that to be Christians, people first had to become Jews and follow all the laws and customs—especially regarding circumcision). This would cause severe damage to the work that Paul had already done for years among the Gentiles (the "race" he was running) and would hurt future missionary efforts of the church. Thus, he would be running in vain. Paul realized the momentous importance of the decision that needed to be made (and *was* made at the Jerusalem council in Acts 15) regarding the relationship of Gentiles and Jews on the common meeting ground of Christianity.

THE TREADMILL
Paul was not a blindly confident man. As sure as he was of the gospel, he was not so certain of his own abilities or the setbacks he might encounter. We cannot guess what Paul might have done if the other apostles had argued with his message or disallowed his ministry. Paul revealed to us his inner turmoil about the encounter and raised a legitimate question for us. Are we running in vain?

When our efforts are intended to promote our own glory, or the glory of anyone or anything other than God, we are running in vain. If our actions attempt to preserve at all costs a man-made policy or institution, we are in fact demonstrating more devotion to human glorification than to the glory of God. Such actions will not stand the test of time or eternity (see 2 Timothy 3:5, 9). We will find ourselves walking a meaningless treadmill that gives the illusion of motion while taking us absolutely nowhere.

For Paul the "race" (see also 5:7) wasn't a figure of speech for the message, but a picture of the life under the message or his ministry. A failed Christian life, or a failed ministry, does not invalidate the truth of the gospel; it merely reflects on the effort or faithfulness of the runner. Paul used this expression elsewhere to depict the functions of carrying out ministry (see 1 Corinthians 9:24-27; Philippians 2:16) as well as to explain the exertion necessary in the Christian life (see 5:7; Philippians 3:14; 2 Timothy

4:7). Paul had no doubts about the message Christ had given him, but he appeared before the other apostles as an equal expecting their wholehearted support.

2:3 But even Titus, who was with me, was not compelled to be circumcised, though he was a Greek.^{NRSV} Paul's message preached among the Gentiles was tested in the treatment of the young Greek convert whom Paul brought along to Jerusalem—Titus. Paul's message to the Gentiles was that God accepted anyone who believes, regardless of race or religious background. Titus's presence gave the entire church an opportunity to practice what they intended to preach. The gospel clearly applied to Titus without requiring his circumcision. The development was a major loss for the Judaizers, for it showed that the Jerusalem church had accepted Paul's policy.

The Judaizers' teaching is summed up in Acts 15:1: "Unless you are circumcised, according to the custom taught by Moses, you cannot be saved" (NIV). Circumcision was a big issue for the Jews because the custom dated back to the days of Abraham and their birth as a nation. God required circumcision for four main reasons: (1) As a sign of obedience to him in all matters. (2) As a sign of belonging to the covenant people. Once circumcised, there was no turning back. The man would be identified as a Jew forever. (3) As a symbol of "cutting off" the old life of sin, purifying one's heart, and dedicating oneself to God. (4) Possibly as a health measure. More than any other practice, circumcision separated God's people from their pagan neighbors. In Abraham's day, this was essential for developing the pure worship of the one true God. Whether the Judaizers were intentionally trying to undermine Christianity with this requirement, or whether they sincerely believed that as an outgrowth of Judaism, Christianity should fulfill Jewish requirements, they were wrong.

> Let this be then the conclusion of all together, that we will suffer our goods to be taken away, our name, our life, and all that we have; but the Gospel, our faith, Jesus Christ, we will never suffer to be wrested from us.
>
> *Martin Luther*

Because of the unusual format of verses 3-5, they have received a great deal of scholarly attention. In the Greek, Paul's wording seems convoluted with unfinished sentences, making it difficult to know whether Paul was saying that he *did* have Titus circumcised as a concession for the sake of the gospel, or that he *did not* have Titus circumcised, thus standing up for the gospel. Both views have the support of various interpreters' studies. Those who believe that Titus was circumcised would paraphrase

these verses thus: "Titus, who was a
Gentile, was circumcised, but the false
brothers did not force me to do it, I
allowed it as a concession."

However, most interpreters read
these verses as the NRSV text above
does; the apostles agreed that Titus did
not need to be circumcised, so Paul
exempted him from the rite. This seems
a more likely view because it would
seem odd for Paul to make any allow-
ances to the Judaizers or any concession on the gospel of "salvation by
grace alone" that he had been preaching
among the Gentiles for so long. If Paul
did, in fact, make the concession and
have Titus circumcised, his later anger
at having allowed this might explain the
excitement and breathlessness of these
sentences in the Greek.

> Galatians 2:1-10 sets
> before us a prototype of
> mutual recognition and
> concern for one another,
> despite our differences. It
> teaches us . . . how to
> distinguish between
> things that really matter
> and things of lesser
> importance . . . , where to
> stand firm and where to
> concede, and even when
> to defy people and
> pressures and when to
> shake hands and
> reciprocate with
> expressions of mutual
> concern.
>   *Richard Longnecker*

If the second view is correct, this
verse records Paul's victory against the
Judaizers' teaching. The apostles, from whom the Judaizers
claimed support against Paul, did *not* demand that Titus *be circumcised, though he was a Greek* and thus a Gentile. Instead, the
apostles agreed with Paul that circumcision was an unnecessary
rite for Gentile converts. Several years later, Paul did circumcise
Timothy, another Greek Christian (Acts 16:3). Unlike Titus, however, Timothy was half Jewish. Paul did not deny Jews the right
to be circumcised; he was simply saying that Gentiles should not
be asked to become Jews before becoming Christians.

**2:4 This matter arose because some false brothers had infiltrated
our ranks to spy on the freedom we have in Christ Jesus and
to make us slaves.**^NIV Titus, brought as a test case, ended up
being the example Paul needed. Titus was a converted Gentile.
This matter refers to the Judaizers' demand that Titus be circumcised; Paul held firmly to his belief that Titus did not need to be
circumcised. (Those who follow the interpretation that Titus was
circumcised translate "this matter arose" as "this concession was
made.")

Here Paul called the Judaizers *false brothers.* They were most
likely from the party of the Pharisees (Acts 15:5), the strictest
religious leaders of Judaism. Although Paul had expressed
astonishment and anger at the Galatians for their turning away to

JUDAIZERS VERSUS PAUL

As the debate raged between the Gentile Christians and the Judaizers, Paul found it necessary to write to the churches in Galatia. The Judaizers were trying to undermine Paul's authority, and they taught a false gospel. In reply, Paul defended his authority as an apostle and the truth of his message. The debate over Jewish laws and Gentile Christians was officially resolved at the Jerusalem council (Acts 15), yet it continued to be a point of contention after that time.

What the Judaizers said about Paul	Paul's defense
They said he was perverting the truth.	He received his message from Christ himself (1:11-12).
They said he was a traitor to the Jewish faith.	Paul was one of the most dedicated Jews of his time. Yet, in the midst of one of his most zealous acts, God transformed him through a revelation of the Good News about Jesus (1:13-16; Acts 9:1-30).
They said he compromised and watered down his message for the Gentiles.	The other apostles declared that the message Paul preached was the true gospel (2:1-10).
They said he was disregarding the law of Moses.	Far from degrading the law, Paul puts the law in its proper place. He says it shows people where they have sinned, and it points them to Christ (3:19-29).

other doctrines (1:6), he still addressed them as "brothers" (*adelphoi,* 1:11). However, these Judaizers were merely acting as brothers; they were not believers in Christ's gospel of grace. Thus they were "false" brothers (*pseudadelphoi,* see also 2 Corinthians 11:26).

It is unclear whether the *ranks* refers to the Jerusalem church or the meeting Paul had with the church leaders (2:2). Whatever the case, some of these Judaizers *infiltrated* and, on Paul's arrival in Jerusalem, immediately forced "this matter" to the forefront. The wording here indicates some subversive action ("infiltrated," "spy"); these people somehow sneaked in or they were planted or smuggled into the Christians' ranks. If they got into the private meeting Paul had with "those who seemed to be leaders," someone of power may have been behind the controversy. Scholars agree, however, that Peter and the apostles were not involved, nor James, the leader of the church. But we do not know how this private meeting was convened. Paul's descriptive words for the group clearly indicate that more were present than the apostles. If "false brothers" were infiltrating the church, it would have been fairly easy to join the believers and pretend to be a part, while in reality having other goals in mind, which became obvious to Paul: (1) *to spy on the freedom we have in Christ Jesus* and (2) *to make us [believers] slaves.*

The Pharisees would have been most interested in observing what was going on in the Christian camp, especially regarding freedom from the Mosaic law. Indeed, their very existence involved detailed obedience to Jewish law and traditions—and making sure everyone else did the same. Apparently the philosophy of the Judaizers was something like, "If you can't beat them or join them, then try to change them by absorbing them." The status quo of Judaism, which Jesus repeatedly confronted during his ministry, did not give up easily. Those still committed to that system decided to "spy on" *(kataskopesai)* the new believers in Christ in order to determine the best way to make slaves of them under the religious legal system. Once they discovered what freedoms the Christians promoted, they hoped to step in with their power and authority and require obedience to the law. Circumci-

---

GUARD THE FREEDOM
Who are the "false brothers" and "spies" in the church today? The role is filled by modern Pharisees who introduce rules, policies, and extra steps that they claim are necessary for salvation or full participation in the Christian life. They may be moralists who have their own hierarchy of values (dos and don'ts), but they may also be those who wish to establish a man-made structure. Motivated by a desire for control over others or for holding a superior status, they promote their own agenda, vision, and purposes. They may elevate nonessentials to the status of salvation theology. They desire to trip people up and catch them in the act of violating a principle of their own choosing.

Grace gives us freedom from the law as a basis for salvation and Christian growth. It also means that no human standards are to enslave us. We must guard our freedom from the law and from those false brothers and sisters who would hinder God's grace.

---

sion, with its inherent significance (see 2:3 above), was a good first step. Obviously they did not see themselves as trying to enslave anyone, but Paul understood that this was the ultimate end of required obedience to all the Jewish laws and traditions. (Paul deals with this topic further, later in this letter. For an extended treatise on the Christian's relationship to the Jewish law, read Paul's letter to the Romans.)

2:5 We did not give in to them for a moment, so that the truth of the gospel might remain with you.^{NIV} The plural *we* proba-bly refers to Paul and his team (Barnabas and Titus). This verse reinforces the conclusion that Paul refused to have Titus circumcised, thus standing for the truth of the gospel. However, some manuscripts omit the word "not," leading some to surmise that Paul did allow Titus to be circumcised, making this concession for the same reason. Facts against this interpretation might include the understanding that circumcision, at least for Titus, could hardly be considered a momentary concession—for Titus it was permanent.

> Now, as concerning faith we ought to be invincible, and more hard, if it might be, than the adamant stone; but as touching charity, we ought to be soft, and more flexible than the reed or leaf that is shaken with the wind, and ready to yield to everything.
>
> *Martin Luther*

The interpretation that Paul *did not* allow Titus to be circumcised agrees with the weight of these matters, for the *truth of the gospel* was at stake. Paul sought to protect the truth that the gospel is for all people who can accept it by faith alone. Titus represented the Galatians. If Paul had allowed him to be circumcised, nothing would have prevented the Judaizers from making the same demand of the Galatians. But Paul was convinced that circumcision, a rite he himself had undergone, was not part of the essential truth of the gospel. And adding any other stipulations or requirements to the essential truth would make the whole into a lie.

We normally think of taking a stand against those who might lead us into immoral behavior, but Paul had to take a hard line against the most "moral" of people. Like Paul, we must not give in to those who make the keeping of man-made standards a condition for salvation, even when such people are morally upright or in respected positions.

Paul fought to protect that gospel for *you*, specifically referring to the Galatian Christians to whom he wrote. But it also applies to any believer today who has not come out of a Jewish background. We have received salvation without having to ascribe to a whole set of Jewish laws because Paul had the foresight and wisdom to fight for protection of the gospel of grace regarding this issue. The early Christians eventually made a wise decision at the Jerusalem council (Acts 15).

TAKING A STAND
We live in a pluralistic society with many kinds of expressions of Christian faith. There is a bewildering array of "stands" inviting our support. Christians can just as easily become unresisting compromisers as they can become belligerent defenders of the faith, who see heresy under every rock or behind every word uttered by someone else. Satan's purposes are as well served by "trigger-happy" Christians as by those who deny we are in spiritual warfare.

During his visit to Jerusalem, Paul realized the very heart of the gospel was under attack. He understood the ground he wanted to defend and guarded it fiercely. We must do the same. Wise military planners choose their targets and positions carefully, and they commit themselves to clear objectives. The truth of the gospel remains under attack today. But we must ensure that we are guarding the gospel, not our own perspectives, pet peeves, or personal issues. Believers are called to active duty. But we must be wise how we involve ourselves in the battle.

2:6 And from those who were supposed to be acknowledged leaders (what they actually were makes no difference to me; God shows no partiality).[NRSV] As noted in 2:2, Paul's wording here was not necessarily meant disrespectfully toward the apostles and church leaders. Paul was walking a fine line between asserting his independence from the apostles, and yet his unity with them. Paul was not in awe of the apostles; who they were made *no difference* to him in that sense. The imperfect tense of these phrases—*those who were supposed to be* and *what they actually were*—most likely referred to the fact that these men knew Jesus during his time on earth, and to this they owed their present position as *acknowledged leaders.* Those in positions of leadership have the responsibility to glorify God. If instead they glorify themselves, they forfeit their authority. Any position we may hold in church should help facilitate the proclamation of the Word of God. If we stop glorifying God, the power of our position vanishes, for at that moment we are seeking our own glory and running in vain (2:2).

Paul wanted to make it clear that both his gospel and his apostleship were of supernatural origin. Because *God shows no partiality* between him and the recognized apostles, then neither should anyone else (see also Ephesians 6:9).

Those men added nothing to my message.[NIV] In other words, the apostles did not correct Paul's message or try to add anything to it (such as the need for circumcision). Instead, they accepted

Paul as an equal and accepted his message to the Gentiles as "gospel truth."

RATING DOESN'T RATE
It's easy to rate people on the basis of their official status and to be intimidated by powerful people. Paul was not intimidated by the acknowledged leaders, however, because he knew that all believers are equal in Christ. We should respect our spiritual leaders, but our ultimate allegiance must be to Christ. We are to serve him with our whole being. God doesn't rate us according to our status; he looks at the attitude of our hearts (1 Samuel 16:7). We should encourage leaders who show humility and a heartfelt desire to please God.

2:7 On the contrary, they saw that I had been entrusted with the task of preaching the gospel to the Gentiles, just as Peter had been to the Jews.NIV What the apostles *saw* (*idontes,* having seen, perceived) that made them understand is unclear. Perhaps the presence, character, and witness of Titus was convincing evidence. Whether this refers to the famine relief visit or the Jerusalem council visit, the convincing factor was the success that God had given to Paul's ministry.

Peter, as one of the leaders of the Jerusalem church, had a dynamic ministry among the Jews (as recorded in the first twelve chapters of the book of Acts). Although Peter had been entrusted (as were many others) with preaching the gospel *to the Jews,* he also had contact with Gentiles (see Acts 10), probably a key point in the approval of Paul and Barnabas's ministry. Peter's encounter with Cornelius had demonstrated God's acceptance of the Gentiles. This prepared Peter to accept the legitimacy of Paul's special call. Peter and Paul represented God's ongoing covenant with all of humanity under the saving grace made possible by Jesus. Each of them had valid ministries, ordained and authorized by Christ. We must be careful not to deprecate those who have been called to ministries different from ours. Those working in the inner city and those in the affluent suburbs are both God's servants. Those who work with professional athletes have as much work to do as those reaching the homeless. Each of us must answer to God for what we do; none of us should reject or put down those who have a different ministry.

At the Jerusalem council, Peter publicly testified about the revelation that God gave to him regarding the Gentiles: "God, who knows the heart, showed that he accepted them [Gentile believers] by giving the Holy Spirit to them, just as he did to us [Jewish believers]. He made no distinction between us and them, for he purified their hearts by faith" (Acts 15:8-9 NIV). The testimony of Paul and Barnabas is contained in one verse: "The whole assembly became silent as they listened to Barnabas and Paul telling about the miraculous signs and wonders God had done among the Gentiles through them" (Acts 15:12 NIV). God had declared his approval of both streams of ministry in Christ's name.

Not only did the apostles accept Paul's message, they recognized the supernatural origin of his message and ministry—that Paul *had been entrusted [by God] with the task of preaching the gospel to the Gentiles.* This meant, not that Paul was exclusively entrusted with this mission (Philip spoke to the Samaritans and to an Ethiopian eunuch—Acts 8; Peter spoke with Cornelius—Acts 10; and Paul continued to speak to the Jews in the cities he visited), but that Paul was spearheading this ministry and that it was his main thrust.

Both Paul and Peter preached the same gospel. Though their audiences were vastly different, the message did not, could not, and would not ever change. The gospel that remains unchanged today is that salvation is by God's grace alone for anyone who believes.

2:8 For God, who was at work in the ministry of Peter as an apostle to the Jews, was also at work in my ministry as an apostle to the Gentiles.NIV This verse repeats the thought of verse 7. The focus here is on the enabler—God. The apostles realized that as God was at work in the ministry of Peter among the Jews, so God was at work in Paul's ministry to the Gentiles. In each case they were able to identify God as the agent, giving great success to both men in their parallel ministries.

The Greek word *energeo,* translated "at work within," refers to the work of the Holy Spirit in and through Paul as well as his work in and through Peter. Peter could not help but grasp the significance of the Holy Spirit's stamp and seal upon Paul's work. In a sense, Paul was carrying on the work of the Spirit among the Gentiles that had been begun by Peter. Peter had first received the vision of the Gentile mission, and the Holy Spirit had authenticated it (Acts 10:47; 15:7-9).

Note that Paul pointedly used the term *apostle* to describe his ministry. The twelve apostles recognized Paul as an equal, as an apostle. The Judaizers and Paul's doubters in Galatia could raise no more objections.

2:9 James, Peter and John, those reputed to be pillars, gave me and Barnabas the right hand of fellowship when they recog-

THE EVIDENCE
How can we identify God's energizing work in someone's ministry? The following indicators help us see God at work:
- *The ministry functions for the glory of God.* Who receives the credit and praise for the results of the efforts? Do others respond as the Christians in Judea did when they heard about Paul (Galatians 1:24)? God received the praise and glory.
- *The ministry finds its roots, purpose, and guidelines in God's Word.* God's call upon Paul's life was personal, but his ministry was the application of the gospel to a group (the Gentiles). Paul defended his ministry and responded to questions and accusations by always relying on the Scriptures (see Galatians 2:2, 6 and 1:10).
- *The ministry finds its power in faith* (see Galatians 2:20). Under the good stewardship of time, talents, and resources, can the ministry still point to a foundation of ministry carried out in faith? Do those involved see themselves as participants in God's work or as the ones to whom credit is due? When God is involved, he makes his presence known.

nized the grace given to me.[NIV] In this verse Paul identified the "they" about whom he had spoken several times: "seemed to be leaders" (2:2 NIV), "supposed to be acknowledged leaders" (2:6 NRSV), and *reputed to be pillars* (*dokountes stuloi einai,* "seeming to be pillars," or "known as the pillars.") The fact that similar wording appears four times in eight verses leads us to wonder what Paul was thinking as he wrote. Those who take the view that Titus was circumcised (see discussion of 2:1-4) point out that Paul's rising indignation against these church leaders can be felt in his word choices. These leaders, Paul realized in retrospect, had handled that situation very poorly; thus, he was disappointed in their leadership. Another consideration involves the following verses (2:11ff.), in which Paul describes his opposition to Peter's handling of a Jew/Gentile situation. Again Paul could have been revealing an underlying disappointment in the leadership of these "pillars" who didn't seem to be "holding up" under pressure from the Judaizers and legalists. Another possibility is simply that Paul was using this wording to silence the Judaizers who had refused to acknowledge Paul as an apostle. In Hebrew writings, Abraham, Isaac, and Jacob were considered the three pillars of Judaism. The Judaizers may have given the same status to James, Peter, and John, thereby disregarding Paul's apostleship. Paul did not show disrespect for the three leaders, but may have disagreed with the position given them by the Jerusalem church.

The men mentioned were *James,* half brother of Jesus and leader of the Jerusalem church, and two of Jesus' original disciples and part of his inner circle of three—*Peter and John.* The James of the original twelve disciples had been executed by Herod (Acts 12:2). This would have occurred about the same time as the famine relief visit (Acts 11:30–12:1) and before the Jerusalem council. It was clear to the Galatians that this was James, Jesus' brother, not James the disciple.

Whether all this occurred in a private meeting during the famine relief visit or after the decision of the Jerusalem council, the important point is that these three noted leaders gave Paul and Barnabas the *right hand of fellowship*—their approval, blessing, and encouragement in their ministry among the Gentiles. The scene must have been wonderful: their joy in God's guidance to two special leaders who preached the same gospel, their rejoicing in God's gracious plan to include the Gentiles, and their excitement over the growth of the church. Clasped right hands signified friendship and trust; this was another blow to the Judaizers.

Paul knew that his words had not persuaded the other apostles to recognize his ministry. The convincing had been done by God *when they recognized the grace given to* him. This "grace" *(charis),* or spiritual gift, to which Paul attributed their acceptance probably pointed in two directions: (1) to the evidence of God's saving grace in Paul's own life and (2) to the results flowing from his ministry among the Gentiles. Paul was a walking, talking advertisement for the gospel.

They agreed that we should go to the Gentiles, and they to the Jews.NIV Paul and Barnabas were sent on their way to continue their dynamic ministry among the Gentiles, while the apostles in Jerusalem and Judea would continue their ministry to the Jews. In other words, the apostles stayed with home missions, while Paul and Barnabas went to foreign fields. This referred to each group's main focus; it was not exclusive. The apostles ministered to many Gentiles; Paul and his team always spoke to Jews, as well. Yet always their message was the same: the gospel of salvation.

2:10 They desired only that we should remember the poor, the very thing which I also was eager to do.NKJV Although the "right hand of fellowship" had been given by the apostles to Paul and Barnabas, the entire issue had not been handled because the Judaizers had not been silenced. It would take the council of Jerusalem to block the efforts to bring the gospel back under the law. In the meantime, much effort would be required to promote unity at the grass roots level between Jewish and Gentile Christians.

The apostles realized that one immediate and practical way to bridge this possible gap would be to care for the poor.

Because the apostles (missionaries to the Jews) had mentioned this to Paul and Barnabas (missionaries to the Gentiles), they were referring to the poor believers in Jerusalem. While some Gentile converts were financially comfortable, certainly there were poor people too. Many of the problems in these churches, confronted by Paul in his letters to them, had to do with fair treatment of rich and poor, and concern that the rich care for the poor among them. In contrast to the general conditions among the Mediterranean churches stood the Jerusalem church that had abject poverty. Besides the effects of a severe famine (see Acts 11:28), there were a series of famines between A.D. 30 and 50 that made food prices rise. Palestine was a poor country, and Jerusalem was an overcrowded city filled with poor people. Add to this the fact that many of the early converts were immediately disowned by their families and became instantly destitute. Thus the bulk of the Jerusalem church was made up of people already in the cycle of poverty.

CALLED TO CARE
Caring for the poor is a constant theme in Scripture.
- Jesus is anointed to preach good news to the poor. (Luke 4:18)
- Jesus said the poor are blessed, for theirs is the kingdom of
- heaven. (Luke 6:20)
- Jesus describes a banquet scene to show the future deliverance of the poor. In it, he is Lord, and the poor are invited to enjoy the banquet. (Luke 14:13-21)
- Jesus told his disciples to sell their possessions and give to the poor. (Luke 12:33)
- Jesus taught that caring for the poor was essential for right living. (Mark 14:7)
    Often we do nothing, however, because we are caught up in meeting our own needs and desires. Perhaps we don't see enough poverty to remember the needs of the poor. The world is filled with poor people, here and in other countries.
    Individuals as well as churches can become aware of specific needs in their area. A giving and missions philosophy should address the question, How are we caring for the poor?

Paul assured them that this *very thing* he *was eager to do*. If this was the famine relief visit, that "very thing" (delivering a gift from a Gentile church to the Jerusalem church) had prompted this visit (Acts 11:27-30), and thus Paul's tone here might be a bit indignant or perhaps amused. Whether Paul "had been" eager or "would be" eager is unclear from the Greek. In any case, Paul never forgot this understanding. He continued to be eager to help the poor believers in Jerusalem. On his missionary journeys (especially the third journey), Paul gathered funds to help the poor Jewish believers in Jerusalem (see Acts 24:17; Romans 15:25-28; 1 Corinthians 16:1-4; 2 Corinthians 8–9).

PAUL PUBLICLY OPPOSED PETER / 2:11-21

With the speed of a remote control switch, the scene changed as Paul began to explain another time when his authority as an apostle had been confirmed. The setting switched from Jerusalem (2:1-10) to Antioch, a Gentile city familiar to the Galatians (2:11-21). In Antioch, Paul had faced another conflict over his authority. At that time, however, he openly opposed the actions of the apostle Peter himself.

The atmosphere must have been electric. Peter had arrived in Antioch and had been warmly welcomed by the church. He, Paul, Barnabas, and the rest of the leadership fellowshiped, taught, and ate together regularly. Though not described in detail, the days must have been eventful and exciting. Then a delegation arrived from Jerusalem, and almost immediately Peter's treatment of the Gentile Christians changed. He kept his distance from them. He began to treat them, in fact, just the same as the Judaizers had treated them, insisting that fellowship was not possible with Gentile Christians until those Gentiles had also converted to Jewish practices. The implied rejection must have stung the Gentile believers in Antioch.

Others, including Barnabas, followed Peter's example. But Paul leaped into the breach with a ringing confrontation. He challenged the inconsistency, even though it was endorsed by a leading apostle. He voiced the uncompromising position that neither he nor Peter were free to set aside the gospel for fear of what others might think. Acceptance of an individual by Jesus makes that person acceptable to every other Christian, without condition. Our allegiance to Christ transcends all other allegiances.

2:11 **When Peter came to Antioch, I opposed him to his face, because he was clearly in the wrong.**NIV This *Antioch* was in Syria (as distinguished from Antioch in Pisidia). Antioch was a major trade center in the ancient world. Heavily populated by Greeks, it eventually became a strong Christian center. In Antioch the believers were first called Christians (Acts 11:26). Antioch in Syria became the headquarters for the Gentile church and was Paul's base of operations.

When *Peter* made this trip to Antioch is uncertain; there is no reference to it in the book of Acts. It may have occurred soon after Paul, Barnabas, and Titus had returned to Antioch from Jerusalem after delivering the famine relief. Perhaps Peter wanted to see for himself the ministry taking place in Antioch. Paul's narrative style does not require this event to be in chronological order with Paul's visit to Jerusalem recorded in previous verses, but it is the most likely conclusion.

In any case, Paul *opposed him to his face.* Paul began his account with the climax of the event. In verses 1-10 Paul had illustrated his unity and cooperation with the other apostles. This one begins with a claim that he was even willing to challenge another apostle. Why he did so is recorded in following verses. Clearly, Paul had already had a great deal of practical experience in applying his theology when it came to dealings with the Gentiles. But Peter's actions were *clearly in the wrong (kategnosmenos en,* "he was condemned"), and Paul, an apostle with the right to speak with authority, had to confront Peter. The event involved an emotional, face-to-face showdown. Peter was caught in a glaring inconsistency that might have gone tragically unresolved if not for Paul's boldness. He always focused on the purity of the gospel truth; whenever it was threatened, Paul acted. The results were dramatic.

CONFRONTATION

All conflicts are not the same. Paul's confrontation of Peter is not meant to be a model for every disagreement in the church. A layperson, questioning a point in the pastor's sermon, probably should not "oppose him to his face" publicly! Conflicts may be similar in emotion and damage caused, but the issues vary greatly in their importance. Churches, families, and friendships can be shattered over trivial matters. Often a simple church decorating or furnishing idea has nearly led to a church split. Such conflicts occur all too often, to the shame of the gospel.

At times, confrontation must take place. The issues ought to be clear and compelling. We must seek to preserve the unity of the body of Christ and faithfulness to God's Word. Whether the issue is a minor disagreement over taste or a major crisis regarding the truth, love must be communicated to all involved.

This instance may be another reason for Paul's usage of seemingly disparaging remarks about the church leaders in 2:2, 6, and 9 (see discussion on 2:9). Although the apostles were to be held in high authority, they were still humans, capable of mistakes, errors in judgment, even hypocrisy. No Christian leader should ever be above correction. No person, no matter what he achieves or how long he serves, should be exempt from rebuke and guidance. We need accountability as much today as it was needed in Paul's day. Paul was not trying to lower their position; he was pointing out to the Judaizers that they were wrong to refuse anyone else (namely himself) the position of apostle. The story itself indicates that their teaching also was incorrect.

2:12 **Before certain men came from James, he used to eat with the Gentiles.**^{NIV} When Peter arrived in Antioch, he saw that Jewish and Gentile Christians enjoyed fellowship at mealtimes without concern over Jewish dietary laws. His setting aside long-established taboos against Jews sharing board and room with Gentiles showed nothing less than his acceptance of freedom in Christ. Peter accepted these practices; he himself had received a vision from God (actually one vision and two instant replays) about food laws and Gentiles in the new world of the gospel. Indeed, Peter had been the first to receive the understanding about God's acceptance of the Gentiles, and he was the first to preach to Gentiles. Acts 10 records Peter's vision of a large sheet falling to the earth, filled with all kinds of animals, reptiles, and birds—many of them on the Jewish forbidden food list. "Then a voice told him, 'Get up, Peter. Kill and eat.' 'Surely not, Lord!' Peter replied. 'I have never eaten anything impure or unclean.' The voice spoke to him a second time, 'Do not call anything impure that God has made clean'" (Acts 10:13-15 NIV).

> The fear of others lays a snare, but one who trusts in the LORD is secure.
>
> *King Solomon*
> *(Proverbs 29:25)*

Peter understood from this vision that he should not look upon the Gentiles as inferior people whom God would not redeem. After Peter had this vision, a Gentile Roman officer named Cornelius asked him to come and share the gospel message with him and his household. Peter did so, without the hesitation he would have felt before the vision, and Cornelius and his household became believers. The Holy Spirit came upon them, they were baptized, and "they asked Peter to stay with them for a few days" (Acts 10:48 NIV). Peter knew firsthand about fellowship with Gentile believers. While he stayed with Cornelius and his family, Peter probably did not adhere to the strict Jewish dietary laws—it would have been difficult and may have insulted these new believers who were his gracious hosts.

Thus, when Peter arrived in Antioch, he already knew that God had broken down the barriers between Jews and Gentiles, and he understood the true meaning of Christian freedom. So he would gladly *eat with the Gentiles.* The imperfect tense of the verb indicates that this was not one occasion but a repeated pattern, meaning that Peter joined with the other Jews in eating with their Gentile brothers and sisters in Christ on a regu-

> How difficult it is to avoid having a special standard for oneself!
>
> *C. S. Lewis*

lar basis. This pattern undoubtedly went beyond sharing common meals and included taking the Lord's Supper together.

But all that was *before certain men came from James.* These men were the legalists, members of "the circumcision group" (see below), and most likely *not* sent by James. The wording here means they came "from James's group," that is, from the Jerusalem church. James, as leader of the Jerusalem church, had a vast range of people to deal with, and these men were part of the legalistic group of his church (almost every modern-day church has its own group of these!). Among the entourage from Jerusalem, there must have been "certain men" who frowned on fraternizing with Gentiles. These may have been rigid and legalistic Jewish Christians, but they were probably associated with the same "false brothers" that had disrupted Paul's visit to Jerusalem.

Though this group probably tried to trade on James's authority, he later firmly denied sending them. In the letter sent back to the Gentile Christians in Antioch after the Jerusalem council, James wrote, "We have heard that some went out from us without our authorization and disturbed you, troubling your minds by what they said" (Acts 15:24 NIV).

But when they arrived, he began to draw back and separate himself from the Gentiles because he was afraid of those who belonged to the circumcision group.NIV Apparently, the mere appearance of this group caught Peter by surprise. When these legalists arrived, they may have expressed shock at Peter's conduct. Peter surely knew these men, as they came from the Jerusalem church, and he was influenced by their presence to the point that *he began to draw back and separate himself from the Gentiles* with whom he had been eating and fellowshiping. The imperfect tense of the verbs indicates a gradual, awkward withdrawal.

Why was this action "clearly in the wrong" (2:11)? By his actions, Peter was implying that there really was a difference between Jewish and Gentile believers—a difference that could not be bridged. The notion that the body of Christ had to be divided between Jews and Gentiles was nothing other than heresy. Peter was being hypocritical. Perhaps he was motivated by the desire to keep peace between the legalists and the law-free gospel group. Peter's error was that he gave in to them. Peter must have known that he had gone against God's revelation. By the very nature of Peter's stature as an apostle, his actions confused and hurt other believers—thus Paul's strong face-to-face opposition to Peter's actions.

FEAR OF FAILURE
Paul identified fear as the motivation behind Peter's erratic behavior in Antioch. Peter's intentions may have been honest or merely confused, but his actions had undermined the gospel. Peer pressure led him to compromise his convictions; in so doing, he compromised the gospel itself (see 2:14). Because personal blunders were such a part of Peter's past, this was probably in some way a response to the fear of making another mistake. Because, in this case, Peter had acted in response to fear, the actions were ill-chosen. How often do we fall into the same trap in order to be accepted by others? Although we recognize that fears of various kinds will usually affect our emotions, we should always base our actions on what God wants rather than the negative motivation of fear of rejection.

What did the *circumcision group* say to Peter to cause him to change his actions for a brief time? One explanation suggests that they may have argued that Peter was encouraging the Jewish believers to disregard their heritage and its laws. They may have played on Peter's emotions; after all, he too was a Jew. It is likely that Peter tried to keep peace by his actions—not wanting to offend these legalistic Christians. After they left, he would resume his fellowship as before. But this sort of playacting was unacceptable to Paul. That was too high a price to pay for peace.

Another explanation points to Peter's pattern of not handling surprises very well. Caught unawares, he tended to overreact (as when he hacked the servant's ear off in John 18:10 or when he denied knowing Jesus in Luke 22:54-62). Circumstances arose in Antioch that he had not faced previously. Up until then, his dealings with Gentile Christians had been totally separate from his dealings with fellow Jewish Christians. Peter was alone with Cornelius and on his own in Antioch, both situations dominated by Gentile Christians. But with the arrivals from Jerusalem, he was suddenly faced with a diversity of extremes. His immediate action was unwise and required Paul's intervention.

But then the question arises, why was someone of Peter's stature *afraid of those who belonged* to this group in the Jerusalem church? That question probably cannot be answered any more than we could answer why he denied Jesus. At times, Peter would act courageously: when he gave the incredible

speech at Pentecost (Acts 2:14-41);
when he and John stood before the
Sanhedrin and refused to follow the
command to stop preaching the gospel (Acts 4:1-20); when he had to
defend to the other apostles his own

> If War is ever lawful, then
> peace is sometimes
> sinful.
>
> *C. S. Lewis*

actions after his visit to Cornelius's home (Acts 11:1-18). Yet
at times, he would seem very weak. How human Peter was!
We should be thankful that Scripture records for us the courage and failings of so many of God's people. Many times we
also find ourselves amazed at our courage in some circumstances and then embarrassed by our weakness in others. Peter
demonstrated the conflict between Spirit and flesh (sinful
human nature) that Paul would discuss in 5:13-26. When Peter
was motivated and led by the Holy Spirit, he was wise and
courageous. When he gave in to the influence of his human
nature, he was fearful, ambivalent, and hypocritical. Everyone
makes mistakes, so we must live each day in close communication with God and under the control of the Holy Spirit.

DON'TS AND DOS

Goal setting and decision making based on "what we *don't*
want to do" rather than "what we want to do" will result in poor
choices. "What we don't want to do" responds to pressure and
tends to avoid discomfort and inconvenience; "what we want to
do" responds to values and convictions. In attempting to avoid
an uncomfortable problem, Peter almost undermined his own
convictions. His instinctive solution to the local conflict over
Jewish/Gentile relations in the church would have opened a
wound in the church that might have never been healed.

Our freedom in Christ must lead us to positive goal setting
and behavior reflecting God's truth. Following Jesus rarely
involves a convenient or comfortable way. In fact, to use
Christ's own words, the way will be narrow and straight. Our
single-minded pursuit of "what we want to do" for Christ will put
most of "what we don't want to do" in its proper place.

**2:13 And the other Jews joined him in this hypocrisy, so that even
Barnabas was led astray by their hypocrisy.**NRSV As Peter acted
on his fear, the other Jews, meaning those not already committed
to the policy of separation, went along with his *hypocrisy.* They,
too, gradually stopped joining with the Gentiles in eating and fellowshiping. These "other Jews" were the Jewish believers who
lived in Antioch and were members of the church there. In that
setting, they were most likely in the minority.

CLOSELY WATCHED
Christians don't live as isolated individuals. Their actions and attitudes affect other Christians. The way Christians treat each other has a particularly strong attractive or repelling effect on outsiders. Jesus said that the world would recognize his disciples by their love for one another (John 13:35). Leaders should be especially careful to be good examples because others may stand or fall because of them.

Paul mentioned *Barnabas* separately, probably because Paul was especially surprised that Barnabas would be *led astray by their hypocrisy*. Barnabas was Paul's traveling companion; together they preached the gospel to the Gentiles, proclaiming Jews' and Gentiles' oneness with Christ. Barnabas was not from the Jerusalem church and would not have had the personal and relational stake in this that Peter had. And Barnabas should have known better (in reality, so should Peter have known better). Yet, like Peter, Barnabas was human, and for some unknown reason he followed Peter's example.

Paul boldly told the truth—this was sheer "hypocrisy." A hypocrite says one thing but does another. Peter, Barnabas, and the Jewish believers knew that God accepted everyone equally, that salvation was available to all, that there should be no separation in the body of Christ. Yet their actions implied just the opposite. If Paul had opted for peace and allowed these actions to go unrebuked, the Christian church would have divided into two distinct groups going their separate ways. But this was not God's plan, nor was it consistent with "the truth of the gospel," as Paul would explain in the next verse.

FACE-TO-FACE
Although Peter was a leader of the church, he was acting like a hypocrite. He knew better, yet he was driven by fear of what the legalistic Christians from his home church would think. Paul knew that he had to confront Peter before his actions damaged the church. At stake were, not only conditions in Antioch, but the future of the gospel in the Gentile world. So Paul publicly opposed Peter. Note, however, that Paul did not go to the other leaders, nor did he write letters to the churches telling them not to follow Peter's example. Instead, he opposed Peter face-to-face. Sometimes sincere Christians, even Christian leaders, make mistakes. And it may take other sincere Christians to get them back on track. If you are convinced that someone is doing harm to himself/herself or the church, try the direct approach. There is no place for back stabbing in the body of Christ.

2:14 But when I saw that they were not acting consistently with the truth of the gospel.^{NRSV} This was the crux of the matter— *they* (Peter, Barnabas, and the Jewish believers there in Antioch) were not behaving *consistently* (*orthopodousin*—walking correctly, being straightforward, acting rightly) with the truth. In other words, their application was in error; their orthodoxy was not leading to orthopraxy. Paul had heard one thing, but then he saw just the opposite!

Paul's agitation was over the *truth of the gospel.* This truth was that Jesus Christ had died and had risen again to offer salvation to all people—Jews and Gentiles alike. Both groups are equally acceptable to God; thus, they must be equally acceptable to each other. Jewish believers separating themselves implied that they were superior because of their race, traditions, or law keeping. The gospel clearly shows, however, that people do not become accepted by God for anything they do but only by God's grace.

Paul was not interested in a power play. He did not oppose Peter in order to elevate himself. Paul recounted this story in this letter to the Galatians to show that he was a full apostle and could speak authoritatively, even in opposition to another apostle if the truth of the gospel were at stake, as was the case at that time. This was not a secondary issue blown out of proportion. The confrontation fit the crisis.

JUST DO IT!
Actions usually speak more loudly than mere words. The goal, of course, must be to have agreement between the way we live and what we say. Hypocrisy exists when what we say professes more than how we live. Paul gave Timothy some effective counsel in this area in 1 Timothy 4:15-16. The following questions can help us avoid hypocrisy:

- Am I participating in behaviors that I know Scripture does not condone?
- What parts of my life would I not want my children to imitate?
- What specific commands in Scripture have I not applied to my life thus far? Why am I refusing to consider their truth?
- Has God given me responsibilities that I have been ignoring?

The recognition and acceptance of God's help often comes when we finally see our own shortcomings.

I said to Peter in front of them all, "You are a Jew, yet you live like a Gentile and not like a Jew. How is it, then, that you force Gentiles to follow Jewish customs?"^{NIV} Paul spoke to Peter publicly, *in front of them all*—that is, in front of the Jewish believers, the Gentile believers, the circumcision group, and Barnabas. Those who want to attribute other motives to Paul might ask why he didn't go to Peter privately. Wouldn't that have been more "peace loving"? more "Christian"? But Peter's actions had started a domino effect; and, because of his authority as an apostle, his actions had confused the believers. A private solution to this problem was not an option. Peter's action was public, with public consequences; thus the rebuke had to be public.

Was Paul acting inconsistently and unbiblically with his treatment of Peter? Some who attack the way Paul handled the issue back up their case by using Galatians 6:1, where Paul urges gentle restoration in dealing with conflict. They raise the possibility that Paul was violating Jesus' teaching in Matthew 18:15-17 regarding the private handling of conflict. They also use 1 Corinthians 9:19-23, where Paul treated people in different ways at different times.

The Bible doesn't say whether or not Paul met with Peter privately; perhaps he did. Paul also wrote, "Those who sin are to be rebuked publicly, so that the others may take warning" (1 Timothy 5:20 NIV). Paul's public confrontation was respectful, forthright, and honest. As a leader of the Jerusalem church, Peter was setting public policy.

CONVICTIONS AND COMPROMISE
The Judaizers accused Paul of watering down the gospel to make it easier for Gentiles to accept, while Paul accused the Judaizers of nullifying the truth of the gospel by adding conditions to it. The basis of salvation was the issue: Is salvation through Christ alone, or does it come through Christ *and* adherence to the law? The argument came to a climax when Peter, Paul, the Judaizers, and some Gentile Christians all gathered together in Antioch to share a meal. Peter probably thought that by staying away from the Gentiles, he was promoting harmony—he did not want to offend the Jewish Christians. Paul charged that Peter's action violated the gospel. By joining the Judaizers, Peter implicitly was supporting their claim that Christ was not sufficient for salvation. Compromise is an important element in getting along with others, but we should never compromise the truth of God's Word. If we feel we have to change our Christian beliefs to match those of our companions, we are on dangerous ground.

Paul recorded his exact words here. Obviously, everyone knew Peter's Jewish background; Paul's wording indicates they also knew that Peter had set aside Jewish rituals and ceremonial laws (especially the food laws that made fellowship between Jews and

Gentiles almost impossible) because of his freedom in Christ, thus living *like a Gentile and not like a Jew.* Certainly the visions Peter had seen and his experience with Cornelius had cured him of any prejudice against Gentiles (see Acts 10).

Paul's actual guidelines for situations like the one in Antioch (see 1 Corinthians 8:1-13; 10:23-33) flowed from the proper role of host and visitor in various cultural contexts. When in someone else's home, a Christian was free to find common ground with that family by accepting their hospitality and food without question. The key to guidance was in keeping the "weaker brother" in mind. Neither Peter nor the Judaizers were in that category in Antioch. In this case, the "weaker brothers and sisters" were being abused.

But how could Paul say that Peter wanted to *force Gentiles to follow Jewish customs?* By siding with the Judaizers who were visiting Antioch, Peter was playing into their hands, appearing as if he agreed with them and actually supported their insistence that Gentiles should follow Jewish customs. By separating himself from the Gentiles, Peter was supporting the Judaizers' claim that Jews still were better than Gentiles.

Alongside the theological problems that Peter's actions caused, a practical question must have surfaced. While Peter's change in policy about having meals with Gentiles was harmful, the change in the policy for the Lord's Supper must have been disastrous. If this group was divided over the sharing of common meals, it is inconceivable that they would be able to assemble together for the Lord's Supper. Without Paul's immediate and forceful intervention, the church in Antioch might have been crippled and destroyed.

Some commentators struggle over where Paul ends his actual self-quotation in the confrontation with Peter. The NIV text ends Paul's speech to Peter with closing quotes at the end of verse 21, making his words fill a couple of paragraphs; the NRSV text puts the closing quotes at the end of verse 14. Based on tone alone, the exact exchange probably ended with Paul's direct question to Peter. What follows summarizes the reasons behind Paul's insistence on consistency. In any case, Paul moves away from the confrontation with Peter and on to a magnificent sketch of the gospel and then back to his concern over the Galatians themselves in chapter 3.

2:15 We ourselves are Jews by birth and not Gentile sinners.NRSV Both Paul and Peter were *Jews by birth,* as were, obviously, all the Jewish Christians. Yet being Jews by birth was not enough for salvation. Paul's phrase *Gentile sinners* was said ironically because this was the scornful name Jews applied to Gentiles. Peter's actions had conveyed some sort of "holier than thou" attitude in line with the teaching that Gentiles were still "sinners" unless they became Jewish. But both Peter and Paul knew better.

2:16 **Yet we know that a person is justified not by the works of the law but through faith in Jesus Christ.**NRSV All people stand as condemned sinners before God: God-fearing, law-keeping Jews, and "Gentile sinners" alike. But all have hope in the same source: *through faith in Jesus Christ.* Paul was speaking from within the context of his Jewish upbringing. He contended with his compatriots that their traditions did not solve the problem of sin. Paul's appeal is similar to Jesus' confrontations with the Pharisees and teachers of the law. Jesus said, "Woe to you experts in the law, because you have taken away the key to knowledge. You yourselves have not entered, and you have hindered those who were entering" (Luke 11:52 NIV).

> Yes, pride is a perpetual nagging temptation. Keep on knocking it on the head, but don't be too worried about it. As long as one knows one is proud one is safe from the worst form of pride.
>
> *C. S. Lewis*

In this verse, three profoundly significant terms occur for the first time in this letter: (1) *justified* (*dikaioo,* in three forms); (2) *works of the law* (*ergon nomou*); and (3) *faith in [of] Christ Jesus* (*pisteos Iesou Christou*).

First, let's look at the word *justified*. In a single word it represents the effect upon us of what Jesus accomplished on the cross. There are two views to interpret its meaning. One view, generally represented in Roman Catholic theology, takes *justified* to mean that people's past sins have been wiped out so that they have been "made righteous" in and of themselves. This approach emphasizes the ethical aspects of a person's relationship to a holy God. It moves from acquittal of past sins to ethical renewal and moral uprightness in the present; final and complete righteousness is not conferred until the last judgment.

The other view, held by many Protestants, takes *justified* as a legal word, literally meaning "to declare righteous" (the opposite being "to condemn"). To use a familiar but helpful explanation, the person who is justified can claim that his condition before God is "just as if I'd never sinned." This view emphasizes the status conferred or relational aspect of God's dealing with us. The reality of past sin, the potential to sin in the present, and the ongoing need for repentance tend to give this view of justification a more intimate and personal sense than the first, which tends to be formal and structured.

When defining theological positions, sometimes alternative views simply emphasize different aspects of a single reality. Recently, scholars show that Paul had in mind both the ethical renewal and the new standing in Christ. One benefit of the first view is that it provides the believers a solid, ethical view of the transaction between themselves and God. But this needs to be held alongside the equally important and probably more foundational understanding of a personal, ongoing relationship with Christ.

Justification, as used in Scripture, always begins with God alone, acting in grace. God justifies people despite their guilt, pardons them, and then makes them his children and heirs.

To be declared righteous could never happen as a result of the *works of* (or by obeying) *the law*—the second term Paul introduced here to the Galatians. The law to which he was referring could mean Jewish Scripture, plus the laws added by the Pharisees. If that were the case, the books of Genesis through Deuteronomy and constant interpretations by the Pharisees would be all that was needed for salvation. The possibility of self-achieved righteousness would mean that Christ did not have to die. But, the *law* could also have a more general meaning—the idea that just by being good and doing good works a person can be justified. While this passage does not conclusively teach how Paul felt about the law itself, there is little doubt about the effectiveness of the "works of the law" *(ergon nomou).* Paul directs the force of his argument toward those who would mistakenly hope to "work" or observe the law in order to merit or earn God's approval. Jesus said, "I have not come to call the righteous, but sinners" (Matthew 9:13 NIV). Those who were righteous in their own eyes did not think they needed Christ; those who saw their true status as sinners could find their hope in him.

Paul, Peter, and the Jewish believers obviously knew this; otherwise, they would not have converted to Christianity. They understood that trying to follow and obey all of God's laws (let alone all the laws the Pharisees heaped on them) could not give salvation. This came "through faith in Jesus Christ" alone. "Faith" is a personal act of commitment; it means believing and accepting that Jesus came, died on the cross to take the punishment our sins deserved, and rose again. This faith opens the way to a relationship with God the Father, and the promise of eternity with him.

LAW AND ORDER
If observing the Jewish laws cannot justify us, why should we still obey the Ten Commandments and other Old Testament laws? We know that Paul was not condemning the law, because in other letters he wrote: "the law is holy" (Romans 7:12 NKJV); "the law is spiritual" (Romans 7:14 NKJV); "the law is good if one uses it properly" (1 Timothy 1:8 NIV). Instead, he was saying that the law can never make us acceptable to God. The law still has an important role to play in the life of a Christian. The law

- reveals God's nature and moral goodness;
- guards us from sin by giving us standards for behavior;
- convicts us of sin, leaving us the opportunity to ask for God's forgiveness; and
- drives us to trust in the sufficiency of Christ because we can never keep the Ten Commandments perfectly.

The law cannot possibly save us. But after we have become Christians, it can guide us to live as God requires.

So we, too, have put our faith in Christ Jesus that we may be justified by faith in Christ and not by observing the law, because by observing the law no one will be justified.NIV The third phrase introduced in this verse by Paul is *faith in [of] Christ (pisteos Christou),* which he used twice (the earlier one being *pisteos Iesou Christou*). The phrase *pisteos Iesou Christou* occurs seven times in the New Testament: twice in 2:16, and once in 3:22; Romans 3:22, 26; Ephesians 3:12; and Philippians 3:9. Scholars differ over an issue of Greek grammar. If "faith in Jesus Christ" is an objective genitive, then it means faith *in* Jesus Christ. If "faith in Jesus Christ" is a subjective genitive, then it means the faith or faithfulness *of* Jesus Christ. The Old Testament word for "faith" is a Hebrew term *emuna,* which can mean either the faithfulness of God or a person's response. If Paul merely substituted *emuna* for *pisteos,* then the evidence would point toward interpreting this phrase as "the faithfulness of Christ that saves us."

The "faith in Christ Jesus" phrase that begins this part of the verse actually translates *eis Christon Iesoun episteusamen* ("in Christ Jesus we have believed"). While all three phrases have often been translated as if they were the same, they clearly are not. The first and last phrases, while difficult to understand, probably describe the *operation* of justification, leading to a suggested translation of "Christ-faith" or "faithfulness of Christ" or even "Christ-centered faith." Meanwhile, the center one of the three phrases describes the *application* of faith on the part of those who allow themselves to be justified by faith. The ambiguity maintains the truth that faith must be exercised but does not "save us." Rather, it is Christ who faithfully applies to us what he provided at the Cross, our justification.

The significance of the different viewpoints can be brought out in this example. Two rock climbers are working together. One person falls and will die if he is not rescued. The top climber drops a rope to save him. The bottom climber responds and grasps the rope. How was he saved? Did his grasp save him, or did the faithful work of his rescuer save him? We are not the source of our salvation. No matter how strong the rope, if you don't grab it, you're dead. No matter how strong your grasp, if there is no rope, you cannot be saved.

Because Paul expected his readers to agree with the "we know" that begins this verse, he could then conclude that *we* have exercised our faith so that the way is now open that *we* might be justified by faith. Whether Paul was still recalling his speech to the group at Antioch, or if he was addressing the Galatians, the truth of this statement remains. Believers today are also part of the "we." Because we believed, because we *put our faith in Christ Jesus,* we have rejected the idea that human endeavor or *observing the law* can make anyone acceptable to God. We have understood that we are *justified by faith*; thus, we know that keeping all the Old Testament laws and trying to do good works could not, cannot, and will not save us.

NO SUBSTITUTE
By studying the Old Testament Scriptures, Paul realized that he could not be saved by obeying God's laws. The prophets knew that God's plan of salvation did not rest on keeping the law. Because all people are sinners, we cannot keep God's laws perfectly. Fortunately, God has provided a way of salvation that depends on Jesus Christ and not on our own efforts. Even though we know this truth, we must guard against using service, good deeds, charitable giving, or any other effort as a substitute for faith.

Paul appealed to the Jewish Scriptures to emphasize his point, for his words echo Psalm 143:2, "Do not bring your servant into judgment, for no one living is righteous before you" (NIV). No one is righteous, nor can they become righteous by doing good deeds and by obeying the law. This was not a new idea, certainly not one created by Paul. The doctrine of justification by faith goes back to Abraham who, "believed the LORD, and [God] credited it to him as righteousness" (Genesis 15:6 NIV).

2:17 If, while we seek to be justified in Christ, it becomes evident that we ourselves are sinners, does that mean that Christ promotes sin? Absolutely not!^{NIV} Because most of Paul's letters were dictated, sometimes one idea springboards to a related point or answers a foreseen, potential problem. In this verse, Paul responds to one objection that might be raised by his opponents. They might say, "How could Paul claim that justification by faith is effective when Christians still sin?" Or, "If you have invalidated the importance of living by the law, how will you escape the charge that you are promoting sinful living? Doesn't that make Christ the founder of an ineffective system (or less effective than the law), and shouldn't the law be added for justification?"

Paul moved directly to his answer. *If we* refers to Jewish believers; the word for *sinners* in the Greek is the same word used in the phrase "Gentile sinners" in 2:15. The NEB translates the first part of the verse, "We ourselves no less than the Gentiles turn out to be sinners." Paul was answering an objection to his message, an objection that would probably be leveled against him by the Judaizers among the Galatians. They claimed that to say the law doesn't matter is to say that standards and morality don't matter. This leaves the door open for people to become believers and then live any way they choose. The freedom that the Gentiles had led them to break some of the legal restrictions and thus, in the eyes of the Judaizers, to "sin."

Of course, Paul did not mean that. If Jewish believers became *justified in Christ,* gained freedom from the law, and then committed a sin, *does that mean that Christ promotes sin?*

Paul's reply is vehement: *Absolutely not!* Sin does not result because people are justified; therefore, Christ is not responsible for promoting sin. Obviously those who have been justified—Christians—can and do sin, for that, unfortunately, is part of our human nature (Paul details his own struggle with sin in Romans 7). But the sin led to the need for justification, not the other way around. The Judaizers saw justification as a "theological" excuse to get out from under Jewish law (that is, changing from Jew to Christian). But Paul (and the Jewish Christians who had experienced justification) knew that while offering freedom from the restrictive law, justification by faith demanded lifestyle and behavioral changes. When God truly gets hold of a life, nothing can remain the same. "Therefore, if anyone is in Christ, he is a new creation; the old has gone, the new has come!" (2 Corinthians 5:17 NIV). At the end of this letter, Paul wrote, "Neither circumcision nor uncircumcision means anything; what counts is a new creation" (Galatians 6:15 NIV). Grace does not abolish the law with its standards and morality; rather, it moves it from an external standard impossible to keep to an inner motivation for living a pure and God-honoring life.

Paul appealed to the Galatian's knowledge that having the law and trying to obey it had not brought assurance of justification. The legalists were doomed to failure, handicapped by human tendency to sin even when they knew better. But the group that Paul was confronting added a twist to the problem. If they agreed with Paul about their inability to be justified by the works of the law, then why did the law remain so important? Because having the law was a label of status and significance. Possession of God's own laws was a matter of great pride. Even if the laws were not obeyed, they were revered.

But Paul could see that the gospel was the way of freedom from the slavery of legalism on the one hand and the pride of ownership on the other. We are still faced with the challenge of following Jesus between these two errors—becoming bound to a set of rules or becoming proud over our spiritual status. Liberation in Christ bears the sign of humility.

2:18 If I rebuild what I destroyed, I prove that I am a lawbreaker.NIV Justification by faith *destroyed* the Jewish "merit system" with all its laws and good deeds that attempted to rack up points with God. To *rebuild* that, to be justified by faith and then return to that legal system as a basis for one's relationship with God, would erroneously imply that Christ's death was not sufficient. The truth, however, is that it was not necessary for the Gentiles to place themselves under the law in order to discover that the law could not add to their justification. Paul saw the situation in Antioch with Peter as a clear illustration of the unnecessary burden that some wanted to place on Gentile believers. Peter, through his act of pulling away from the Gentile fellowship, was giving law a place of authority that it no longer held.

Justified people will sin, but they are moving onward and upward. The real sinner is the one who is justified and then returns to the law. Ironically, that person is actually a *lawbreaker.* People under the law are more precisely described as lawbreakers than as law-keepers! The law cannot give salvation because no one can keep it perfectly. The best the law can do is *prove* our sinfulness and how much we need the Savior and his gracious offer of justification by faith.

2:19 For through the law I died to the law so that I might live for God.NIV Paul changed his wording from "we" to *I* here, relying

again on his personal experience. His phrase *through the law*
embodies much of what he would write regarding the law's purpose several years later in his letter to
the Romans. The law itself could not
save because no one can keep its perfect standards. The law thus cannot give
eternal life; instead, it offers only failure and death. So what is its usefulness? The law was a necessary
instrument to show people the ultimate
futility of trying to live up to God's standard on their own. But
that very hopelessness created by the law can have a positive
impact if it leads a person to the true hope, Christ himself. Christ
took upon himself that death penalty—the death we deserved for
being lawbreakers. His action freed us from the jurisdiction of
Moses' law. When Paul understood that the law was completely
incapable of giving salvation, and when he embraced the one
who could give salvation, he knew he could never go back to the
law. Paul felt this so intensely that he expressed it in terms of
death, *I died to the law.* Paul went from a law-centered life to a
Christ-centered life.

> The law's purpose was to work itself out of a job and point us beyond itself to a fuller relationship with God.
> *Richard Longnecker*

Years previously, Paul had been at the height of his determined
service of the law when Christ had interrupted his life on the road
to Damascus. His efforts were weighed and found lacking. Seeking to pursue "spiritual justice," in reality he had been persecuting God's Son. "Death" may well have been the most appropriate
description Paul could choose to capture the effect of that encounter. But it was a death that opened the way for new and real life!

Paul knew he had to die to the law before he could *live for
God.* There can be no middle ground. It makes no sense to accept
salvation by faith and then work for it, just as it makes no sense
to accept a gift and then offer the giver money for it. We must
deny that our own efforts can accomplish anything in order to be
able to humbly accept the gift that Christ offers. By identifying
with Christ, we can experience freedom from the law that he pro-
cured for us by dying on our behalf.

Some scholars think the next phrase should actually be
attached to this verse in order to round off Paul's thought, rather
than place it at the beginning of verse 20. Thus Paul would have
been saying, "In order that I might live for God I have been crucified with Christ." This parallels other passages such as 2 Timothy
2:11, "If we died with him, we will also live with him" (NIV).

**2:20 I have been crucified with Christ; it is no longer I who live, but
Christ lives in me; and the life which I now live in the flesh I**

live by faith in the Son of God, who loved me and gave Himself for me.NKJV In several short phrases the apostle captured the breathless wonder believers experience as the realization dawns that we are no longer living "our" lives, but have surrendered to the author of life, who now lives his life in and through us.

Paul continued his thought from verse 19. The perfect tense of the verbs indicates something that happened in the past but influences the present. Paul "died to the law" by being *crucified with Christ.* Christ completely fulfilled the law (past tense); this act influenced Paul in the present (who, as an imperfect human, could not keep the law). Yet because of Christ's death, the law no longer had a hold on either of them. What profound relief Paul must have felt! He no longer needed to fear that, after spending his entire life studying and trying to keep the law, somehow he might still miss God. The Cross of Christ shows that although the law had to be kept, it was fulfilled by a perfect human. Christ paid sin's penalty for imperfect humans.

Being crucified with Christ refers to the conversion experience, a once-for-all transaction that has ongoing results. We do not have to be crucified with Christ again each day. As Christians, we must daily take up our cross to follow him, but this refers to the responsibilities of discipleship. We are required to daily withstand our sinful human desires. (This will be discussed in detail in 5:16-25.)

Scholars have looked at Paul's phrase "I have been crucified with Christ" in different ways. This could mean that

- all believers participate in the benefits of Christ's death and resurrection;
- all believers experience death and new life because Christ did so on their behalf;
- all believers will have experiences like those Christ endured (Romans 8:17; Philippians 3:10); or
- all believers actually participate in Christ's death and resurrection because of the mystical union that believers have with the Lord (see also Romans 6:4-8; Colossians 2:12-14, 20; 3:1-4).

This statement holds in its simplicity the incomprehensible depth of each believer's union with Christ. Each of the above suggestions actually emphasizes an aspect of the workings and benefits of Christ's death on our behalf. Our biggest danger is in trivializing Christ's death. Being a part of the "body of Christ" means more than just church membership. Union with Christ means that believers share his death, burial, and resurrection.

Believers are so united with Christ that Christ's experiences
become their experiences. Paul would later write to the Romans:

- *Don't you know that all of us who were baptized into Christ
  Jesus were baptized into his death? We were therefore buried
  with him through baptism into death in order that, just as
  Christ was raised from the dead through the glory of the
  Father, we too may live a new life. If we have been united with
  him like this in his death, we will certainly also be united with
  him in his resurrection. (Romans 6:3-5* NIV*)*

Paul claimed he had been "crucified," but he found himself
still alive. Paul had died with Christ, but it was his "old self" that
had died: *it is no longer I who live.* The self-centered, Jewish
Pharisee, Christian-persecuting, law-abiding, violent, and evil
Paul "no longer" lived. That person's sinful life had been crucified with Christ on the cross when Paul was saved. This is the "I"
of the flesh (see 5:13-24), of sinful human desires, of works and
pride. Paul was released, not only from the tyranny of the Mosaic
law, but also from the tyranny of self. Thus, this verse could read,
"I no longer live I myself" or "I no longer I the old self in the
flesh live."

Instead, Paul was a "new creation" (2 Corinthians 5:17)
because, he explained, *Christ lives in me.* In other words, Paul
had turned over his life to Christ. Each of the phrases is a crucial
aspect of the sequence of salvation: We relinquish our old life
and turn to Christ for his life. The self-centered self now becomes
the Christ-centered self. It is as if Paul was saying, "My old life,
my old goals and plans, even old relationships were nailed to the
cross with Christ. Now I have a new life because Christ came in
and filled the empty spaces all those old pursuits could not fill.
Now he lives in me and is the focus of my life." To accomplish
this, there must be a radical cleansing of our old selfish nature.
But there must also be a turning to the empowering of Christ.
Just as in repentance we turn away from sin and toward Christ,
we must turn from the self in the flesh to the self hidden in Christ.

Mystical? Yes. Difficult to understand? Certainly. True?
Beyond a doubt—ask any Christian. And that is precisely Paul's
point in the following section. Although mystical, this resurrection life is not beyond anyone's reach, for the key to living it is
by faith.

Paul no longer focused his life on trying to please God by
obeying laws; instead, with Christ in him, *the life which I now
live in the flesh I live by faith in the Son of God, who loved me*

and gave Himself for me. Believers' lives are still lived "in the flesh" (in their bodies prone to sin) while they remain on earth. But with Christ in charge, they are new creations, living life "by faith." This faith is not a one-shot deal—have faith, be saved, end of story. Rather, it is an attitude, a lifestyle. This new life is lived every day, every moment, through every situation "by faith." (For more on "gave Himself," see the notes on 1:4. See also Mark 10:45; Romans 5:6; and 1 John 4:10.)

What is the object of that faith? Our Lord Jesus Christ. We have faith in his act of loving us and giving himself (dying) for us. In other words, "Because he loved me and died for me, he can live in and through me."

DYING TO LIVE
How have we been crucified with Christ? *Legally,* God looks at us as if we had died with Christ. Because our sins died with him, we are no longer condemned (Colossians 2:13-15). *Relationally,* we have become one with Christ and identified ourselves with him, and his experiences are ours. Our Christian life began when, in unity with him, we died to our old life (see Romans 6:5-11). *In our daily life,* we must regularly crucify the sinful desires that keep us from following Christ. This too is a kind of dying with him (Luke 9:23-25).

And yet the focus of Christianity is, not dying, but living. Because we have been crucified with Christ, we have also been raised with him (Romans 6:5). *Legally,* we have been reconciled with God (2 Corinthians 5:19) and are free to grow into Christ's likeness (Romans 8:29). And *in our daily life,* we have Christ's resurrection power as we continue to fight sin (Ephesians 1:19-20). *Relationally,* we are no longer alone, for Christ lives in us—he is our power for living and our hope for the future (Colossians 1:27).

2:21 I do not set aside the grace of God, for if righteousness could be gained through the law, Christ died for nothing!^{NIV} Paul returned to his argument with the legalistic and "labelistic" false teachings begun in chapter 1. Paul's message of salvation by faith (without works of the law) did not *set aside the grace of God.* Instead, that is exactly what the Judaizers' teaching did—they "set aside" or "nullified" God's grace. For if people have to follow laws in order to earn their salvation—*if righteousness could be gained through the law*—then the logical conclusion is that *Christ died for nothing.* Christ did not need to die if we could have obtained salvation by obeying the law. However, it was because no one could obey God's law perfectly that Christ came to both obey it and then set it aside as a means to salvation. That was the ultimate picture of God's love and grace for sinful humanity. The basis of Christianity is God's grace and Christ's death for sin. Without these there is no faith, no gospel, and no hope of salvation.

LEGAL EAGLES
Believers today may still be in danger of acting as if Christ died for nothing. How? By replacing Jewish legalism with their own brand of Christian legalism, they are giving people extra laws to obey. By believing they can earn God's favor by what they do, they are not trusting completely in Christ's work on the cross. By struggling to appropriate God's power to change them (sanctification), they are not resting in God's power to save them (justification). If we could be saved by being good, then Christ did not have to die. But the Cross is the only way to salvation.

Galatians 3:1–4:7

With the heartfelt words affirming his personal commitment to the Galatians, Paul spoke of his ministry with his Galatian friends. He remembered how clearly he had shared the message and how openly they had responded. Since they had been launched so beautifully in the Christian faith, how could they have run aground so quickly? Paul was convinced that those who influenced the Galatians acted like friendly harbor pilots. They promised to guide the Galatians' faith by adding to their under-standing of Christ an "essential component" of the law. But, instead, these pilots put the Galatian ship of faith in great danger.

Paul used six rhetorical questions to present his arguments in this section:

1. Who has bewitched you?
2. Did you receive the Spirit by doing the works of the law or by believing what you heard?
3. Are you so foolish?
4. Are you now trying to attain your goal by human effort?
5. Have you suffered so many things in vain?
6. Does God give you his Spirit and work miracles among you because you observe the law, or because you believe what you heard?

Paul used a rhetorical method often used by orators of his day called a *diatribe* (using ironic, satirical, and sometimes even abusive speech to make a point). This common Greco-Roman technique was intended to rebuke the listener. The Galatians would have been familiar with this approach.

Paul's arguments from Scripture refuted those who undercut the gospel by making Jewish standards a prerequisite for salvation. But they also struck a blow against those who accepted the gospel, then added legal requirements. To differentiate them from the legalists, these have been called nomists or labelists. In essence, this group allowed Gentiles to respond to the gospel of Christ, but then insisted on *adding* legal requirements to "complete" the salvation of these new believers. The legalists presented Gentiles with the law as a gate for salvation; the nomists accepted the gospel as a door, but just as one component in a system of salvation that kept believers busy meeting all sorts of legal requirements in order to be truly saved. Legalists stressed earning one's salvation. Labelists stressed trying to do the right forms of piety. They congratulated themselves for having the right symbols, experiences, and methods.

Paul was adamant in his response to all of this. Whatever role the law might play in a believer's life, it did not add to or improve the salvation provided freely in Christ. To be acceptable to God, we must be justified by faith in Jesus Christ alone. The point needed to be hammered home, and Paul did this repeatedly in this letter.

> When I survey the
>   wondrous cross,
> On which the prince of
>   glory died,
> My richest gain I count
>   but loss,
> And pour contempt on all
>   my pride.
>   Hymn *"When I Survey
>   the Wondrous Cross"*

3:1 You foolish Galatians! Who has bewitched you?[NRSV] In 1:11 Paul had called the believers in Galatia "brothers and sisters" (NRSV); in this verse, he used a much more impersonal *Galatians* to address his converts in the region. He preceded it with a strong adjective reprimanding their behavior—they were *foolish*. The Greek word does not mean that they were mentally deficient; rather, *anoetos* suggests the behavior of people who are intelligent yet are not using that intelligence to perceive the truth (the same Greek word is used in Luke 24:25; Romans 1:14; 1 Timothy 6:9; and Titus 3:3). The Galatians had shifted from believing in the death and resurrection of Christ for salvation to believing that they must obey the law in order to be fully saved. Such illogical thinking implied that "Christ died for nothing" (2:21 NIV). This was inconsistent, contradictory, nonsensical—all summed up in the word "foolish."

Paul used a sarcastic rhetorical question to highlight their problem—perhaps they'd been *bewitched*. Paul's question *Who has bewitched you?* did not mean he wanted to know who had taught the false doctrine; the emphasis was on the word *bewitched*. The Galatian believers had become fascinated by the false teachers' arguments, almost as though they had been hypnotized. Magic was common in Paul's day (Acts 8:9-11; 13:6-7). Magicians used both optical illusions and Satan's power to perform miracles, and people were drawn into the magician's mysterious rites without

BEWITCHED!
Paul's question, "Who has bewitched you?" carries a strong second meaning. He was upset with those who taught false-hoods, but he was astounded at the Galatians, who were so easily fooled. Paul might have also rebuked the twentieth-century church.

When believers are swept into cults and heretical teaching, who is to blame? Poor leadership or lack of clear doctrinal teaching may be partly at fault, but consider an even more basic reason. Jesus warned his disciples, "I am sending you out like sheep among wolves. Therefore be as shrewd as snakes and as innocent as doves" (Matthew 10:16 NIV). Too often, Christians act a though they are little more than sitting ducks! They lack thought and discernment. Their faith is charac-terized by naive assumptions, intellectual laziness, and practi-cal shallowness. Instead of being alert sheep, watching for danger, they wander in ignorance. Are you shrewd and wise, or is your faith largely secondhand and rarely analyzed—vulnera-ble to the slightest challenge? Have you thought through your faith, or are you susceptible to every wind of doctrine (Ephesi-ans 4:14-16)? Can you stand against the charming anti-Chris-tian arguments?

recognizing their dangerous source. Paul ironically suggested that perhaps some magician had cast a spell on the Galatian believers so that they took leave of their reason—how else could this nonsense be explained? He was questioning, not their intelli-gence, but their lack of discernment. They were being fooled by arguments that they should have been able to refute.

It was before your eyes that Jesus Christ was publicly exhib-ited as crucified!NRSV At first reading one might think these people were present at the crucifixion of Jesus. While that was not the case, Paul's preaching of Christ crucified was so clear and vivid, it was almost as if they had seen it with their own eyes.

The phrase *publicly exhibited* in Greek literally means "plac-

THE MESSAGE
Paul's concern was not so much over the quantity of knowl-edge possessed by the Galatians, but rather over the quality of that knowledge. Hearing biblical messages every Sunday in church and on the radio every day means little if they don't become internalized in our thoughts and actions. The gospel we share with others must be our own story, not an endorse-ment of someone else's belief. Before others can hear "Jesus died for you," they will have to hear you explain why you believe that "Jesus died for me."

arded." In other words, Paul's preaching to them about the Crucifixion was as clear as if it had been posted on a huge billboard by the roadside; it could not be missed or misunderstood.

The tense of the verb *crucified* is perfect passive, denoting a past action with a continuing effect or result. Christ had been crucified; Paul had clearly explained the significance of that crucifixion to the Galatians. Yet they were missing the ongoing benefits of the Crucifixion—namely that it alone brings salvation to anyone who believes and that the mercy and love displayed there affect every believer, every day of his or her life. "Christ crucified" was a compressed term referring to the entire gospel message (see 1 Corinthians 1:23; 2:2; 2 Corinthians 13:4). By turning their eyes from the Cross to the law, they were confusing the very simple facts of salvation. This action was foolish and inexcusable; thus, Paul expressed his astonishment in 1:6.

> An open mind, in questions that are not ultimate, is useful. But an open mind about ultimate foundations either of Theoretical or Practical Reason is idiocy. If a man's mind is open on these things, let his mouth at least be shut.
> *C. S. Lewis*

LEARN TO DISCERN
Though the Galatians had the benefit of excellent teaching, they still lacked discernment—the ability to distinguish sound and true teaching from error (Hebrews 5:14; Philippians 1:10). In their abundance of knowledge, they had lost the central point that God's grace and Jesus' death were sufficient for salvation. At this point they could have profited from James's counsel "If any of you lacks wisdom, he should ask God" (James 1:5 NIV).

We must ask God for help. We must depend on his assistance as we seek to discover and apply the truth from his Word. If you have questions about the effectiveness of grace in your life or the basis for assurance of your relationship with God, begin by asking God to show you his wisdom.

3:2 The only thing I want to learn from you is this: Did you receive the Spirit by doing the works of the law or by believing what you heard?NRSV To rectify the Galatians' confused thinking, Paul returned to the basics. Four simple questions in the following verses will reveal their foolishness.

Paul's first question was most basic, for it focused on how their Christian life had begun. From their answer, Paul would hear *the only thing [he wants] to learn.* The Galatians' shift to following the law for salvation was completely contrary to their initial experience of the Christian faith at Paul's preaching. So he asked, *Did you receive the Spirit by doing the works of the law or by believing what you heard?* The Galatians had accepted the gospel and had received the Holy Spirit (see also 4:6). According to 6:1, some understood the spiritual life. Did this happen because they obeyed the law or because they believed the gospel Paul preached to them? The Galatian believers, mostly Gentile in background, didn't even

> The law requires works of human achievement; the gospel requires faith in Christ's achievement. The law makes demands and bids us obey; the gospel brings promises and bids us believe.
>
> *John Stott*

have or know the law, so the answer was painfully obvious. Their salvation began by faith. Law keeping had nothing to do with it.

BACK TO BASICS
We may live in the age of "new and improved," but Paul realized the benefits of relying on the "old and proved." He was alerting his Galatian friends to the dangers of the "most recent thinking" on any subject, especially regarding salvation itself.

Nevertheless, we are constantly exposed to "new teaching." How are we to discern when a challenging message clarifies our faith and when it is nothing more than human speculation? The following questions may be of help:
- To what degree do I find this new teaching present and illustrated in Scripture?
- Does this new teaching emphasize faith instead of works for salvation?
- Does the life of this new teacher consistently model, not only what he/she teaches, but what Christ taught?
- Does this new teaching advocate the appropriation of the Spirit by believing the Word of God?

Paul mentioned as an indisputable fact that the Galatians had received the Spirit *(to pneuma elabete)*. The apostle could point to their receiving the Spirit at the time of their conversion (see "having begun" in 3:3) as proof that God had accepted them based solely on their acceptance of the gospel message. They had believed what they had heard, and the evidence had been plain in their lives. God's Spirit had been within them long before the Judaizers had entered the scene.

Paul pointed out the error of their thinking by contrasting two explanations for the presence of the Spirit in the Galatians. Had God's indwelling come as a result of strenuous legal efforts or by a simple believing response? What were these "works of the law"? The teachers offered people the chance to earn God's respect and admiration by keeping the law. This resulted in pride.

COMPARISON OF HUMAN EFFORT VS. LIFE IN THE SPIRIT
It's easy to try to attain maturity in Christ the wrong way. Much of devoted and dedicated service is in reality human effort. All of our service and good work must flow out of a life of faith and the enabling power of the Holy Spirit.

	Religion by Human Effort	Life in the Spirit
Goal	Please God by our own good works	Trust in Christ and then live to *let* ~~please~~ God *flow*
Means	Practice, diligent service, discipline, and obedience in hope of reward	Confess, submit, and commit yourself to Christ's control
Power	Good, honest effort through self-determination	The Holy Spirit in us *causes* ~~helps~~ us do good work for Christ's kingdom
Control	Self-motivation; self-control	Christ in me; I in Christ
Results	Chronic guilt, apathy, depression, failure, constant desire for approval	Joy, thankfulness, love, guidance, service, forgiveness

---

The phrase "works of the law" refers to the legalistic system that the Judaizers used to try to win God's favor by observing the law. Paul's point was unmistakable: Long before the Galatians could even think of meeting God's standard, God had accepted them on his terms. Those terms were simply "believing what [they] heard." Paul's phrase could mean the act of the Galatians' "hearing" or the content that they heard. Paul emphasized believing the gospel message (see John 2:22; Romans 10:16-17). The Galatians had listened attentively to the point of believing the gospel. At that point, he emphasized, the Spirit was given.

3:3 Are you so foolish? After beginning with the Spirit.[NIV] The Galatians would have responded to Paul's indictment for foolishness by agreeing that they had received the Spirit not by law keeping but by faith. "Receiving" the Holy Spirit was the startling result of their trust in Christ. The book of Acts repeatedly describes the life-changing effect of receiving the gospel. These results come from the Spirit's work in the lives of new believers: exclamations in unknown tongues, public praise to God, moral transformation, healing, and the expulsion of demonic influences in certain lives (see Acts 10:44-47; 14:8-10; 16:16-18; 19:1-7)— in short, almost everything except circumcision and Jewish food restrictions! Paul appealed to these experiences brought by the Holy Spirit to highlight how completely inconsistent it was to receive a gift and then try to earn it. But Paul had heard that those

in Galatia were attempting just that—trading freedom in Christ
for slavery to tradition. He was astounded! How could anyone
trade the Spirit for circumcision and Jewish food laws?

EVIDENCE
Though many people experience an immediate effect when the
Holy Spirit enters their lives, the most lasting changes are subtle. The reality of forgiveness, the wonder of eternal life, and
the end of fears may lead to profound feelings. But the Holy
Spirit does not concern himself so much with our temporary
feelings as with the facts of moral and spiritual change. The
very desire to grow in Christ, to find guidance in the Scriptures,
and to tell others about Christ demonstrate the Spirit's presence in us (see Romans 8:1-11).

Are you now trying to attain your goal by human effort?^{NIV}
Paul's comment presupposed that they had accepted the teaching
of those who were undermining the original gospel: "So that
being the case," Paul said, "it is utterly foolish to think you begin
your Christian life with the Spirit and then are made perfect
(grow in Christian maturity) *by human effort.*" There are two
ways to falsely understand our relationship with God: (1) to
believe that we can be saved by works, or (2) to believe that we
can grow by our works. Both are dead ends.

How ludicrous it would be for a modern airline passenger to
entrust his life to a jet aircraft but still insist on flapping his arms
to help the plane stay in the air. Paul stressed that just as the Galatian believers had begun their Christian lives in the power of the
Spirit, so they should grow by the Spirit's power. The Galatians
had taken a step backward when they had decided to insist on
keeping the Jewish laws. Paul used contrasting Greek words to
show the complete contradiction in their thinking: They began
with the Spirit *(pneumati),* but they were then trying to attain the
goal of Christian maturity in the "flesh" *(sarki),* or through their
own effort. As in verse 1, this was inconsistent, contradictory, and
nonsensical—utterly foolish.

The Judaizers had led the Galatians to believe that keeping the
law would help their spiritual growth and maturity. But Paul's
point was that faith is all that is needed, both for salvation and for
each believer's everyday growth toward maturity. Grace is precisely what makes Christianity so unique. Every other religion in
the world demands that people earn whatever reward they are
offered; Christianity uniquely offers the sinner the grace of God,
salvation, and eternal life through faith alone. Our minds balk at
this realization because submission, humility, and trust are so con-

trary to our sinful human desires. When we attempt to earn what
God has already given, we treat Christ's death as though it were
nothing. Trying to grow on our own strength will stunt our
growth. To grow into Christian maturity, to be "made perfect,"
we must grow in faith and rely on the Holy Spirit (see Philippians
1:6; Galatians 5:25).

ESSENTIAL COMPONENTS
As Paul himself made clear, there are plenty of opportunities for
service available to the believer. He wrote to the Ephesians:
"For we are God's workmanship, created in Christ Jesus to do
good works, which God prepared in advance for us to do"
(Ephesians 2:10 NIV). The problem in Galatia and elsewhere
was not about the place of personal effort in the context of a
relationship with God. Rather, it was an argument over what
were the essential components of peace with God. Do our
efforts contribute in some way to establishing grounds or merits
for God's acceptance? Or does the relationship have its only
root in our reception by faith of God's grace? For Paul, the
answer was a thundering cry for grace! Our efforts in obedience and in carrying out spiritual disciplines must rest on the initial reality that God has fully accepted us by grace.

**3:4 Have you suffered so many things in vain—if indeed it was in
vain?**NKJV Paul's next question asked the Galatians to apply their
past experience to their immediate situation. The words *have you
suffered so many things* probably included actual suffering at the
hands of nonbelievers.

Paul and Barnabas certainly had faced great suffering as they
preached in the region of Galatia on the first missionary journey.
In Antioch of Pisidia, the Jews talked abusively to them (Acts
13:45) and caused them to be expelled from the region (Acts
13:50). In Iconium, the Jews again caused trouble, first talking
against them, then even plotting to stone them so that they had to
flee the city (Acts 14:2, 5-6). In Lystra, Paul was stoned and left
for dead (Acts 14:19-20). After preaching in Derbe (Acts 14:21),
Paul and Barnabas retraced their steps through those same cities,
"strengthening the disciples and encouraging them to remain true
to the faith" through many hardships (Acts 14:22 NIV). It may be
that the new believers in each of these cities had been treated the
same. Thus Paul's question here: "If you were willing to suffer so
much for your newfound faith at the hands of the Jews, why
would you now turn back to obeying the Jewish laws? All your
suffering (and ours) was *in vain* if the new teaching you are following is true." "In vain" means "to no purpose." If the Galatians

turned to the Judaizers, they would empty their suffering of all meaning. They would be saying, "The Jews were right to persecute us"!

CHALLENGE IN THE ORDINARY
The Holy Spirit gives Christians great power to live for God. Some Christians want more; they want to live in a state of perpetual excitement. The tedium of everyday living leads them to conclude that something is wrong spiritually. Often the Holy Spirit's greatest work is teaching us to persist, to keep on doing what is right even when it no longer seems interesting or exciting. The Galatians quickly turned from Paul's Good News to the teachings of the newest teachers in town; what they needed was the Holy Spirit's gift of persistence. If the Christian life seems ordinary, you may need the Spirit to stir you up. Every day offers a challenge to live for Christ.

This verse can also be translated, "Did you experience so much for nothing?" (NRSV). While Paul was probably referring to suffering and persecution, at least some of the Galatians' experiences may also have been positive—such as the miracles they witnessed (Acts 14:3, 8-10) and the salvation they received (Acts 13:46-48; 14:1, 21, 23). Paul's question might then be paraphrased: "After seeing so many miracles and hearing so many wonderful assurances, why would you now turn back to obeying the Jewish laws? If you grow in the faith by obeying the Jewish laws, then those experiences meant nothing."

In either case, Paul knew that this too was foolish. Even as he said it, he was unwilling to believe it, for he added: *if indeed it was in vain.* Paul did not feel it was hopeless to try to bring the Galatians back to true faith. Paul was pointing out their double mistake if they rejected what God had done for them. Not only would their faith be in vain, since they would be effectively denying it, but they would also be forfeiting the added endurance and confirmation their experiences had offered them. Instead, they were listening to false teaching in how to have a right relationship with God. Note, for example, the encounter between Jesus and the young rich man (Mark 10:17-23). Although the man did not hesitate to claim that he had kept the law since he was a child, his original question ("What must I do to inherit eternal life?") betrayed the inadequacy of legalism to provide assurance of acceptance by God.

3:5 Does God give you his Spirit and work miracles among you because you observe the law, or because you believe what you

heard?NIV Paul had yet another rhetorical question. By asking these questions, Paul hoped to get the Galatians to focus again on Christ as the foundation of their faith. While this seems to repeat Paul's first question (3:2), there are key differences. Paul's question in verse 2 focused on the Galatians' point of view (receiving): "Did you receive the Spirit by doing the works of the law or by believing what you heard?" (NRSV). This question restates the question in verse 2, but it reflects God's point of view (giving): *Does God give you his Spirit and work miracles among you because you observe the law, or because you believe what you heard?* Verse 2 is in the past tense, reminding the Galatians of their initial response of salvation and what happened because of that response. This verse, however, is in the present tense, focusing on what God continued to do for the Galatians. He "gives" his Spirit and "works" miracles among them every day. Perhaps Paul was even urging the believers to examine the effectiveness of their own evangelistic impact: Why were people continuing to respond to the gospel? Was this happening because the Galatians were carefully observing the Jewish law or because they believed in Christ and proclaimed that opportunity to others? Again, the answer was painfully obvious. God's continual blessings come just as salvation came—through faith, not through law keeping.

ALL YOU NEED
The Galatians knew that they had received the Holy Spirit when they had believed, not when they had obeyed the law. People feel insecure in their faith because faith alone seems too easy, so they try to get closer to God by following rules. The Holy Spirit may use various spiritual disciplines (such as Bible study and prayer) and service as tools to develop our holiness. These tools must not take the place of the Holy Spirit in us or become ends in themselves. They may be components of the Christian life, but they are not, in themselves, sources of life. Don't look for extra steps, improved features, or enhancing supplements; the Holy Spirit is all you need.

Paul developed his argument in four concentric circles, each one encompassing more of the Galatian experience than the last.

1. In verse 1, Paul reminded them of the original message he had preached to them—Christ crucified.
2. He asked them to consider how they had received the Holy Spirit.
3. He pointed out how ridiculous it was to jump from freedom and life in the Spirit back to the slavery of works.

4. He presented the positive evidences of the Spirit's presence
among them. In this last concentric circle, Paul reminded the
Galatians to take another look at the miracles the Spirit was
doing among them right then.

Paul would not accept compromise; he expected the Galatians
to agree that all of the evidences of God's work in their lives had
flowed from their faith in Christ rather than as a result of their
effort. His argument presented the choice to the Galatians (and
us): Would you rather enjoy the results of your own efforts to
please God or revel in the results of God's Spirit working in you
by faith?

GOD WORKS MIRACLES
Miracles are the outward manifestation of the Spirit's activity as
mentioned in 1 Corinthians 12:7-11. In Scripture, words used
for miracles convey divine wonder, power, and significance as
he sovereignly works out his plan. But all aspects of God's
activity, wonder, power, and significance occur in his creation
as well as in his special acts (see Romans 1:20). Miracles in
the New Testament were associated with the coming of Christ,
the proclamation of the gospel, and the coming of the Spirit
(Acts 2:43; 2 Corinthians 12:12; Hebrews 2:4). But God is the
author of miracles, and his power is not limited to any time or
place. While God still does miracles, we are not to stop our service and efforts and wait for a miracle. Paul stressed the activity of the Holy Spirit as producing fruit in our moral lives
(Galatians 5:22). This is the miraculous work God wants to do
in us today.

**3:6 Consider Abraham: "He believed God, and it was credited to
him as righteousness."**[NIV] The previous questions pointed to the
Galatians' experience; then Paul turned to an example from Scripture to support his teaching of salvation by faith alone. As such,
3:6-14 answers the questions Paul posed in 3:1-5. What had happened to the Galatian believers resonated with what had happened hundreds of years earlier to others who had served God.
Paul mentioned Abraham as an example.

For the Jews, there could hardly be a more important and influ-
ential person than Abraham, the father of their nation. But how
did the Galatian Gentiles know about Abraham? It could be that
the Galatian converts had heard about Abraham from the Gentile
converts to Judaism in the church (there were many Jews in
southern Galatia). Another possibility is that the Judaizers were
hammering away at the need for Gentiles to become "descendants of Abraham" (3:7 NRSV) through circumcision (see notes

on 2:3). The Judaizers would focus on passages like Genesis 17:1-14 (where God gave Abraham the covenant of circumcision) and Genesis 22:9-18 (where Abraham sacrificed a ram instead of his son Isaac) to teach that only those who were circumcised and kept Jewish laws would be acceptable to God. Thus the Gentile believers knew Abraham's name, but with a legalistic association.

But Paul asked the Galatians to *consider Abraham* in a whole new light. Leave it to Paul to put a twist on the Judaizers' argument and expose its flaws. Abraham did not have Moses' law, for Moses would not come along until hundreds of years later! The covenant of circumcision was given to Abraham (Genesis 17). This happened *after* the words quoted in this verse, Genesis 15:6, where Abraham *believed God, and it was credited to him as righteousness.* For Jews, the weightier argument preceded the lighter argument; so Paul was arguing that Abraham's belief had precedence over legal circumcision. The Judaizers argued for good works in order to be saved and grow spiritually; Abraham, the founder of the Jewish nation, was considered righteous, not by works, but because he "believed God." Therefore, the revelation of God's grace anteceded Abraham's specific act of obedience in circumcision.

NO EXCUSE!
In the same way that we claim Jesus' death as God's provision for our salvation, Abraham believed in God and his promises, although they would not be made fully evident until centuries later on the cross. God promised, and Abraham answered in faith, even during the trial of God asking him to sacrifice his son. This is the heart of Christian faith. God promises to save us when we trust in Christ and take him at his word, just as Abraham did. We know in greater detail how God worked out his plan of grace in Christ. We have much less excuse for our unbelief!

Several years later, Paul would write to the Romans and explain this concept in more detail:

■ *Is this blessedness only for the circumcised, or also for the uncircumcised? We have been saying that Abraham's faith was credited to him as righteousness. Under what circumstances was it credited? Was it after he was circumcised, or before? It was not after, but before! And he received the sign of circumcision, a seal of the righteousness that he had by faith while he was still uncircumcised. So then, he is the father of all who believe but have not been circumcised, in order that righteous-*

*ness might be credited to them. And he is also the father of the
circumcised who not only are circumcised but who also walk in
the footsteps of the faith that our father Abraham had before he
was circumcised.*

*It was not through the law that Abraham and his offspring
received the promise that he would be heir of the world, but
through the righteousness that comes by faith. . . .*

*Therefore, the promise comes by faith, so that it may be by
grace and may be guaranteed to all Abraham's offspring—not
only to those who are of the law but also to those who are of
the faith of Abraham. He is the father of us all. (Romans 4:9-
13, 16* NIV*)*

To be credited with righteousness means that we are accepted
by God. We don't deserve this righteousness; God graciously
gives it to us. God reckons, or gives to us freely, his own righteousness (see 2 Corinthians 5:21). Abraham did not have Moses'
law, nor did he have the cross of Christ, the gospel, or salvation
as offered in the New Testament. But he was God's servant, acceptable to God and considered righteous because he believed
what he knew of God. "Righteousness" is an aspect of God's
character, his standard of behavior, and a description of all that he
wishes to give to us. God gives righteousness to those who
believe—it is his provision for justifying sinners. When God
declares us righteous, we have been made right with him. Just as
when in a court of law the judge pronounces the accused innocent, we are declared righteous by God's act on our behalf. Abraham was not made right with God by works of the law, nor by
circumcision (for God hadn't told him about circumcision yet),
but simply by his faith.

**3:7 So, you see, those who believe are the descendants of Abra-
ham.**NRSV The conclusion is obvious—and the rug has been
pulled out from under the Judaizers. They had argued that to be a
Christian a person had to first become a Jew, a descendant of
Abraham, and subsequently obey the Jewish laws. Jews, including these Judaizers, were extremely proud of their lineage traced
back to Abraham. At the heart of Jewish salvation theology was
the concept of being a "descendant of Abraham." The Jews
believed that they were automatically the people of God because
of their heritage. But from Abraham's own example, Paul showed
that true *descendants of Abraham* were not part of a national heritage or keepers of the ancient custom of circumcision. Rather,
they are all *those who believe* in God and, with the advent of
Christ, those who believe in Christ and the salvation he offers. As

Abraham was saved by faith, so each person is saved by faith. As Abraham was declared righteous because of his faith in God, so both Jews and Gentiles who believe are declared righteous because of their faith in Christ. Belief is the first and only step to salvation.

GOOD CREDIT RATING
You may have received in the mail those tantalizing notices of "Pre-approved Credit—Immediate Acceptance" as advertisements for charge cards. Someone is assuming your trustworthiness to pay your debts (plus a substantial interest fee), so they extend you credit. The gospel, on the other hand, offers us "righteousness credit" based on Jesus Christ and his faithfulness. We have not earned this righteousness that is credited to our account, nor is it based on our weak or imperfect faith. It is by God crediting or imputing his righteousness to us that we are saved. If it weren't for his imputation, our faith wouldn't be enough to save us. When we feel our faith is small or weak, remember that Christ's perfect faith saves us, not our own faith. God bases his credit rating on Christ, not on us.

3:8 And the Scripture, foreseeing that God would justify the Gentiles by faith, preached the gospel to Abraham beforehand, saying, "In you all the nations shall be blessed."NKJV Although Paul had made his point, he added a further devastating application of the Old Testament against the Judaizers' false teaching: Not only are Gentiles and Jews saved by faith, but this had been God's plan from the very beginning!

Paul's wording sounds as though *the Scripture* is a separate entity from God, as if it foresaw what God planned and wrote itself thus. However, the opposite is true. Paul was using a figure of speech. He saw Scripture as truly God's words; what Scripture said, God meant. The wording simply shows Paul's understanding of the Word of God. "Scripture" is not the actual subject of the sentence; "God" is the subject. By "the Scripture," Paul was referring to part of the Abrahamic covenant (see, for example, Genesis 12:3). It was God who planned from the beginning to *justify the Gentiles by faith,* and it was God who *preached* (announced or declared) that to Abraham.

But Abraham lived hundreds of years before Christ. How could the *gospel* have been preached to him? Abraham was considered a prophet, and through these promises to him God may have revealed some of his incredible plans for the future. The essence of the gospel is salvation by faith to all who believe. Thus Abraham heard the gospel through the promises he

received. Christ would be born into the Jewish race—the nation
that would begin with Abraham and his miracle baby, Isaac.
God's promise to Abraham encompassed God's plan for the ages
and his incredible acts in human history. Thus "all the nations"
would be blessed in Abraham because his descendant, Christ
Jesus, would bring salvation to all who believe.

THE TRUST COMPANY
As used in contemporary language, "belief" takes on two distinct meanings. On the one hand, people use the term merely
to denote recognition or to admit existence. Phrases such as "I
believe in UFOs"; "I believe in God"; and "I believe in doing the
right thing" employ the term *believe* for little more than to con-
cede the possible reality of the object, being, or action
described. The speaker may actually harbor quite a negative
personal attitude toward what is described. "I believe in God"
may well be followed by the sentiment "and I want to have nothing to do with him," or "I believe in God—why can't he be satisfied with that?" Such would be the perspective of those whom
James describes in James 2:19. Intellectual assent requires no
submission, trust, or obedience.
  On the other hand, the belief response required by the gospel means active trust or commitment. We must not merely
believe about Christ, but we must personally rely on him. Christian belief involves a total personal response to what Jesus has
done for us. We begin a lifelong process of commitment to
Christ. Those who come to Christ in this way parallel the
response of Abraham, who trusted implicitly in what God had
revealed about himself. As in Abraham's belief and our own, no
law, circumcision, or any other act of symbolism or personal
devotion and no personal merit can make us acceptable to
God. We can only trust in God's boundless grace.

Here Paul quoted from Genesis 12:3. Just prior to that verse,
God had told Abraham, "I will bless you" (Genesis 12:2 NIV).
Just as Abraham was blessed, so *all the nations shall be blessed.*
Paul made two key points in quoting this verse: (1) The blessing
promised to Abraham was intended, from the beginning, to be
given by God to all nations, not just to the Jews, and (2) this
blessing, both to Abraham and to the nations, was promised by
God before any laws or works were given or required. Paul's
opponents might have used this same passage, but they would
have applied it differently. Their assumption was that God had
limited his blessing only to Abraham's direct or adopted offspring. They taught, therefore, that one had to "prove" (by doing
the works of the law) that one was worthy to be considered Abraham's offspring. But Paul was using the passage to illustrate that

in Abraham God had established a precedent of relating personally to those willing to trust him.

How are the nations blessed? What is the nature of the blessing of the nations? If the nations had to become Abraham's offspring before being eligible for the blessing, the verse doesn't make sense. Paul was driving home the point that God's grace could reach the nations without requiring that they abandon their identity as nations. The identity of the blessing becomes clear in 3:14—"He redeemed us in order that the blessing given to Abraham might come to the Gentiles through Christ Jesus" (NIV). The one who provided the blessing (retroactive in Abraham's case and foreordained in ours) was born in the family line as the human offspring of Abraham. In this way, through Christ, God made the blessing available through Abraham to the entire world. Those of any nation who imitate Abraham's obedient belief in God receive the blessings—salvation and all its benefits.

FAITH
Because of what it ushers into the lives of those who exercise it, faith has several benefits:

- *The superiority of faith:* Christ's faithfulness makes possible our response of faith. Faith is the sole means whereby Christ's grace and forgiveness are applied to our lives. Faith has no substitute. The response of faith remains the only effective basis for our relationship with God. All other proposed methods—obedience to the law, human efforts at righteousness, and various forms of legalism and pietism ultimately fail.

- *The simplicity of faith:* Jesus described faith as dynamic even when it is small (see Luke 17:5-6). Mustard-seed faith claims effectiveness, not by its inherent power, but because of the power and character of the one in whom that tiny faith rests. It is the faith of Christ and our trust in him that save us. Therefore, simple faith is all we need, even if it is small and weak. We never claim a gigantic faith in a tiny God; but a minuscule faith in the awesome Maker of heaven and earth, who demonstrates his grace by loving us.

- *The sufficiency of faith:* The Galatians were being told that faith needed to be bolstered by certain works; faith was not enough—action had to be added to faith. But Christ's faith is all-sufficient for our salvation, and our faith in him is sufficient to receive salvation. It is also the sufficient means for us to receive the Spirit and fully participate in Christian growth.

Thus, God would justify the Gentiles, not by works of the law, not by circumcision, but by faith. Salvation is the ultimate blessing, a gift simply to be believed and received. All believers in

every age and from every nation share Abraham's blessing. This
promise comforts us, gives us a great heritage, and provides a
solid foundation for living.

**3:9 For this reason, those who believe are blessed with Abra-
ham who believed.**NRSV Faith did not begin in the New Testament; rather, it has been the key requirement for all believers
from the beginning. God's relationship with his children has
always been based on faith. Abraham, the father of the Jewish
nation, exemplified faith in God, even though his faith faltered
at times. He well deserves to be called *Abraham who believed*
("the man of faith" NIV). Hebrews 11, aptly called the "Roll
Call of Faith," identifies four specific times in Abraham's life
when he responded in sheer faith under trial (see Hebrews 11:8-
19). Abraham clearly stands out among those before and after
him who lived by faith. Those of us *who believe* in God, in
Christ, and in the salvation we have been so graciously offered,
are indeed *blessed with* Abraham, for we, too, receive a relationship with God and all of God's promises.

Another point must be noted: While it is true that "all the
nations" would be blessed, there is a qualifier—only the people
in those nations *who believe* would receive the blessing of salvation. To this degree the blessing relates to the opportunity for salvation extended to all people. Also, those who do not believe but
rely on works will not be "blessed with Abraham," as Paul will
clarify in 3:10.

The question arises: Was Paul reading some kind of remote
idea back into the Old Testament by claiming that the Gentiles
had always had a part in God's plan, or can his claim be substanti-
ated from Scripture? One of the most eye-opening studies of the
Old Testament occurs in reference to the Gentiles. God clearly
refers to the non-Jews as an essential part of his plan. The entire
books of Jonah and Ruth provide key examples. See also
Deuteronomy 32:43; 2 Samuel 22:50; Psalm 18:49; 117:1; and
Isaiah 11:10; also see Romans 15:9-12. Once a reader begins to
approach the Old Testament with the Gentiles in mind, the fre-
quency of their inclusion in the text is quite remarkable.

**3:10 For all who rely on the works of the law are under a curse;
for it is written, "Cursed is everyone who does not observe
and obey all the things written in the book of the law."**NRSV
Having shown that justification by faith is true according to the
Scriptures, Paul here made the opposite point, that justification
by the law is false according to the Scriptures—in fact, according
to the law itself. Paul quoted Deuteronomy 27:26 to prove that,

contrary to what the Judaizers claimed, obeying the law cannot justify and save—it can only condemn. Those who place themselves under the authority of the law place themselves under the curse. This curse, incidentally, concludes the list of twelve curses recited annually by the Levites in commemoration of the covenant between Israel and God. *All who rely on the works of the law are under a curse* because no one can obey the law perfectly and because breaking even one commandment brings a person under condemnation. Trying to achieve salvation through obedience to the law is a no-win situation. No one can perfectly *observe and obey all the things written in the book of the law.* The law demands perfection—an impossibility for sinful humans. Many people struggle with this Old Testament principle, but the fact is that we all regularly break the first and foremost commandment, failing to put God first and have no other gods before him. Thus, everyone has broken the commandments and everyone is *cursed.*

The law cannot save; neither can it reverse the condemnation (Romans 3:20-24). But Christ took the curse of the law entirely upon himself when he hung on the cross (Deuteronomy 21:23). He did this so we wouldn't have to bear our own punishment. The only condition is that we accept Christ's death on our behalf by faith as the means to be saved (Colossians 1:20-23). There are only two ways to approach God. The first is to come through Christ, humbly realizing our complete inability to do anything on our own to merit God's favor. The only other alternative is to come on the basis of our works—our merits and achievements. Unfortunately, that approach leads to judgment using the standard of the law, ultimately resulting in condemnation.

Popular religion has usually settled for symbol over substance. Faced with their repeated failures to meet even their own codes of behavior, people have often resorted to strategies intended to appease God or the gods. Not even the great rabbis could perfectly keep the law. Thus, we find it no surprise how tightly the Jews of Jesus' and Paul's time held on to the idea that being genetically connected with someone great like Moses or Abraham and having the mark of circumcision would lead to inherited merit (see John 8:31-59). Jesus challenged their claim to merit from Abraham by questioning why they didn't also share some of Abraham's faith and character. But he was confronting people almost blinded by their zeal to depend on their pedigree and their pride in having God's law and in being God's chosen people.

REALITIES
Before we can deride the people in Paul's day for their blind-
ness, we might ask how we make the same mistakes. Do we
ever rely on works rather than faith? Do we replace genuine,
informed faith with the trappings of faith? Do we cling to or
reject certain labels (evangelical, conservative, fundamental, liberal) without really thinking about what they mean? Do we
make membership in a certain church, a certain form of baptism, years of service, or certain theological systems the "test"
for measuring our own and other people's acceptance with
God?

**3:11 Clearly no one is justified before God by the law, because, "The
righteous will live by faith."**NIV Even from the first century, this has
been interpreted in two ways: (1) The righteous will live by faith in
God, or (2) the righteous will live by God's faithfulness (see note on
2:18). Either way, we need to depend on God for our justification.
Trying to be *justified before God by the law* (right with God by our
own effort) doesn't work. Sinful humans cannot attain the perfection
demanded by the law. And good intentions, such as "I'll do better
next time" or "I'll never do that again," usually end in failure. Yet
there always was hope for those who lived before Christ, and those
who believe in Christ have the same hope. The law could not save,
but faith could. Paul pointed to Habakkuk's declaration in Habakkuk
2:4, *"The righteous will live by faith,"* to show that by trusting
God—believing in his provision for our sins and living each day in
his power—we can break this cycle of failure.

JUSTIFIED OR UNDER A CURSE?
If we can't be justified by keeping God's law, surely we can't be
justified or *sanctified* by any human law. Yet so many still try.
Some are burdened by the rules of a cult; some strive to obey
church or institutional rules that have been added to the gospel; some labor under specific "shepherding" restraints. Nearly
all of us struggle with family rules or expectations that have
nearly the status of God's laws.
   The oppressive feeling of trying to fulfill man-made laws is
like the curse of those who don't keep all the law (3:10). Whose
laws are you trying to obey? While we may freely adopt certain
restrictions out of love (Romans 14:15) or for purposes of evangelism (1 Corinthians 9:19-23), we must not do so for justification or for spiritual growth.

Righteousness by faith was not a new idea—it is found in the
writings of the Old Testament prophets. Even though Paul was
proclaiming the gospel to Gentiles, he was determined to hold up

its connection with the plan and promise God had begun with the Jews. "The righteous" refers, not to those who are keeping the law, but to those who are in a right relationship with God. There are two ways to understand the statement "The righteous will live by faith": (1) People's faith in God makes them righteous before God, and as a result, they have eternal life; or (2) those made right with God live their Christian lives by remaining faithful to God. In summary, this expression means Christians will live because of God's faithfulness and because of their response of faith in God; as a result, they will have eternal life and experience fullness of life. Faith does not exist in a vacuum. Faith has value only if the object of its focus is true and dependable. Faith in a false god or a broken chair have this in common: Both will cause us to fall. The faith by which the righteous live has a very definite object—God himself.

What then is this faith?

- Faith is personal trust in God's faithfulness.
- Faith is the source of the believer's new life in Christ.
- Faith justifies us, saves us, and gives us new life and a new lifestyle.

GRACE-FULL
How can Christian parents teach their children about grace when so much of child rearing involves rules and law? Dos and don'ts are essential to teaching children self-discipline and keeping them safe. The "law" has an important function in teaching children right from wrong (see discussion of 3:21-25). But long before they can actually understand the difference between rules and grace as a concept, children should be experiencing God's love and grace and our love for them. At some key point, we must explain that rule keeping doesn't earn parental love, nor does rule breaking mean parents withdraw love. When children understand this, we have communicated grace.

3:12 **But the law does not rest on faith; on the contrary, "Whoever does the works of the law will live by them."**NRSV Some might then ask, "Maybe both faith and law are needed for salvation?" But here Paul explained that faith and law are mutually exclusive: When we have faith, we do not need the law. The law, by its very nature, excludes faith. While Paul knew the real but limited value of the law (a point that must be remembered in Paul's writings), he made clear that it had no value for salvation. Quoting again from the law (Leviticus 18:5), Paul supported his statement *"Whoever does the works of the law will live by them."* The law itself says that only perfect performance of the law can gain approval from God—one can "live" by the law only by doing "the works of the law." The problem is, no one can do the law perfectly—it is humanly impossible. To "live" by doing the works of the law may be an objective, but one that can never be fully accomplished on our own. Obviously, the law cannot help us. Is the human condition hopeless? No, for another has fulfilled the law's requirements for us.

3:13 Christ has redeemed us from the curse of the law, having become a curse for us (for it is written, "Cursed is everyone who hangs on a tree").^{NKJV} All people are cursed by the law, as illustrated in the previous verses. Because the law sets forth requirements that are impossible to fulfill, it sets us up for failure; we are under its *curse* (see also 3:10). Yet there is hope. *Christ has redeemed us.*

To "redeem" (*exegorazo,* deliver, redeem) a person meant to buy that person out of slavery. But the term carries added meaning—the process proves costly to the one who accomplishes the delivery. Christ redeemed "us" (that is, all people who believe, Jews and Gentiles) by buying us out of slavery to sin and to the law. But his generosity came dearly. He paid the price with his life. "For you know that it was not with perishable things such as silver or gold that you were redeemed from the empty way of life handed down to you from your forefathers, but with the precious blood of Christ, a lamb without blemish or defect" (1 Peter 1:18-19 NIV; see also Matthew 20:28; Acts 20:28; 1 Corinthians 6:20; 7:23; 1 Timothy 2:6; 2 Peter 2:1; and Revelation 5:9).

The law demanded obedience while implying dire consequences for disobedience. Given our inevitable failure to meet the demands of the law perfectly, the law serves as *a curse.* Taken alone, the law becomes a hopeless treadmill from which we may fall at any moment. In fact, by the time we realize the impossible demands of the law, we have already fallen. Because the law expresses perfect justice, it includes no remedy for those who fail to meet its demands. Unless we receive help, we have no hope. We cannot redeem ourselves; we need a redeemer.

But how did Christ *become a curse for us?* Paul answered the question by yet another Old Testament quotation, *"Cursed is everyone who hangs on a tree"* (Deuteronomy 21:23). The quotation meant not that a person was cursed by God because he was hanged; rather, that to be hanged on a tree signified to the Jews that a person had been cursed. Christ was not cursed because he was crucified; rather, he willingly allowed himself to become cursed for all humanity, and thus endured the Crucifixion. At the Cross, the curse of the law was transferred from sinful humanity to the sinless Son of God. During his crucifixion, Christ cried out, "My God, my God, why have you forsaken me?" (Mark 15:34 NIV). God forsook his Son for a short time, the time when Christ took on himself the penalty for sin—and God, in his holiness, could not look upon that sin. He endured for a short time what we would have experienced for eternity otherwise.

Both the magnitude of our separation from God and his responding grace require radical language. That Christ became loathsome to his Father in order to provide us with a way of salvation shows how much love God has for us.

IT IS FINISHED!
Our tendency to sin and our sins make us liable to the full impact of the law's consequences. As we await the crushing judgment that we deserve, Christ absorbs that blow in himself for us. He did this on the cross by becoming "a curse" (though he in no way deserved it) so that he might in turn offer us a way of escape from the fate we justly deserve. He carried all our sin, guilt, and obligation. It is finished. So if you have trusted in Christ, you don't need to feel guilty any longer. All your guilt has been removed!

3:14 **He redeemed us in order that the blessing given to Abraham might come to the Gentiles through Christ Jesus, so that by faith we might receive the promise of the Spirit.**NIV This second use of the term "redeemed" does not appear in the Greek text, but is implied in such a way that the translation reads more smoothly with it. Verse 13 introduced the idea of redemption, stating its reason (our being under the law's curse) and its method (Christ becoming a curse in our behalf). This verse states two outcomes of Christ's redeeming work. These two clauses started by the Greek word *hina,* translated "in order that" and "so that," summarize all of 3:1-14 and state the major themes of the whole section.

Christ *redeemed us* (delivered us) from the curse of the law (3:13) *in order that the blessing given to Abraham might come to the Gentiles.* This "blessing" refers to justification by faith and not by the law (as discussed in 3:8-9), to be offered to Gentiles as well as to Abraham's descendants, the Jews. How do we receive God's blessing? Through trust in Christ's redemption on the cross, God's promise to Abraham (see 3:8) could be made a reality to all who believe—the blessings are salvation and the benefits of salvation.

Certainly the Jews were among the descendants of Abraham, but the great patriarch himself was a Gentile. We find significant insights in God's dealing with Abraham. God counts as righteous those who trust in him, and God made specific promises touching the fate of the whole world to be accomplished through Abraham's descendants. By being born into Abraham's line, and then dying for even the Jews, Jesus showed that his work on the cross could be applied to any person's life.

By faith we might receive the promise of the Spirit. Then "we" (Jews and Gentiles together), having been justified by faith, will by faith receive the promised Holy Spirit. If all persons are eligible to benefit from Christ, then the Holy Spirit, God's deposit, must also be available to all (see Ephesians 1:13-14).

Paul taught about the Holy Spirit clearly in Romans 8. In Romans 8:2, Paul calls him the Spirit of life. The Holy Spirit was present at the creation of the world as one of the agents in the origin of life. He is the power behind the rebirth of every Christian and the one who helps us live the Christian life. The Holy Spirit sets us free, once and for all, from sin and its natural consequences. Romans 8:4 tells us that we must live according to the Spirit. The Holy Spirit provides the power to help us do what the law requires of us externally. The Holy Spirit directs the entire course of our lives, our actions, our daily behavior, and our moral direction. Romans 8:6 says that to set the mind on the Spirit is life and peace. Choosing to follow the Spirit's leading brings us full life on earth, eternal life, and peace with God. Romans 8:9 says we are controlled by the Spirit if the Spirit of God lives in us. The Holy Spirit lives in us, taking control of our sinful human desires. Romans 8:14-15 says that we have received the Spirit of sonship. The true sons of God are not those of Jewish birth but those who are led by the Spirit of God as evidenced in their lifestyles. Romans 8:16 says, "The Spirit Himself bears witness with our spirit that we are children of God" (NKJV). The Holy Spirit not only adopts us as God's children, but he also assures us of our family status. Romans 8:26 says the Spirit also helps in our weaknesses. The Holy Spirit strengthens us and sustains us through times of trial. These wonderful benefits of the Holy Spirit come to believers by faith, not by keeping the law.

CHANGES
When we accept Christ's redemptive work in our lives, much more changes than our legal standing before God. The following passages describe a new relationship that exists between ourselves and God (Joel 2:28; Ezekiel 36:26; 37:14; 39:29; John 14:16-17; Ephesians 1:13). In short, God's Spirit takes up residence in a person who has trusted God and is now living by faith. What evidences of the Spirit's presence can you find in your life?

THE LAW AND THE PROMISE / 3:15-22

Paul turned to an illustration from the Galatians' daily experience
to help them understand the principles of law and grace. He
found parallels in the making and executing of human wills or
covenants to the way that God deals with us. In 3:15-18 he used
the Judaizers' own arguments against them. They had argued that
the Mosaic law was a fuller and more complete expression of the
covenant given to Abraham. Paul reversed their train of thought
and showed that God's promise to Abraham was a promise made
prior to Moses, thus it was more authoritative.

**3:15 Brothers and sisters, I give an example from daily life: once a
person's will has been ratified, no one adds to it or annuls
it.**^{NRSV} Paul began this chapter addressing his audience with an
impersonal "Galatians"; here he returned to the tone of 1:11 by
calling them *brothers and sisters*. Paul anticipated a question the
Judaizers might raise at this point and summarily answered it.
While the Judaizers might go so far as to agree with Paul that
Abraham was justified by his faith, they would then add that the
coming of the law changed the basis for gaining salvation. Paul
wanted to clarify that nothing would change the promise that
God made to Abraham.

Paul turned to *an example from daily life*. Citing a human contract, a person's will, he noted that once a person's will is ratified
(*kekuromenen*—approved, confirmed, signed), it cannot be
changed by anyone. It cannot be added to, nor can any part of it
be annulled (or removed). If that is the case with human contracts, how much more is it true of divine contracts? God's promises always stand, no matter what changes occur. He always
keeps his promises.

Scholars have discussed the specific kind of will or covenant Paul
might have had in mind—whether it was Roman, Greek, or pat-
terned after Old Testament treaties. Scholars have determined that
this agreement was not a treaty or covenant but a will or testament
generally used to deal with inheritance to children. Roman law per-
mitted the originator to cancel or modify the will after it was drawn
up at any point during his lifetime. Some scholars think Paul
referred not to a Roman-style will but to a Greek one that would be
familiar to the Galatians. In the Greek world, once a will was registered at the records office, not even the originator could change it or
reverse the basic intent. It was irrevocable. But these discussions
seem inconsequential since Paul's main point was the irrevocability
of a will. But Paul was not basing his illustration on the right of a
maker to change the will but emphasizing the fact that as long as the

PROMISES MADE TO ABRAHAM

Genesis 12:1-3, 7	The promises of inhabiting a new land, becoming a great nation, being blessed, having a great name. Through Abraham all families of the earth would be blessed.
Genesis 15:1-5, 18	The promise of an heir and descendants too numerous to count, and the promise of inheriting the land.
Genesis 17:1-8	The promise that Abraham would be the ancestor of many nations, kings would be among his descendants, the covenant would be eternal, and the land would belong to his descendants forever.
Genesis 22:16-18	The promise of descendants as numerous as the stars of heaven and the sand on the seashore. The promise that through him all nations of the earth would be blessed.

will was unchanged by the maker it remained in force. His point was not that God couldn't change his covenant with us, but that God *didn't* ever change the covenant established between himself and us, as illustrated by his specific dealings with Abraham. God's divine promise was made to Abraham long before the giving of the law to Moses. As such, it was a binding agreement not to be changed or annulled.

3:16 The promises were spoken to Abraham and to his seed. The Scripture does not say "and to seeds," meaning many people, but "and to your seed," meaning one person, who is Christ.NIV This verse would probably make more sense in the flow of the text if it appeared in parentheses. But the point is important. *The promises* that Abraham received from God *were spoken to Abraham and to his seed.*

Now, if the promises were meant for Abraham and his many descendants alone (to all his *seeds*), then it might appear that the promises had already been fulfilled, and that the law had come as a new phase in God's dealing with his people. But the promises had been given to the "Seed"—that is, Abraham's most famous descendant, who came many years after both Abraham and the law. The law has an important function, but salvation by grace through faith was God's promise from the beginning of time until the judgment day.

While language experts argue that "seed" can also be a plural ("The farmer plants seed" certainly refers to more than one seed), Paul correctly applied the singular form of the word in this

instance. The Jews had always believed that God's promises
would be fulfilled in a single person, the Messiah. God's promise
remained intact even though Abraham himself only had one
descendant through Sarah. Further, the promises were not fulfilled prior to the giving of the law, nor by the giving of the law.
Instead, they were fulfilled when Christ came as Abraham's
"Seed." Christ alone fulfilled the messianic aspects of God's covenant and showed that God's promises are in effect for all time.

Many claimed to be rightful heirs to God's promises to Abraham by their being his offspring, but Paul pointed out the only
true, rightful heir was Jesus. The covenant that God shared with
Abraham had been reaffirmed many times, but only Christ fulfilled the Abrahamic covenant as the unique Seed. The Jews certainly enjoyed many privileges and responsibilities as part of the
Abrahamic covenant, but blessing the nations was the Messiah's
role. The promises to Abraham go just to Christ. (They don't
reside in the Jewish people.) In and through Christ they go to individual believers. Christ is our hope of blessing.

3:17 **What I mean is this: The law, introduced 430 years later, does
not set aside the covenant previously established by God and
thus do away with the promise.**NIV Moses received the law and
gave it to God's people *430 years later.* This number comes from
Exodus 12:40, which says that Israel's captivity in Egypt lasted
430 years. Genesis 15:13, however, has 400 years for the period
of slavery. Rabbis solved the problem by taking 430 as the time
between Abraham's covenant and Moses receiving the law at
Mount Sinai. They took 400 years to mean the time Israel served
as slaves in Egypt.

While there is debate about the exact period of these 430
years, the point is not the number of years, but rather that the law
came "later" than God's promise to Abraham. For four centuries
God had been blessing Abraham and his descendants on the basis
of their faith, not by the Mosaic law, for there was no law. When
the law was given, it did not *set aside the covenant previously established by God;* neither did it *do away with the promise.* The
giving of the law itself was an integral part of God following
through on his covenant. God had preserved his people in Egypt
and had overseen their Exodus. Then, through Moses, God had
provided the law as a written standard of his own legitimate
expectations of those in covenant with him.

The law neither replaced nor improved the covenant of promise (by faith through grace). As Paul would later develop (see
3:23-25), the law's main function is to demonstrate how crucial
the covenant of faith is in allowing people any hope at all. As a

paragraph in God's gracious covenant, law provides guidance; but taken alone the law becomes a grinding foe, constantly pointing to our shortcomings. In other words, the Judaizers were wrong. The promise of justification by faith is still in effect; the law does not set that aside or annul it.

THE PROMISE KEEPER
God kept his promise to Abraham; he has not revoked it, though thousands of years have passed. He saved Abraham through his faith, and he blessed the world through Abraham by sending the Messiah as one of Abraham's descendants. Circumstances may change, but God remains constant and does not break his promises. He has promised to forgive our sins through Jesus Christ, and we can be sure that he will do so.

3:18 **For if the inheritance depends on the law, then it no longer depends on a promise; but God in his grace gave it to Abraham through a promise.**[NIV] There is yet another reason why salvation cannot be through law, or through faith plus law. The words *law* and *promise* are opposites in nature. Like oil and water, they cannot be combined. *Inheritance* here refers to believers' enjoyment of what they receive through the promise: salvation, eternal life, and removal of the curse. Thus, if our salvation and enjoyment of God's gifts depend on obeying the law, then they cannot depend on a promise, for it cannot be both ways. People do not need to work to attain what has been promised to them.

Instead, *God in his grace gave it to Abraham. Grace* means "undeserved and unearned favor." God gave the promise because he loved Abraham, not because Abraham deserved it. God "gave" the promise—the verb implies something that is both free (or unearned) and permanent. God gave Abraham the inheritance *through a promise.* That way of salva-

> The Law is a court of justice, but the Gospel a throne of grace.
> *George Swinnock*

tion was still in effect in Paul's day, as well as in our own. God in his grace gives us salvation by our faith alone. He grants graciously and generously, not reluctantly; in love and compassion, not in judgment; abundantly and without reservation. We have an advantage over Abraham; we "know whom we have believed" in a way that Abraham did not know. We have been given the record of how God secured our salvation.

3:19 **What purpose then does the law serve?**[NKJV] In the previous verses, Paul made four distinct observations about the law:

1. The law could not give the Holy Spirit (3:1-5).
2. The law could not give righteousness (3:6-9).
3. The law could not justify; it could only condemn (3:10-12).
4. The law could not change the fact that righteousness always comes by faith in God's promises (3:15-18).

Paul's opponents, and especially the Judaizers, could still be expected to raise the questions "Why did God give the law?" and *"What purpose then does the law serve?"* Paul's arguments could sound as though he believed the law had no purpose whatsoever and that he was actually opposed to it. So Paul explained the true purpose behind God's giving of the law and its place in the plan of salvation.

It was added because of transgressions, till the Seed should come to whom the promise was made.NKJV The law had two functions. First, it had a negative function: *It was added because of transgressions* (meaning that God had given the law to punish sin). Second, it had a strong positive function: The law reveals the nature and will of God, and it shows people how to live. Thus, it had been given to restrain transgressions by helping people recognize wrong behavior and thus refrain from it. Negatively, the law points out people's sins and shows them that it is impossible to please God by trying to obey all his laws completely. It was given to reveal transgressions, causing people to realize their sinfulness and their desperate need of a Savior. God's intent was that by starkly spotlighting sin, the law would drive us toward Christ (see 3:23). This is the positive function. Elsewhere Paul wrote, "Where there is no law there is no transgression" (Romans 4:15 NIV), for "through the law we become conscious of sin" (Romans 3:20 NIV). The phrase "it was added" implies that the law was supplementary to God's promise because it came into effect after the promise made to Abraham.

The little word *till* indicates that the law was meant as a temporary measure, and certainly not as the permanent and final means of salvation. The law was in place until *the Seed should come to whom the promise was made.* When Jesus Christ ("the Seed") came, the law was finally fulfilled. (See Matthew 5:17-20, where Jesus explained that he came, not to abolish the law, but to fulfill it.)

God's promise to Abraham dealt with Abraham's faith; the law focuses on actions. The covenant with Abraham shows that faith is the only way to be saved; the law shows how to obey God in grateful response. Faith does not annul the law; but the more we know God, the more we will see how sinful we are. Then we will be driven to depend on Christ alone for our salvation.

OUTLAWS
Christ has set us free, but as we attempt to live by faith, we are still in danger of falling into certain traps. Wanting the security of being able to earn our salvation, we add human traditions, standards, and rules to our faith. We slip back into performing a certain way, serving, or doing good works as if we need to impress God or earn his approval. And wanting to feel good, we let ourselves be directed by our ever-changing emotions. The security trap makes us prisoners just as surely as the law had held us in its grip. The emotional trap can result in our becoming "outlaws," deciding for ourselves what is right and wrong. Either way, we rob ourselves of the true joy and security we share with all who have accepted God's promise of salvation by faith alone.

The law was put into effect through angels by a mediator.^{NIV}
To show the inherent inferiority of the law, Paul explained that while God personally gave the promises to Abraham, the law *was put into effect through angels* and *by a mediator.* This was not a new idea made up by Paul; it was already a Jewish belief. Although it is not mentioned in Exodus, Jews believed that the Ten Commandments had been given to Moses by angels. Stephen, in his speech before his death, said, "You who have received the law that was put into effect through angels . . . have not obeyed it" (Acts 7:53 NIV). The writer of Hebrews called the law "the message spoken by angels" (Hebrews 2:2 NIV). The "mediator" was undoubtedly Moses, who acted as the mediator between God and his people (read Exodus 19:1–20:21; also Deuteronomy 33:2 and Psalm 68:17-18).

3:20 Now a mediator involves more than one party; but God is one.^{NRSV} To have a *mediator* obviously means that *more than one party* is involved. A mediator works between two or more parties to aid in communication, effect an agreement, or settle a dispute. Moses, implied in 3:19, was the mediator who communicated between God and Israel. God (through angels) mediated the law to Moses, who then gave it to the people. The law could be compared to a contract, which is valid only as long as both sides keep their sides of the agreement. While God kept his, the people of Israel could not keep theirs.

However, when God gave the promises to Abraham, he did so directly, without any mediator. The promises were given and would be kept by God, regardless of the actions of people. Thus, the promise is superior to the law because the promise is from God alone, meant for eternity, and would not be broken. The law and its mediator, Moses, were temporary, preparatory arrangements designed to confirm the truth of God's ultimate desire to relate directly with his creatures. Paul did not put down Moses, but showed the primacy of Christ's way of faith over the law.

> The Mosaic law was not designed to be the final code of the religious life, but to prepare the soil of the human heart to receive Jesus Christ in all the fullness of his salvation.
>
> *F. B. Meyer*

What is the significance of the phrase *God is one?* Paul seems to have intentionally used a double meaning. On one hand, "God is one" refers to the unity of his person. He is one being, and that truth is the theological foundation for both Jews and Christians. But also, "God is one" refers to his unity in dispensing his sovereign will. He needs no auxiliaries to accomplish his decrees in the world.

It is true that Christ is called a mediator between God and people: "There is one God; there is also one mediator between God and humankind, Christ Jesus, himself human" (1 Timothy 2:5 NRSV); yet Jesus is himself God, so even while dealing through Christ, God himself is dealing with his people. In addition, the phrase "God is one" was part of the great Hebrew creed (Deuteronomy 6:4), basic to their belief about God. No Jew would argue with Paul here.

God revealed the doctrine of the Trinity to the one people on earth most passionately convinced of the oneness of God. We who live centuries later are so used to thinking in triune categories that we are in danger sometimes of completely separating the Father, Son, and Holy Spirit. But the perfect single-mindedness of God must be included in our understanding of his dealings with us. The three-personed God worked in flawless harmony to bring about our salvation by grace. When God saved us, he acted on his own. No angel, apostle, pastor, or priest is qualified or able to stand in his place.

3:21 Is the law, therefore, opposed to the promises of God? Absolutely not! For if a law had been given that could impart life, then righteousness would certainly have come by the law.NIV Having answered the question "What purpose then does the law serve?" (3:19), Paul raised another question that might have been troubling his listeners: "Are the law and God's promises in conflict? If they're like oil and water, doesn't that mean one is against the other?" The Judaizers might have even concluded that

Paul was inferring that the law was evil. Paul answered with an emphatic *Absolutely not!* Both the promises and the law were given by God; both are important, but for different reasons. God offered eternal life through the promises. Paul's use of the phrase *could impart life* refers to spiritual life as illustrated by such other passages as John 6:63; Romans 8:11; 1 Corinthians 15:22, 36; and 2 Corinthians 3:6. The law's purpose was never to give that kind of life (as explained in 3:19). If a law could have been given that people could obey perfectly, then the law would have given life and *righteousness would certainly have come by the law.* The law is not evil; it is very good. But not for salvation.

> No man has ever appreciated the gospel until the law has first revealed him to himself. It is only against the inky blackness of the night sky that the stars begin to appear, and it is only against the dark background of sin and judgment that the gospel shines forth.
>
> *John Stott*

EXCHANGING GRACE FOR LAW
This passage in Galatians explains how we exchange life under the law for life under grace:

- We realize that we can't obtain righteousness and eternal life by keeping the law (3:21).
- We discover the sufficient grace of God given through faith in Christ (3:22).
- We abandon our own efforts for trying to gain merit with God (3:24-25).
- We become accepted, rightful heirs in the heavenly Father's family (3:26, 29).
- We clothe ourselves with Christ (3:27).
- We practice unity without discrimination with all others who also believe in Christ (3:28).

3:22 But the Scripture declares that the whole world is a prisoner of sin, so that what was promised, being given through faith in Jesus Christ, might be given to those who believe.[NIV] Sin affects all of humanity without discrimination; *the whole world* is permeated by sin, making each person *a prisoner of sin.* By *Scripture,* Paul may have had in mind Deuteronomy 27:26 or the series of verses that he later quoted in Romans 3:10-18, which describe the universal sinfulness of mankind (Psalms 5:9; 10:7; 14:1-3; 36:1; 140:3; and Isaiah 59:7-8). Or he may have been thinking of the Pentateuch as the biblical context of the law itself, filled with the record of unrelenting rebelliousness against God. What must be understood, however, is that the Scriptures speak with one voice when describing the human condition—we are sinners.

Describing the action accomplished by Scripture, Paul used the term *sunekleisen* (consigned, made prisoner, confined) to indicate our imprisonment to the power of sin. All people are prisoners without parole, prisoners on death row. We broke the law. By the time we were old enough to acknowledge right and wrong, we already had added to our account a great deal of wrong. Through Scripture we discovered that we could not earn a right relationship with God by our good works because our works were not good enough—they were always tainted by sin. But just like a dot of light shining into a dark prison cell, a ray of hope shone for us. The law showed us our hopelessness on our own, caused us to look elsewhere for hope, and directed us to the Savior, Jesus Christ. We missed the promises by trying to keep the law, but we can receive the promises by believing.

SINNERS ALL

People naturally recoil at being labeled sinners. Even when they accept the term, they usually state conditions, such as: "I'm not that bad of a sinner," or "Well, since no one is perfect, I guess I'm a sinner too." The resistance stems from two serious errors about the human condition:

The Error of Comparing: When we view our moral state by comparing ourselves with others, we may feel a mixture of despair (in seeing others who are "better" than we are) or pride (in noting those who are failing worse than we are). Suppose, however, that God's standard of perfection were the distance from earth to the moon; then squabbling over who is closer to perfection, those in the gutters or those at street level, would make no sense. We can't excuse ourselves because somebody is worse than we are. We are unable to gain a proper sense of our common lost condition before God by comparisons with others.

The Error of Using Scales: When people think of good and bad actions as weights added to one or the other "side" of life, they are not thinking as God thinks. In this distortion of reality, people visualize God keeping a record of the balance of good and bad in our lives and allowing people into heaven based on which outweighs the other. This is truly a terrible way to live and a terrifying way to die. For if every good action is nothing more than what is expected of us, then there is no "extra merit" from our good actions that could be charged or "weighed" against the evil we do. Our good deeds would have no effect on the balance. Jesus described this very problem to his disciples. When we have done everything we have been told to do, we still have only done our duty (see Luke 17:5-10). Only Jesus Christ can eliminate the terrible weight of sin.

In the terms of the Abrahamic covenant, *what was promised* refers to the blessing of the nations accomplished by the seed. Placed in context of the gospel, the promise includes salvation. Note, however, that Paul mentioned the Spirit in this connection in verse 14. The arrival of the Spirit indicates that salvation has taken place, but picturing the fulfillment of the promise in this way adds the ongoing presence of the Spirit to the picture.

The promise becomes effective in our lives *through faith* to *those who believe.* Both these phrases translate related words in Greek, *pisteos* (faith) and *pisteuousin* (believers, those who trust or believe). Both terms are necessary. The first indicates how God gives the promise; the second refers to how we receive the promise. As this letter elsewhere makes clear (2:16), "those who believe" are those whose faith is in Jesus Christ.

PRISONERS
Before faith in Christ delivered us, we were imprisoned by sin, beaten down by past mistakes, and choked by desires that we knew were wrong. God knew we were sin's prisoners, but he provided a way of escape—faith in Jesus Christ. Without Christ, everyone is held in sin's grasp, and only those who place their faith in Christ ever get out of it. Place your complete trust in Christ, because he is reaching out to set you free.

SONS OF GOD THROUGH FAITH / 3:23–4:7

While maintaining that the law was useful, Paul pointed out what a severe taskmaster it could be for those who failed to learn about grace received through faith. At this point in the letter, he shifted from a legal to a familial point of view. This change is not sudden, for though he began this chapter with his dismayed cry "Foolish Galatians!" he has already softened his language to "brothers and sisters" (3:15 NRSV) in preparation for the profound and universal message about what faith in Christ can do for relationships between people. Once we have gained a right relationship with God, our dealings with people will be entirely different.

3:23 Before this faith came, we were held prisoners by the law, locked up until faith should be revealed.ᴺᴵⱽ *This faith* refers to the faithfulness of Jesus Christ and to our response of faith in Jesus Christ. Clearly, Paul was not claiming that the capacity to believe had originated with the arrival of Christianity— people have managed to "believe" many things. They have also managed very often to be wrong in what they believed. Faith, as spoken of in the Scriptures, does not refer to some innate human power that, when used to its greatest capacity, gives us merit with God no matter what the actual content or object of that faith. The central point of the gospel is not belief, but who we believe and how we believe in him. Paul did not hesitate to display the vulnerability of Christianity in the claims about Jesus Christ. The system proves true or false in its foundational statement: "If Christ has not been raised, your faith is futile; you are still in your sins" (1 Corinthians 15:17

> Man, blinded and bowed, sits in darkness and cannot see the light of heaven unless grace with justice comes to his aid.
> *Bonaventure*

NIV). Abraham was justified by his faith and, along with other Old Testament believers, had to trust in God's grace without knowing much of God's plan; but "this faith" was faith in what *should be revealed*—Jesus Christ.

We were held prisoners by the law means that the law held people in bondage. Not only was the whole world "a prisoner of sin" (3:22), but the law also held all people as prisoners. The phrase could also be interpreted to mean that the law guarded us, or held us in protective custody. In a sense, it kept us out of trouble, kept us away from the evil into which our natures might otherwise have led, until faith in Christ would be revealed. That faith then sets us free from the law but leads us into the desire to obey God wholeheartedly out of love for him.

3:24 Therefore the law was our disciplinarian until Christ came, so that we might be justified by faith.NRSV The Greek word *paidagogos* is difficult to translate into English, but educational terms like *pedagogue* (tutor or basic instructor) and *pedagogics* (the science of teaching) have been derived from it. The NIV renders the word as "put in charge," and the NKJV says the law was a "tutor," while the NRSV best translates it *disciplinarian.* In Greek culture, a "pedagogue" was a slave who had the important responsibility for the children in a family. A wealthy family might have one pedagogue for each child. This slave strictly disciplined the child, conducted the child to and from school, cared for the child, taught the child manners, and gave the child moral training. He reviewed "homework" but was not a teacher as such. Or to put it another way, the ancients understood better than we that a child needs far more direct instruction in life skills than merely learning educational content. The pedagogue's role was temporary— he or she was responsible for the child until the child reached adult age (probably age sixteen).

WHAT IS THE LAW?

Part of the Jewish law included those laws found in the Old Testament. When Paul says that non-Jews (Gentiles) are no longer bound by these laws, he is not saying that the Old Testament laws do not apply to us today. He is saying that certain types of laws may not apply to us. In the Old Testament there were three categories of laws.

Ceremonial law	This kind of law relates specifically to Israel's worship (see, for example, Leviticus 1:1-13). Its primary purpose was to point forward to Jesus Christ. Therefore, these laws were no longer necessary after Jesus' death and resurrection. While we are no longer bound by ceremonial laws, the principles behind them—to worship and love a holy God—still apply. The Jewish Christians often accused the Gentile Christians of violating the ceremonial law.
Civil law	This type of law dictated Israel's daily living (see Deuteronomy 24:10-11, for example). Because modern society and culture are so radically different, some of these guidelines cannot be followed specifically. But the principles behind the commands should guide our conduct. At times, Paul asked Gentile Christians to follow some of these laws, not because they had to, but in order to promote unity.
Moral law	This sort of law is the direct command of God—for example, the Ten Commandments (Exodus 20:1-17). It requires strict obedience. It reveals the nature and will of God, and it still applies to us today. We are to obey this moral law not to obtain salvation, but to live in ways pleasing to God.

The picture of the law serving as a "pedagogue" shows that the law was a temporary measure meant to "lead us to Christ" (NIV). Paul summed up the role of the law in this verse with a single word, *eis* ("to," or "until"). The word could be used in Greek to refer to both place and time. Thus, the phrase *eis Christon* forces a translation choice between stating that the "law instructed us until Christ" or that the "law guided us to Christ." Paul may well have meant to include both nuances, although the context leans more strongly in the direction of the law's temporal and supervisory (not educational) work. This leading was meant in the sense of the law watching over us until we could receive our "adulthood," our full relationship with the Father, through Christ's coming.

What was the ultimate purpose of the law? Paul repeated it in the last phrase, *that we might be justified by faith.* The law, through imprisonment and discipline, taught us (though negatively) that justification with God really is through faith alone. Paul did not hesitate to repeat crucial facts, and justification by faith was one of his constant themes. In fact, it represents in brief what he offered to the Galatians as the alternative to any other "gospel" or system that might appeal to them. The law had its usefulness in pointing out the wrong and providing constant reproof.

3:25 Now that faith has come, we are no longer under the supervision of the law.[NIV] *The supervision of the law* is like the supervision given by the pedagogue to the young child (3:24). Once the child came of age, he or she no longer needed the preparatory services of the pedagogue. After Christ arrived, offering salvation by faith alone, people no longer needed the supervision of the law. The law teaches the need for salvation; God's grace offers us that salvation.

The Old Testament still applies today. In it God has revealed his nature, his will for humanity, his moral laws, and his guidelines for living. The law still serves as a demanding instructor to those who have not yet believed. But we cannot be saved by keeping that law; *now that faith has come,* we must trust in Christ. The word *now* is important. The law super-

> We must take care lest, by exalting the merit of faith, without adding any distinction or explanation, we furnish people with a pretext for relaxing in the practice of good works.
>
> *Ignatius of Loyola*

vised us until Christ came; but Christ has come, so we can now respond to God through faith. We are no longer bound by legalism or guilt-ridden by perfectionism.

As Paul will immediately demonstrate, the arrival of faith was not a static experience. Living does not come to an end when we are no longer under the authority of the law. Faith comes first, then we lay aside the supervision of the law. Many would like to do away with the supervision of the law, but they also don't want the requirements of faith. Now we must live by faith in Christ. Paul had already addressed this issue in 2:20-21. Faith had its most basic work in our being "crucified with Christ," but it immediately pursues its ongoing task: "The life I live in the body, I live by faith in the Son of God" (2:20 NIV). This living by faith will be the theme of much of the remainder of this letter.

3:26 For in Christ Jesus you are all children of God through faith.[NRSV] The change to *you* shows Paul's return to focusing on the Galatian believers. They did not need to be children under the care of the pedagogue (the law); instead, they *are all children of God.* They received this status *in Christ Jesus* and *through faith.* Those who are truly God's children have been justified by faith

in Christ and receive a new relationship with God—that of
adopted children.

LAW BREAKING
One reason that we fail in our attempts to present the gospel to
others is our hesitancy to bring the law to bear on their lives.
We assume that their consciences will admit to sinfulness
enough to lead them to acknowledge their need for a divine
solution. So we end up debating with someone whose confidence rests on the hope that they are not nearly as bad as
many other people whom they are willing to name. They may
even claim that their understanding of God assures them that
they are making a passing moral grade.

But going through the Ten Commandments, one at a time,
asking them to measure their lives against God's standard,
may well create a new openness to the gospel. People are
often not ready for freedom in Christ until they have a deeper
awareness of their slavery to sin and judgment under God's law.

The phrase "in Christ Jesus" strikes a dominant responsive
chord for those who are trusting him as Savior and Lord. In this
context, the phrase expresses the alternative to being "under the
supervision of the law" (3:25 NIV). Just as the use of a life instructor in the ancient Greek world assumed a distance between the
slave and the child under his care, the alternate arrangement "in
Christ Jesus" assumes a personal relationship. Paul made this
clear by reminding the Galatians that their relationship with
Christ means that they are "children of God."

The actual expression "in Christ" appears eight times in Galatians. Paul used the expression in every one of his letters to
churches. He found it just as easy to say, "Christ lives in me"
(2:20). For some, the idea of being "in Christ" contradicts the
idea of Christ being "in us." But the
terms describe a relationship like no
other. They help us understand much
without allowing us to claim that we understand everything. The picture of
being "in Christ" establishes the reason
or basis of our relationship with God.
Christ's righteousness, sacrifice, and
faithfulness are all regarded by the
Father to stand in our place. From the
perspective of grace, when God views
us who are "in Christ," he sees Christ.
The picture of Christ being "in us" identifies the actual experience of relation-

> Being "in Christ" is the
> essence of Christian
> proclamation and
> experience. One may
> discuss legalism,
> nomism, and even
> justification by faith, but
> without treating the "in
> Christ" motif we miss the
> heart of the Christian
> message.
>
> *Richard Longenecker*

ship. To the Colossians, Paul spoke of Christ being "in you" as the essence of the mystery of God revealed in the gospel— "Christ in you, the hope of glory" (Colossians 1:27 NIV). Yet in the next verse he wrote of his goal to "present everyone perfect in Christ" (Colossians 1:28 NIV). Or perhaps to put it another way, "in Christ" and Christ "in us" convey two aspects of our family relationship. Our membership in the family of God flows from being "in Christ," just as our biological connection with our earthly family derives from having been literally "in" our father and mother. Our constantly changing experience of having Christ "in us" varies as much as the fellowship that flows from day to day among the various members of an earthly household (see also comments on 4:19, where Paul speaks of Christ being "formed in you").

What does it mean to be "children of God"? As he did in most of his letters, Paul was moving from the initial section of teaching passages to the application of what he had been developing. Here the first application is unmistakable: Our relationship with each other has its common principle in how we are related to God. We are children of the same family if we have the same heavenly Father. Paul wrote to the Romans, "Now if we are children, then we are heirs—heirs of God and co-heirs with Christ, if indeed we share in his sufferings in order that we may also share in his glory" (Romans 8:17 NIV). What a privilege! Because we are God's children, we share in great treasures as co-heirs. From this point, Paul will first develop applications regarding how we should see ourselves and others. Later in the letter he will discuss how we should treat each other.

3:27 For all of you who were baptized into Christ have clothed yourselves with Christ.[NIV] The reference to baptism here does not mean that Paul was replacing the rite of circumcision with baptism. Baptism does not save anyone any more than circumcision would. If Paul was referring to water baptism, he was recognizing the fact that, in the early church, new converts usually were baptized (see Acts 2:41; 8:36-38; 9:18; 10:47-48; and 16:33 for some examples of new converts being baptized). Baptism demonstrated their faith—people "believed and were baptized"— not the other way around. It also demonstrated identification with the body of believers, the Christian church.

Paul may have been referring to the baptism of the Holy Spirit. When a person believes, the Holy Spirit comes to dwell within. Jesus promised this: "And I will ask the Father, and he will give you another Counselor to be with you forever—the Spirit of truth. . . . He lives with you and will be in you" (John 14:16-17

NIV). The Holy Spirit also supernaturally makes us a part of the body of Christ: "The body is a unit, though it is made up of many parts; and though all its parts are many, they form one body. So it is with Christ. For we were all baptized by one Spirit into one body—whether Jews or Greeks, slave or free—and we were all given the one Spirit to drink" (1 Corinthians 12:12-13 NIV).

Most likely Paul referred to the theology behind water baptism expressed as an early form of liturgy. Paul restated for emphasis his claim to the Galatians that they were children of God. The purpose of baptism ultimately confirms the connection between us and Christ. We are "baptized into Christ." Those who would use a text like this as proof that babies who have been baptized are somehow acceptable to God (unlike babies who are not baptized) must do so with caution. The context certainly implies an active, informed faith whose object is Jesus Christ. Our faith rests, not on any form of baptism, but in Christ.

NEW CLOTHES
In order to grasp the long-term effects of "putting on Christ," we might be helped by seeing the robe he gives us as a full-size, adult set of clothing. It is a seamless robe of characteristics, attitudes, and intentions modeled by Jesus himself. At first, because we are no more than spiritual children, the clothing doesn't fit. The more we grow, the better we fit into what Christ has already given us.

However, we carry out the disciplines of the spiritual life or train in holiness, not under the threat of failure or judgment, but under the loving guidance of God's Spirit. We do not seek merit with God; rather, we desire to experience fully all that God has given to us in Christ. In what areas of spiritual life do you find your "clothing" still not fitting? What parts of God's Word have you found that give you directions for growth in those areas?

The expression *enedusasthe* (put on, clothed yourselves) recalls a specific ancient rite of passage. In Roman society, a youth coming of age laid aside the robe of childhood and put on a new toga. This represented his move into adult citizenship with full rights and responsibilities. Likewise, being "in Christ" leads to our ongoing experience of clothing ourselves with Christ. Paul combined this cultural understanding with the concept of baptism. By becoming Christians and being baptized, the Galatian believers were becoming spiritually grown up and ready to take on the privileges and responsibilities of the more mature. Paul was saying that they had laid aside the old clothes of the law and had put on Christ—that is, Christ's robe of righteousness (see

2 Corinthians 5:21; Ephesians 4:23-24). The person who did so became a "new" person, with a new lifestyle and new aspirations. Clothing ourselves with Christ is not passive; it is an action we must take. Have you put on the attitudes, characteristics, and intentions of Jesus Christ?

UNITY
Christians do not have permission to discriminate against other believers. The emphasis must always be, not on unity for unity's sake, but on unity in Christ. Where Christ is not recognized as Lord, all unity will be superficial, if present at all. But remarkably divergent people who recognize in Jesus their common life will find deep unity and fellowship.

Those who seek unity as their only goal will find their objective elusive. Those who seek others who also name Jesus as Lord will find themselves yoked with any number of unusual characters. Unity flows out of being "in Christ," not the other way around. Where do you tend to discriminate (culture, background, gender, racial issues)?

3:28 **There is neither Jew nor Greek, there is neither slave nor free, there is neither male nor female; for you are all one in Christ Jesus.**^{NKJV} In the first part of this verse, discrimination and barriers are eliminated. In the second part, unity is established. If all believers have put on Christ, if all believers have professed faith and joined the body of Christ, then this unity sets aside all other superficial distinctions. While it is true that in the body of Christ, Jews, Greeks (meaning Gentiles), slaves, free people, men, and women do still have individual identities, Paul exalts their unity *in Christ Jesus.* All labels become secondary among those who share Jesus in common.

Some Jewish males would greet each new day by praying, "Lord, I thank you that I am not a Gentile, a slave, or a woman." The prejudice toward all three categories was real and strong. As discussed throughout this letter to the Galatians, a Jew who believes in Christ is no different from a Gentile who believes. Unity in Christ transcends racial distinctions. Next is the barrier of social status. Slaves and free persons treat each other like brothers and sisters in the body of Christ. To take it even further, when it comes to faith and God's promises, there really is no gender distinction. Both male and female alike are acceptable in the body of Christ. Women were not treated well in Paul's day. Both the Gentile and the Jewish culture placed women in inferior positions—almost as property. The ancient Jewish historian Josephus pointed out that "woman is inferior to man in every way"

(*Against Apion* 2.24). Christianity liberated women as God's creations with worth and abilities that could be used for God's kingdom. Just to announce that barriers have been removed does not mean that all prejudice has been overcome. This requires faith and being clothed with Christ. More than tolerance and superficial harmony, it requires a real change of heart and actions.

Christians have debated the application of this verse. Some would contend that the equality applies only to salvation. They interpret the verse to mean that we all have equal access in Christ to God's grace without discrimination. They would limit the application of equality to salvation and not see it as a basis for social equality in the life of the church (such as allowing women to hold offices). Others see this verse to mean the stripping away of all barriers to God's use of people to do his will based on their position in Christ. Thus, it does clear the way to full equality for all people. Paul seems to imply both. Our equal standing in Christ gives us equal access not only to salvation but to the full gifts of the Spirit and to all avenues of service.

The barriers broken down in this verse may not seem so radical to our day, but they were astounding in ancient Roman culture. This made Christianity unique and attractive—it valued each individual, yet it provided a unified body. All believers are one in Christ Jesus. All are equally valuable to God. Differences arise in gifts, in function, in abilities, but all are one in Christ (Ephesians 2:15).

COMMON GROUND
It's natural to feel uncomfortable around people who are different from us and to gravitate toward those who are similar. But when we allow our differences to separate us from our fellow believers, we are disregarding clear biblical teaching. Make a point to seek out and appreciate people who are not just like you and your friends. You may find that you have a lot in common with them.

3:29 And if you are Christ's, then you are Abraham's seed, and heirs according to the promise.NKJV Besides becoming God's children (3:26) and one in Christ (3:28), believers (those who *are Christ's*) also become *Abraham's seed.* Abraham was the prime element in Jewish thought about salvation. Jews believed that they were automatically God's people because they were "Abraham's seed." Paul concluded that Abraham's spiritual children are not the Jews, nor are they those who have been circumcised. Abraham's children are those who respond to God in faith as

Abraham had done. The only difference is that our response is to Christ as Savior. Because we have responded, we are *heirs according to the promise.* The original promise (see 3:16), though given to the Seed (Christ), was fulfilled in the believers, who are "in Christ." Since they are "the body of Christ," they are heirs to God's eternal kingdom.

WHO ARE YOU?
Christians often fail to live up to the identity they have been given in Christ. They live passive, defeated lives, appearing in almost every respect to still be living with the curse of the law hanging over their heads. We may be heirs in Christ, but we appear to have missed the reading of the will.

God's Word inspires us to confidence—not in our own ability to live the Christian life, but in God's infinite ability to help us grow into Christ. If you believe in Christ, then you are in him and truly belong as a member of his family.

By responding to Christ in faith, we have followed in the ancient way of Abraham, one of the early ones justified by faith. He trusted God, and so do we. But to us has been added the opportunity to appreciate what price Christ paid to ensure our share in the promise.

4:1 My point is this: heirs, as long as they are minors, are no better than slaves, though they are the owners of all the property.NRSV To further illustrate the spiritual immaturity of those who insist on remaining under the law, Paul used an example from Roman law and custom. In ancient times, the "coming of age" of a son carried tremendous significance. This did not occur at a specific age (such as twelve or thirteen), as it did among Jews and Greeks; rather, the "coming of age" was determined by the father. In Rome this event was usually marked on March 17 by a family celebration known as the *Liberalia.* During this event, the father formally acknowledged his son and heir. The son received a new "grown-up" toga and entered into adult responsibilities.

Paul pointed out, however, that while this son and heir was still a minor (not yet of age), he really was no better off than a slave, for he had no rights and little freedom. Although he was the future

> We cannot come to Christ to be justified until we have first been to Moses to be condemned. But once we have gone to Moses, and acknowledged our sin, guilt and condemnation, we must not stay there. We must let Moses send us to Christ.
>
> *John Stott*

owner of an estate and a fortune, while he was young, he had no claim to it nor any right to make decisions regarding it. In the eyes of the Roman law, the young heir was no different from a slave.

Paul's application of the illustration reveals that when we were under the law, we were no better off than slaves. Though the law regards the child as the *kurios* (master, owner) of the estate, his experience resembles that of the servants. He lives under rules and discipline until he has achieved adulthood.

4:2 But they remain under guardians and trustees until the date set by the father.NRSV In this analogy Paul focused on the legal rights and status of the son, so he used the words *epitropous* (guardians, those who watch over the child) and *oikonomous* (trustees, those who watch over the inheritance), instead of *pedagogue,* as in 3:24. But Paul's meaning was the same. The law performed its function of "keeping us out of trouble" and disciplining us during our "immaturity" until God offered us "maturity" through our acceptance of salvation by grace. Paul's words imply that the time of this "coming of age" differed for every son. In Rome, the father set the time for his son's coming of age and adulthood. So, too, God set the time for terminating our guardianship under the law and making us his children and heirs by faith. The *date* is the time of Christ's coming into the world.

Faith, then, initiates the believer into maturity and full rights. Paul was dumbfounded that the Galatians would choose to revert to the state of discipline when Christ had given them freedom. They were behaving like a child who had inherited an estate but still insisted on remaining in a dependent, servile role.

SLAVERY
Religious slavery (trying to please God by legalism or works) is particularly devastating to people because it offers false hope. Thinking they will gain freedom, they instead get trapped in a cycle of effort and failure leading to more effort and failure.
Opportunities to return to religious slavery occur almost every day. When we have fallen short of our expectations, we are tempted to try harder and be more disciplined. But when we fail in the Christian life, we should apply grace, not renewed effort, as the primary means for becoming right again.

4:3 So also, when we were children, we were in slavery under the basic principles of the world.NIV Paul alluded to slavery in order to show that before Christ came and died for sins, people were in bondage to whatever law or religion they chose to follow. Thinking they could be saved by their deeds, they became enslaved to trying—and failing—to follow even the basics. Applying the illustration directly to the Galatian believers, Paul pointed out that when they were immature spiritually (when they were *nepioi*—children, infants), they were like slaves (see 4:8). The *basic principles of the world (stoikeia tou kosmou)* has also been translated "elements of the world" (NKJV). This phrase has three main interpretations:

1. Some have interpreted "basic principles" to refer directly to the law of Moses, for Paul's focus in this letter has been on the law and the believers' relationship to it. While this interpretation agrees with Paul's view that the law taken by itself leads only to slavery, the meaning must be much broader. As in Romans 2:12-16, Paul pointed to the conscience as a general means for God to reveal his standards. The Galatian believers had come from heathen backgrounds and had not grown up under the Jewish law. Although they had not been in slavery, they were becoming enslaved by turning from grace to the law.

2. Others have interpreted "basic principles" or "elements" to mean the four basic elements of Greek philosophy—earth, air, fire, and water. Later, these elements became associated with the gods and then with the stars and planets as well. Many pagan religions (and, at times, the Jewish people) worshiped stars and planets because of their supposed effect on human destiny. Thus, Paul may have lumped both pagan and Jewish religions under one banner by saying that when the people followed these "principles" or "elements" of the world, they were actually in slavery under Satan's influence. This idea would parallel Paul's claim regarding the real source of our struggles in the Christian life (see Ephesians 6:12). Yet this view is unlikely because of the context. Paul spoke about people who are under the law.

3. A third interpretation explains "basic principles" or "elements" as the elementary stages of religious practice, whether under the law of the Jewish religion, or the rites and rituals in any heathen religion (see also 4:9 and Colossians 2:20). In other words, the statement referred to any religious experience prior to accepting Christ as Savior.

The third interpretation seems most plausible. Paul was pointing out that trying to reach God through any religion or any worldly plan brings failure. The "basics" of the world (whether religious or moral) suggest that a solution is needed, but do not offer that solution. In fact, these "basics" can be used by demonic powers to give slavery a strong "religious" flavor. Paul compared religious rituals to *slavery* because they force a standard that people can never achieve. But, with the proclamation of the gospel, grace in Christ replaced those worldly religious practices.

GROWN-UPS
The illustration of slavery demonstrates that the law, apart from Christ's death for our sins, keeps us in bondage. It holds us accountable to a standard we can never hope to meet on our own. But, as Paul wrote in 3:26, through faith in Jesus Christ we who were once slaves become God's very own children. Because of Christ, we no longer have any reason to fear our heavenly Father. We can approach him as his treasured children, not as cringing slaves. What is your relationship with the heavenly Father? Have you experienced the freedom he wants you to have?

4:4 But when the fullness of the time had come, God sent forth His Son, born of a woman, born under the law.^{NKJV} Everyone was enslaved under the "basic principles of the world," *but . . .* That little word offered hope to humanity. God's intervention into human history changed the world.

When the fullness of the time had come, God sent Jesus to earth. Why did Jesus come when he did? The "why" may be unanswerable, except that God knew it was the right time, the "fullness." Several factors present in the Roman Empire certainly aided the quick spread of the message of the gospel. The Greek civilization provided a language that had spread across much of the known world as the main language for all people. The Romans had brought peace throughout their empire and built a system of roads that made land travel quicker and safer than ever before. The Jews were expectant, eagerly awaiting their Messiah. Messianic fervor was at its height. Into this world came Jesus.

Ultimately, the term "fullness of time" refers more clearly to the time of Christ's arrival rather than to a climate caused by other events that somehow made Jesus' birth inevitable. Just as a Roman father would set the date for his son to reach maturity and attain freedom from his guardians (4:2), so God had set the date when he would send *forth His Son* to free people from the law, to become his children (see 4:5). Guided by a sovereign God, historical events worked in harmony to prepare for the predecided moment of Jesus' arrival on earth. God chose the exact time (see also Psalm 102:13; Mark 1:15; and Ephesians 1:10).

TIMING IS EVERYTHING
For centuries the Jews had been wondering when their Messiah would come—but God's timing was perfect. We may sometimes wonder if God will ever respond to our prayers, but we must never doubt him or give up hope. At the right time he will respond. Are you waiting for God's timing? Trust his judgment, and trust that he has your best interests in mind.

The reference to Jesus as "sent" indicates his preexistence as well as his endorsement by God in the overall plan of salvation. The sending also clarifies the relationship between God the Father and God the Son. The former lovingly sends, while the latter obediently goes. This act of divine sending is mentioned forty-one times in the Gospel of John (for example, see John 3:16-17; 17:18; see also Romans 8:3-4 and 1 John 4:9-10). At the conclusion of that mission, Jesus prefaced his own "sending" of us into the world by claiming, "All authority in heaven and on earth has been given to me. Therefore go . . ." (Matthew 28:18-19 NIV). Jesus successfully submitted to his Father's authority. Therefore, God gave him authority over us, both to rescue us and to send us out into the world.

Jesus was *born of a woman*—he was God yet also human (Genesis 3:15; Luke 1:26-38; John 1:1, 14). Paul balanced his amazing claims about Jesus' divine nature with his reminder of Jesus' human character. *Born under the law,* Jesus was a human; thus he was voluntarily subject to the structured universe that he had created (John 1:3-5) and that had been marred by human rebellion. More significantly, Jesus lived as a Jew, subject to God's revealed law. In keeping with this, Jesus was both circumcised and presented at the temple (Luke 2:21-32). Yet while no other human being has been able to perfectly fulfill God's law, Jesus kept it completely (Matthew 5:17; Hebrews 4:15). Thus, Jesus could be the perfect sacrifice because, although fully human, he never sinned. His death bought freedom for us who were enslaved to sin, offering us redemption and adoption into God's family.

4:5 To redeem those under the law, that we might receive the full rights of sons.[NIV] Jesus was himself born "under the law" (4:4) so that by his living and dying he could accomplish two purposes: (1) *to redeem those under the law* and (2) to allow those "redeemed" people to *receive the full rights of sons.*

To "redeem" means "to buy back" (see 3:13). "Redemption" was the price paid to gain freedom for a slave (Leviticus 25:47-

54). Through his life, Jesus demonstrated his unique eligibility to be our Redeemer. Through his death, Jesus paid the price to release us from slavery to sin. When Christ redeemed "those under the law," he did not redeem the Jews alone. His death set people free from bondage to any law or religious system (see 4:3)—offering, instead, salvation by faith alone. But because the law was God's clearest revelation of his justice, being born under the law and keeping it perfectly proved that Jesus was the perfect sacrifice. He took upon himself the curse the law required in order to set believers free of that curse.

In these verses, Paul continued to respond to the foolishness of the Galatians. If Christ had fulfilled the law, taking upon himself the curse of the law, and had freed people from the law, why would the Galatians try to keep requirements already fulfilled by Christ? The question appears again plainly in 4:9. Meanwhile, Paul was building a case that would make the question entirely rhetorical.

FULL RIGHTS AND PRIVILEGES
The scope and value of our "sonship rights" in Christ accumulate almost beyond our comprehension. These rights, given to us freely through faith in Christ, include:
- We are no longer debtors, nor cursed (3:13).
- We have received "new life" (2:20).
- We are part of a new family (4:5).
- We have received the Spirit (4:6; 5:25).
- We have experienced a supernatural birth (John 1:12-13; Galatians 4:28-29).
- We have the promise of future resurrection of our bodies (Romans 8:23).
- We have the promise of a place in the future (John 14:2).
- We will be with Christ in eternity (John 14:3).
- We enjoy the same special relationship with God previously limited to Israel (Romans 9:4; Galatians 3:28).
- We receive inestimable riches predestined for us by God through Jesus Christ (Ephesians 1:5).
  Do you know your rights? In your relationship with God through Jesus Christ, they are yours to claim.

Redemption had an ongoing purpose—"that we might receive the full rights of sons." Until Christ redeemed us (that is, paid the ultimate price by taking the penalty for our sins), we could never have been acceptable to God. In our sinful state, God could have nothing to do with us. Even our good works or religious rituals could bring us no closer to a relationship with him. But when Christ "bought us back," he gave us freedom from the slavery we

faced before and brought us into a new relationship with God the
Father. Our new position in Christ goes beyond mere acceptance
by God. So close is that relationship that Paul called it *huiothes-
ian* (sonship) or "adoption as children" (NRSV) or "full rights of
sons." In Roman culture, a wealthy, childless man could take a
slave youth and make that slave his child and heir. The adopted
person was no longer a slave. He became a full heir to his new
family, guaranteed all legal rights to his father's property. He was
not a second-class son; he was equal to all other sons, biological
or adopted, in his father's family. That person's origin or past was
no longer a factor in his legal standing. Likewise, when a person
becomes a Christian, he or she leaves the slavery of trying to
please God through works and gains all the privileges and responsibilities of a child in God's family.

4:6 **Because you are sons, God sent the Spirit of his Son into our
hearts, the Spirit who calls out, "Abba, Father."**[NIV] This verse
and the next are central in the apostle's entire argument. Focusing
again on the Galatians, Paul added *you are sons,* that is, God's
children, part of God's family. Paul almost seems to say,
"Because you're God's kids, start acting that way!" Despite their
doubts and confusion at that time, God still regarded the Galatian
believers as his children. How did Paul
know this? How could the Galatian
believers claim this? Because *God sent
the Spirit of his Son* into their hearts. As
God had sent the Son, so he had sent
the Spirit (Paul used the same Greek
word for "sent," *exapes-teilen,* in 4:4).
God sent his Son to bring redemption
(4:4-5); God sent his Spirit to mark us
with his seal as "the pledge of our inheritance toward redemption as God's own
people" (Ephesians 1:14 NRSV). The
Spirit cannot be earned or obtained, as
if he were the result or reward of some
system of works or discipline. Instead,
God sends the Holy Spirit as a gift. It is
through the Spirit that Christ can live in
believers' hearts:

■ *But you are not in the flesh; you are
in the Spirit, since the Spirit of God
dwells in you. Anyone who does not
have the Spirit of Christ does not*

> There is often a sense of
> failure among professing
> Christians that is sadly
> out of keeping with their
> rightful position in
> Christ. Do not be over-
> anxious. Live in your
> Father's house in con-
> stant freedom of heart.
> Remember that you are
> under the same roof as
> Christ, and are therefore
> allowed to avail yourself
> of all his grace and help.
> Refuse no task, however
> irksome, that God sets
> before you; and do not
> worry about irksome
> rules or petty vexations.
>
> *F. B. Meyer*

*belong to him. But if Christ is in you, though the body is dead
because of sin, the Spirit is alive because of righteousness. If
the Spirit of him who raised Jesus from the dead dwells in you,
he who raised Christ from the dead will give life to your mortal
bodies also through his Spirit that dwells in you. (Romans 8:9-
11 NRSV)*

Having the Spirit of Christ means that we belong to Christ.
Faith in Christ includes the reception of the Holy Spirit as part of
the same transaction between us and God (see Ephesians 1:13-
14). We do not experience Christ's redemption apart from receiving his Spirit. "The Spirit of his Son" is a unique expression for
Paul. It appears only in Galatians and shows Christ's full deity
and the total interaction of the Trinity.

WE HAVE THE SPIRIT
When Jesus described the Holy Spirit to his disciples during the
Last Supper (John 13–17), he used the term *parakletos* (com-
forter, counselor, encourager). The actual ministry of the Spirit
outlined in John 15:26–16:15 also shows his work as a "discom-
forter"—convicting the world of sin. But in Galatians we see the
Spirit in his strengthening, helping, indwelling role.
- He confirms our identity (4:6).
- He comes into our hearts, bringing the character of Christ
  (4:6).
- He assists in the control of our human nature (5:16).
- His presence creates certain by-products: steadfastness, intimacy with God, unity, and those character traits called the
  fruit of the Spirit (5:22-23).

A person cannot have a personal relationship with laws or rituals. But believers have an intimate relationship with God. *Abba* is
an Aramaic word for "father." It was a very familiar, endearing
term used by a child when addressing his or her father at home,
perhaps like the English "Daddy." Christ used this word in his
prayer in Mark 14:36. Paul may have added *pater* (Father) simply as a translation of the word *Abba,* but he may have also been
pointing to deeper issues than simply the freedom to be familiar
with God. Before, when we were enslaved to the "principles"
(4:3), we had no access to God. But now, as God's adopted children, we can approach him with love and trust. Notice that it is
the Holy Spirit, not we, who calls out *Abba,* Father. The Spirit
cries out to the *Abba* on our behalf (Romans 8:26-27), and we cry
to the *Abba* with the Spirit (Romans 8:15). Taken together, the
two terms convey the delightful fearlessness of a little child with
the honor of a respectful son. He gives us the Spirit, not for us to

display our spirituality, but so that we may witness to our adoption into his family. As God's adopted children, we share with Jesus all rights to God's resources. As God's heirs, we can claim what he has provided for us—our full identity as his children.

How do the sending of the Spirit and adoption work together? Neither one occurs logically or chronologically prior to the other. God's work of adopting us and sending his Spirit is an interwoven relationship, reciprocally entwined.

THE FEAST
A young missionary couple with several children boarded an ocean liner, traveling economy fare on their way to a South American country. Finding their way to the dining room the first evening, the family was astonished at the sumptuous feast that was laid out on the serving tables. The family felt out of place; they were certain that there must be an "economy" dining room, or that perhaps they needed to look at a menu to decide if they would be able to eat at all. A discreet question to the purser produced a chuckle and an explanation. "You folks aren't the first to be impressed by our cook. But everything you see here is for you. It's all part of the ticket when you sail with us."

How many Christians look for meager fare when God has already given us the best of everything?

The doctrine of the Trinity implicit in these verses must not be missed. Salvation is accomplished through the work of all persons of the Trinity. God the Father sent both God the Son and God the Holy Spirit. God the Son, by his death on the cross, allowed us to have the position as God's children; God the Holy Spirit, by entering into believers' hearts, gives us the assurance of that experience. The Galatians were being encouraged by the Judaizers to pursue what they in fact already had. No wonder Paul was astonished. It was as if the Galatians were believing door-to-door salesmen who were offering to sell them tiny shares of the inheritance they had already received!

4:7 So you are no longer a slave but a child, and if a child then also an heir, through God.NRSV To conclude his argument from this analogy, Paul explained briefly that each Galatian believer was *no longer a slave* to any law or religious ritual or even to Satan. Instead, each person had entered into God's family, being adopted as a *child.* Belonging to God as his child also means being an *heir,* for God has promised the inheritance of eternal life and his riches and blessings to all his children. We need no further preparation. No system can fill in or stand in for Christ.

Being a child and being an heir are inseparable realities in God's family. Paul wrote to the Romans:

■ *For you did not receive a spirit of slavery to fall back into fear, but you have received a spirit of adoption. When we cry, "Abba! Father!" it is that very Spirit bearing witness with our spirit that we are children of God, and if children, then heirs, heirs of God and joint heirs with Christ (Romans 8:15-17* NRSV*).*

Note the change from the plural in 4:6 to the singular in this verse. The focus on each individual believer drives the point home. Not the Galatians only, but all believers, including you who read these words, can claim this incredible promise: You are no longer a slave but a child, and an heir of all God's promises! For a Galatian to follow the Judaizers would be the same act as if a son and heir removed his birthright and returned to slavery.

The two words *through God* emphasize Paul's source for his teaching and his assurances. The promises come through God and God alone. Paul's teaching of these doctrines also came through God and God alone. Believers who trust in Christ's sacrifice have the Holy Spirit and thus can have the same assurance. Our privileged position comes through God.

FREE!
When by faith we receive Christ, God gives us everything we need to be fully saved. We need no further act of repentance or submission to complete our salvation. Christ does all the work to redeem and cleanse us, and none of our work adds anything.

Some teach that sin has so polluted our nature that even the death of Christ cannot cleanse us. They imply that Christians must continually work to achieve a greater degree of righteousness and acceptability before God. But this is false. Because of our love for Christ and as a grateful response for his saving us, we serve him and battle the world, the flesh, and the devil—but none of these efforts contributes an ounce to our salvation. Salvation comes completely and utterly free!

Galatians 4:8–5:1

What do Christians mean when they claim to "know God"? As strange as the concept may sound to modern ears, the Scriptures speak confidently of our ability to know God intimately. Jeremiah recorded a significant verbal confrontation issued by God himself:

▪ *Thus says the Lord: Do not let the wise boast in their wisdom, do not let the mighty boast in their might, do not let the wealthy boast in their wealth; but let those who boast boast in this, that they understand and know me, that I am the LORD; I act with steadfast love, justice, and righteousness in the earth, for in these things I delight, says the Lord. (Jeremiah 9:23-24 NRSV)*

We ought to be so confident of our personal acquaintance with God that we border on boasting. Indeed, for us to boast of wealth, wisdom, or personal accomplishment (none of which can be ours permanently) would be foolish. All of these are insignificant in comparison to knowing God.

Jesus later underscored this statement in Jeremiah when he prayed: "Now this is eternal life: that they may know you, the only true God, and Jesus Christ, whom you have sent" (John 17:3 NIV).

In the light of these facts, Paul turned to the Galatians' seeming denial of their relationship with God. Though they had met God, their present course of action (living by the law) amounted to a sad betrayal of God's grace.

4:8 Formerly, when you did not know God, you were enslaved to beings that by nature are not gods.NRSV As in 3:23 and 4:1, Paul reiterated the former enslaved condition of the Galatians. The "beings" (or "ones") who were enslavers could come from any of three possible spheres of authority.

1. Before they came to know the one true God, the Galatians believed in other *beings* (gods such as Zeus and Hermes—read about Paul's experience in Lystra, a city in Galatia, in Acts 14:8-

18). These "beings" may have been gods, but they had no divine power.

2. The "beings" may have been demonic powers, attractive for their supernatural control or strength but bent on the destruction of those under their control.

3. The "ones" may have been the principles and pursuits of life that so easily change from being our possessions to possessing us.

KNOWING GOD
On certain important topics, English words don't communicate as well as other languages. The extensive overuse and trivialization of the word *love* may be the clearest example. The word *know* shares a similar fate. Many languages use one word to convey personal or relational knowledge while using a different word to mean factual or static knowledge. For example, in Portuguese, when you "know" someone, you *conhecer* them. But when you "know" certain facts or skills, you *saber* them. You never *conhecer* facts, or *saber* a person. Greek, though having two terms that are translated "know" *(oida and ginosko),* nevertheless tends to make use of the words interchangeably. Paul used a form of *oida* in 4:8 and two forms of *ginosko* in 4:9, always referring to personal knowledge in relation to God. The context makes this clear.

Whatever terms are used, Scripture encourages us to know God intimately and personally. The Bible provides us with factual knowledge about God, giving us a basis for a relationship with our Creator. God's Spirit confirms to us the reality of that relationship in such a way that we know God and are his children (see Romans 8:16). How well do you know God?

Whether these beings were demonic powers, Greek or Roman idols, or the "principles" (as explained in 4:3 and 4:9), the people's ignorance of God made them slaves of something less than God. There is only one God; to worship anything else means false worship and slavery to sin. As Paul explained in 4:1-7, anyone who has not discovered freedom in Christ remains a slave. In this verse, Paul was simply restating the preconversion predicament of the Galatians.

4:9 But now that you know God—or rather are known by God—how is it that you are turning back to those weak and miserable principles?[NIV] The Galatian believers had been enslaved, but then Paul introduced them to God. They came to *know God.* The Greek word for "know" used here *(ginosko)* refers to knowing intimately and on a personal level. They had gotten to know God personally, to understand his grace and love toward them. Yet Paul, not wishing to make it sound as if the Galatians had done

some work or gotten to know God on their own merit, clarified
his thought by saying *or rather are known by God*. God initiates
the "knowing"; we know him only because he first knew us.

THE MASTERS
Although our lives may be quite different from the lives of the
Galatians, the potential for slavery to sin remains the same.
The names of the deities may change, but the wrongful worship
continues. Which of the following slave masters exert the great-
est control on your life?

- Accomplishment—the lure of personal fulfillment
- Approval of others—measuring up to peer expectations
- Autonomy—the craving to do it my way or no way
- Chemical addictions, accompanied by denial
- Knowledge and technology—the faith that lends divinity to
  human abilities
- Pleasure—entertainment as the ultimate pursuit
- Sexual addiction—slavery to pornography of every kind
- Success—the drive to reach the top, to be number one
- Wealth—security promised through the accumulation of
  money, power, and possessions

Those who have never believed in the one true God remain in
slavery to sin. Paul has already established that. And while that
was true of the Galatians at one time, Paul was astonished that
after getting to know God personally, the Galatians would return
to the very conditions that had held them in bondage. Were they
still completely ignorant of God? Who, after tasting freedom,
would return to slavery? Why, after meeting God, would the
Galatians turn back *to those weak and miserable principles?*
These "principles" are the "basic principles of the world" as
described in 4:3. Whether "principles" referred to the Jewish law
or to pagan rituals, Paul declared them to be *asthene* (weak, powerless, unable to save or set free) and *ptocha* (miserable, bankrupt, unable to offer an inheritance).

The "weak and miserable principles" that lured the Galatians
away from freedom in Christ continue to entice us. They take
many forms, but their essential character remains unchanged;
they offer what they cannot provide. Even when disguised by religious language and formality, these "basics" lead to continued
slavery. The "gospel" of religious busyness and the mindless
keeping of endless rules rob us of our freedom in Christ and keep
us enslaved.

Do you wish to be enslaved by them all over again?[NIV] Certainly the Galatians had no intention of returning to slavery;

indeed, as they had listened to the false teachers, they had not realized that this was what was happening. But Paul explained the inevitable consequences of their return to legalism and label-ism (see the chart in the Introduction). Whether they were attempting to gain additional merit before God by following the law or returning to the idolatry of their past, the Galatians were going to be *enslaved* again. Is this what they truly wanted?

DEFECTORS
What causes people to turn away from freedom in Christ to legalism and labelism?

- *Fear of going alone.* Placing our trust in Christ alone may be offensive to family and friends. They may think the gospel is too simple or easy, preferring their own way. Faced with this response, some revert to a life of effort.
- *Fear of grace/love.* The idea of being "masters of our fate," or "doing it our way," may entice some to work for righteousness.
- *Fear of intimacy with God's Spirit.* The Spirit-filled life may be threatening because of its spontaneity. Legalism provides the "security of busyness."
- *Fear of losing the benefits of the old system.* Legalism has its own rewards with status and respect for those who advance in it.
- *Fear of the unfamiliar.* For some, such as slaves who have been emancipated, the familiar life seems safer. The very idea of spiritual freedom in Christ may seem terrifying. The past for-mulas, lifestyles, patterns, and programs were comfortable, secure, and predictable.

We must continue to teach the freedom we have in Christ so that all believers can walk in newness of life.

4:10 You are observing special days, and months, and seasons, and years.^{NRSV} As an example of this law keeping the Galatians had been attempting, Paul pointed out their observance of special holi-days. The *days* referred to keeping the Jewish Sabbath or other specified dates in the Jewish calendar. The observance of *months* would be the new moon celebrations of the Jews. *Seasons* would refer to the festivals that lasted several days. For the Jews this could be the three main feasts: Unleavened Bread, Pentecost, and Tabernacles. *Years* of celebration for the Jews were the Year of Jubilee and Sabbath years.

Paul did not condemn the celebration of the Jewish events—for he himself kept the Sabbath and still traveled to Jerusalem for certain festivals (see also Colossians 2:16). He would have con-demned the Gentile Galatians celebrating the Jewish holidays in order to somehow receive more merit before God or fulfill some legal duty in doing so. The God-honoring festivals were not bad in themselves; but when used as a way to earn salvation or "score points" with God, they became nothing more than slavery.

CHURCH YEAR
Christians approach the celebration of traditions in the church year in three different ways: (1) ignorantly, (2) automatically, or (3) intentionally.

Those who keep the traditions in ignorance know nothing of the church's yearly calendar or have been told that the church year is meaningless. Those who keep the traditions automatically go through church events without any thought or with a vague belief that repetition somehow gains merit for them. But the meaning behind the actions is lost. Paul would have questioned both of these attitudes because they fall far short of a vibrant and growing faith in Christ.

Those who keep the traditions intentionally know the reasons behind the seasons of advent and lent. They "keep" those seasons with genuine study and reflection on the aspects of our faith that those seasons highlight.

Christians today remain largely ignorant of the history of their faith. Helpful lessons can be learned from both the failures and the successes of believers over the last two millennia. How well have you educated yourself in the history of Christianity?

4:11 I am afraid that my work for you may have been wasted.^{NRSV} If the Galatians continued in their law-centered approach to Christianity, setting aside God's grace in order to obey codes, customs, and rituals (or if they allowed their pagan roots to invade their newfound faith), then Paul feared that all his work among them and his suffering on their behalf (see 3:4 explanation) would be wasted effort. Paul was not saying that the Galatians would lose their salvation but that their very turning away from the truth would render them unfruitful and their faith "dead," as if Paul had never visited them at all.

4:12 Friends, I beg you, become as I am, for I also have become as you are.^{NRSV} After his lengthy theological discussion, Paul's true personal concern for the Galatians resurfaced, for he again called them *friends* (see also 1:11; 3:15). His appeal is concerned and personal. It also softens the effect of the negative outlook he has just expressed.

Several explanations have been given for the phrase *become as I am, for I also have become as you are.* This could refer to attitudes, as if Paul were saying, "Put yourselves in my place, for I have put myself in yours." Or, "Be as honest and loving with me as I have always been with you." Or he might also have been referring to a spiritual state, "Become free from the law as I am,

for I became as you are after my conversion—a Gentile who had never been
enslaved to Jewish law."

The Greek gives us little to work
from, but perhaps the best explanation
of the phrase would be a combination
of the above. Paul may have been
appealing to the Galatians in this way:
"Become as I am (regarding my Christian faith and freedom from the law),
for I also have become as you are
(I brought the gospel to you without
requiring anything of you—such as
becoming Jewish first)." Paul's
attitude toward evangelism was
always to meet people on their own
ground and then to present them with
the gospel:

> How great a loss is it when we allow ourselves to be diverted from the simplicity of faith to trust in ceremonies, rites, and a prescribed routine! Let us therefore not pay slavish attention to the outward, but seek to have Christ within, and from within he will become the energy and passion of a new life. Each time we yield to the prompting of his Spirit, there is less of self and more of him.
>
> *F. B. Meyer*

■ *For though I am free with respect to
all, I have made myself a slave to all, so that I might win more
of them. To the Jews I became as a Jew, in order to win Jews.
To those under the law I became as one under the law (though I
myself am not under the law) so that I might win those under
the law. To those outside the law I became as one outside the
law (though I am not free from God's law but am under Christ's
law) so that I might win those outside the law. To the weak I
became weak, so that I might win the weak. I have become all
things to all people, that I might by all means save some.
(1 Corinthians 9:19-22 NRSV)*

Paul had become like the Galatians in the sense that he had
met them on common ground in order to win them to Christ.
They had accepted the gospel; here Paul asked that they simply
remain in the faith and in the freedom they had learned from him.
He was convinced that they would realize in an instant the folly
of what was being offered to them if they would only reflect on
the change that had actually occurred in their lives when they had
trusted Christ. In a sense, Paul was reminding them, "We have
traveled too far and too well together for you to now question the
map we have been using!"

You have done me no wrong.NRSV This phrase actually ties in
with the following verses where Paul reminisced about how the
Galatians had received him on his first visit to them (see Acts 13–

14). They had done him no wrong, even receiving him in his physical weakness. Paul was generous in reassuring the Galatians that they were neither his "project" nor his "pets." They had become his brothers and sisters, his traveling companions in the journey of faith. He had depended on them in ways that were as important as their own dependence on the gospel that he had delivered to them. His present concern for them was real, but not such that he took their struggles as a personal offense.

4:13 As you know, it was because of an illness that I first preached the gospel to you.^{NIV} Many attempts have been made to identify the *illness* to which Paul referred here. Some commentators suggest that Paul's illness was some sort of handicap, perhaps an eye disorder (inferred from the reference to eyes in 4:15). Others think that Paul may have contracted some form of malaria on the coast after landing in Perga in Pamphylia (see Acts 13:13). Or he may have had epilepsy, so he and his traveling companions had headed for the highlands where Paul could recuperate. Still others point to the physical abuse and beating Paul had received in Lystra and the resulting care of the believers as his wounds had healed (Acts 14:19). Whether this "illness" was the same as Paul's "thorn in the flesh" referred to in 2 Corinthians 12:7 is also unknown. Whatever the illness, it did not completely incapacitate Paul, for while in Galatia, he had *preached the gospel* to the Galatians.

GOD'S STRANGE WAYS
How strange that God would use an illness as an opportunity to preach the gospel. But Paul's own confession was that his greatest personal struggles and "weakness" were used by God to display his greatest strength (see 2 Corinthians 12:7-10). Whatever Paul was doing, he had no illusions about who was accomplishing the mighty works. He could say, "That is why, for Christ's sake, I delight in weaknesses, in insults, in hardships, in persecutions, in difficulties. For when I am weak, then I am strong" (2 Corinthians 12:10 NIV).

We can turn our weaknesses to great advantage if we remember Paul's discovery. Weaknesses can make us more compassionate as we relate to others. They can make our faith more attractive as others see our vulnerability. They certainly can produce greater patience and dependence upon God. Instead of becoming disheartened over our struggles, we should simply ask God to use those very weaknesses to display his strength.

While it would be interesting to identify this illness, we can know for certain from Paul's words that he remembered the illness as the cause of his encounter with the Galatians. Their relationship with each other had not begun with Paul as a confident herald of the gospel but rather as a weak person in need of help. Paul had depended on the Galatians before they had come to depend on his message and his Lord.

WHO CARES?
Paul's physical infirmity was a sickness that he had endured while he visited the Galatian churches. The world is often callous to people's pain and misery. Paul commended the Galatians for not scorning him, even though his condition had been a trial to them. Such caring was what Jesus meant when he called us to serve the homeless, hungry, sick, and imprisoned as if they were Jesus himself (Matthew 25:34-40). Do you avoid those in pain or those facing difficulty, or are you willing to care for them as if they were Jesus Christ himself? When you are in need, do you allow others to minister to you even though it requires vulnerability and humility?

4:14 Even though my illness was a trial to you, you did not treat me with contempt or scorn.[NIV] The Galatians could have refused Paul any reception because his illness *was a trial* to them. Apparently his need had been a genuine imposition; he was shamelessly in their debt. Perhaps Paul's resulting appearance had made him difficult to look at, or his weakness had made him an extra burden on those who cared for him. The trial may simply have been the temptation to treat him with contempt or scorn because of his illness.

Instead, you welcomed me as if I were an angel of God, as if I were Christ Jesus himself.[NIV] To the Galatians' credit, they welcomed the ill Paul with open arms, ready to care for him and to listen to his words. Paul compared their reception to how they might have received someone more obviously powerful—such as *an angel of God* or even *Christ Jesus himself.* The Galatians had respected Paul very highly, although they had never met him before. Paul had been touched by their welcome and described it in the highest possible terms. Paul was not equating himself with Christ or an angel, but he was applauding the Galatians' hospitality. And they had been correct in receiving Paul in this way, for he had come to them as God's messenger bringing the gospel

> All joy (as distinct from mere pleasure, still more amusement) emphasises our pilgrim status; always reminds, beckons, awakens desire. Our best havings are wantings.
> *C. S. Lewis*

of salvation. They never minded his physical infirmities, his obvious human weaknesses. The Galatians had refused to make judgments on appearances. They had listened to the life-changing message Paul had given, and they had received it joyfully.

4:15 What has happened to all your joy? I can testify that, if you could have done so, you would have torn out your eyes and given them to me.[NIV] The Galatians had received Paul with open arms, had cared for him, had heard and accepted his message, and had been joyful that he had come and preached among them. The Greek word *makarismos* (joy) can also be translated "blessed." The Galatians had considered themselves blessed

> Truth may make some enemies, yet some people are so bent on making enemies that they don't even need the truth to do it.
>
> *Bruce B. Barton*

with Paul's ministry and had expressed the benefits of the gospel message and the presence of God's Spirit among them. But that had changed. Their capitulation to the Judaizers was a denial of their previous joy. This was the conclusion Paul reached as the only reason for what could have caused them to turn to other "answers."

So Paul asked, *What has happened to all your joy?* The Galatians loved and respected Paul greatly. Paul knew they would have given him their eyes if they could have. This may be a reference specifying Paul's particular illness, or it may be a figure of speech meaning that the Galatians would have given their most precious possessions to Paul out of love and respect for him. When Paul was among them, the Galatians did Paul no wrong (4:12); but in his absence, their joy had ebbed away and they were regarding Paul as if he were an enemy (4:16).

LOST AND FOUND
Have you lost your joy? Paul sensed that the Galatians had lost the joy of their salvation because of legalism. Legalism can steal joy because

- it makes people feel guilty rather than loved;
- it produces self-hatred rather than humility;
- it stresses performance rather than relationship; and
- it points out how far short we fall rather than how far we've come because of what Christ did for us.

If you feel guilty and inadequate and your joy is gone, check your focus. Are you living by faith in Christ or by trying to live up to the demands and expectations of others?

THREE DISTORTIONS OF CHRISTIANITY

Almost from the beginning there were forces at work within Christianity that could have destroyed or sidetracked the movement. Of these, three created many problems then and have continued to reappear in other forms even today. The three aberrations are contrasted to true Christianity.

Group	Their definition of a Christian	Their genuine concern	The danger	Application question
Judaized Christianity	Christians are Jews who have recognized Jesus as the promised Messiah. Therefore, any Gentile desiring to become a Christian must first become a Jew.	Having a high regard for the Scriptures and God's choice of Jews as his people, they did not want to see God's commands overlooked or broken.	Tends to add human traditions and standards to God's law. Also subtracts from the Scriptures God's clear concern for all nations.	Do you appreciate God's choice of a unique people through whom he offered forgiveness and eternal life to all peoples?
Legalized Christianity	Christians are those who live by a long list of "don'ts." God's favor is earned by good behavior.	Recognized that real change brought about by God should lead to changes in behavior.	Tends to make God's love something to earn rather than to accept freely. Would reduce Christianity to a set of impossible rules and transform the Good News into bad news.	As important as change in action is, can you see that God may be desiring different changes in you than in others?

4:16 Have I now become your enemy by telling you the truth?[NRSV] He who had been the object of affection and respect was being treated like an *enemy.* Why? The only possible reason would be that the Galatians didn't want to hear the truth. Paul may well have had two ideas in mind regarding this "truth." One possibility is that the Galatians were suddenly rejecting Paul and instead were turning to new teachers. He had become a *persona non grata,* an "enemy." Another possibility is that in confronting the wavering faith of the Galatians, Paul was placing himself and his relationship with them in jeopardy.

In both possibilities, what was really at stake was the truth, and the Galatians needed to realize that they were in real danger of believing a lie rather than the truth of the gospel. Whether they

Group	Their definition of a Christian	Their genuine concern	The danger	Application question
Lawless Christianity	Christians live above the law. They need no guidelines. God's Word is not as important as our personal sense of God's guidance.	Recognized that forgiveness from God cannot be based on our ability to live up to his perfect standards. It must be received by faith as a gift made possible by Christ's death on the cross.	Forgets that Christians are still human and fail consistently when trying to live only by what they "feel" God wants.	Do you recognize the ongoing need for God's expressed commands as you live out your gratitude for his great salvation?
True Christianity	Christians are those who believe inwardly and outwardly that Jesus' death has made possible God's offer of forgiveness and eternal life as a gift. They have accepted that gift through faith and are seeking to live a life of obedient gratitude for what God has done for them.	Christianity is both private and public, with heart-belief and mouth-confession. Our relationship to God and the power he provides result in obedience. Having received the gift of forgiveness and eternal life, we are now challenged to daily live that life with his help.	Avoids the above dangers.	How would those closest to you describe your Christianity? Do they think you live so that God *will* accept you or do they know that you live *because* God has accepted you in Christ?

rejected the message or the messenger, the effect remained the same—Paul would then have been treated as an enemy.

4:17 Those people are zealous to win you over, but for no good. What they want is to alienate you from us, so that you may be zealous for them.[NIV] While Paul had spoken only the truth from pure motives (to bring the Galatians to salvation), the Judaizers had less than honorable motives. *Those people* refers to the false teachers who were claiming to be religious authorities and experts in Judaism and Christianity. Appealing to the believers' desire to do what was right, they drew quite a following. Their teaching about following laws and customs seemed sensible because it promoted actions that supposedly would make them even "holier."

Paul pointed out, however, that the false teachers had selfish motives. They were *zealous* but for the wrong reasons and the wrong cause. Zeal can be positive, but in the wrong hands it can cause much damage. The false teachers' only desire was to win the people over to their side—and at the same time

> If you're lost in the wilderness and travelling in circles, it really doesn't matter how much ground you cover each day!
> *Anonymous*

alienate the people from Paul, and thus from Christ. Their zeal was misdirected; it was not for God, but only to support their own cause.

HUMBLE PIE
Paul did not gain great popularity by rebuking the Galatians for turning away from their faith in Christ. Human nature hasn't changed much; we still get angry when we're scolded, even when someone tells us the truth. Don't write off someone who challenges you. There may be truth in what he or she says. Receive his or her words with humility, and carefully think them over. If you discover that you need to change an attitude or action, take steps to do it.

The legalizers' motives were even more insidious. They sought to form their own following and alienate the Galatians from Paul and from Christ. The Galatians might have enjoyed the attention and concern paid by these "teachers," but Paul knew what would happen. Once the Galatians became committed to the false teachers, the roles would be reversed and the Galatians would be forced to pay attention to and even provide money and lodging for them. They would be in bondage to the false teachers and all their wrong teachings.

Jesus' response to this kind of zeal was uncompromising: "Woe to you, teachers of the law and Pharisees, you hypocrites! You travel over land and sea to win a single convert, and when he becomes one, you make him twice as much a son of hell as you are" (Matthew 23:15 NIV).

Paul had no such motives. He did not preach a message that would make people feel good—he spoke the truth. He did acquire followers, but he did not create a following. Paul did not compete with other preachers and teachers—his goal was simply to bring the message of the gospel to as many as possible. Paul's disciples belonged not to him but to Christ.

4:18 It is fine to be zealous, provided the purpose is good, and to be so always and not just when I am with you.NIV Paul acknowledged that zeal helps, *provided the purpose is good.* Paul himself passionately preached the gospel. But passion or zeal does not limit itself. It needs a dependable goal or object. And Paul worried that his Galatian friends were becoming zealous over the lie that human moral and ethical efforts can satisfy God's perfect standard.

PASSION
The capacity and desire for passionate commitment appears to be a basic human trait. We will be passionate about something or someone. Young people often exhibit this trait clearly, seeking to find meaning by investing their energy in a cause. For them, the truth of the cause may take second place to the excitement, zeal, and passion they feel about an idea or a leader.

But our zeal can be misdirected. As believers in Christ, our zeal must be for those ideas and actions for which he demonstrated zeal. Make sure your cause centers on Christ and honors him before you put yourself behind it (see John 2:17).

The false teachers were zealous to win over the Galatians in order that the Galatians would be zealous in support of them. This was not a good use of zeal. Instead, Paul wished that the Galatians could again have the zeal they once had for the true gospel, and that they could keep that zeal alive *always and not just when [Paul was] with them.* Our zeal should not diminish when our leaders are out of sight. Nor should we allow ourselves to be influenced by those who would court us to their point of view when other teach-

> If ministers wish to do any good, let them labour to form Christ, not to form themselves, in their hearers.
>
> *John Calvin*

ers are away. We should hold firmly to the truth at all times.

4:19 My little children, for whom I am again in the pain of child-birth until Christ is formed in you.[NRSV] While the false teachers simply sought a larger following, Paul saw these believers as his *little children.* (Paul used this term of endearment only this time in all his letters, although John used it quite frequently.) Obviously his motives differed from those of the false teachers, for he loved the Galatians dearly, as a mother loves her children. Paul compared the pains of childbirth to the pain he felt at their turning from the faith. He had watched them "be born again" into the faith; the pain he felt at their apparent defection from that faith was agonizing.

Paul mixed his metaphors in this verse—how could he have labor pains as the believers have Christ formed in them? Often

Paul's imagery is complicated because what he is describing (God's supernatural work) is impossible for humans to fully understand. Despite the difficulty of the metaphor, Paul expressed his concern for his children in the faith.

Paul's goals would always be the same—*until Christ is formed in you.* Paul wanted each of his children to reach spiritual maturity in the faith. They would do so by having the likeness of Christ portrayed in their lives. "Formed in you" refers to a mother carrying an embryo until it is developed enough to be born. God desires for Christ to live in and through each believer. As Paul wrote in 2:20, "I have been crucified with Christ; it is no longer I who live, but Christ lives in me; and the life which I now live in the flesh I live by faith in the Son of God, who loved me and gave Himself for me" (NKJV). Becoming conformed to the image of Christ (Romans 8:29) emphasizes the personal changes necessary to become like Jesus. At the same time, Paul said that Christ takes form in us. As a Christian becomes conformed and transformed (Romans 12:1; 2 Corinthians 3:18) in relation to Christ, Christ's attitudes and character are "formed" in him or her (Philippians 2:5-9; 3:10). We become like Christ even as his life and teaching become visible in us.

FOLLOW-THROUGH CARE
Paul led many people to Christ and helped them mature spiritually. Perhaps one reason for his success as a spiritual father was the deep concern he felt for his spiritual children. He compared his pain over their faithlessness to the pain of childbirth. We should have the same intense concern for those to whom we are spiritual parents. When you lead people to Christ, remember to stand by them to help them grow. Their spiritual welfare should be as much a concern to us as was our desire to see them trust Christ.

4:20 I wish I were present with you now and could change my tone, for I am perplexed about you.^{NRSV} As with any confusion or misunderstanding, face-to-face talk accomplishes more than written correspondence. (Paul didn't even have a telephone, although doubtless he would have also considered that to be inadequate.) For some reason, Paul could not pick up and dash off to Galatia (perhaps for the same reasons many of us cannot drop everything and go to be with someone we care about—expense, time, previous commitments, health, or simply God not allowing the circumstances to come together). If he could go, he might change his tone but not his message or his expectations—those would always remain the same, for they were true and correct.

But Paul's tone might be different because he could ask questions and get answers; he could read faces; he could find out exactly how far the heresy had gone and why. In other words, Paul could discover what was behind it all. Instead, Paul wrote this one-sided letter to express how *perplexed* he was over the Galatians.

KEEP LOVING
Paul had every right to be angry with the Galatian Christians. They had turned away from the truth that he had worked so hard to teach them, and they had returned to the empty religion that had formerly enslaved them and robbed them of so much joy. But Paul cared enough about the Galatians to grieve over their condition. He was their spiritual brother because he, too, was one of God's adopted sons, and he was their spiritual father because he had led many of them to Christ. Paul's great love made it impossible for him to turn his back on them or to act selfishly to further his own ends. That kind of love could only come from God. And because God loves us, we should keep loving others even when they let us down.

ABRAHAM'S TWO CHILDREN / 4:21–5:1

The final paragraph of Galatians 4 records an extended allegory by Paul. Using the allegorical method known to most Greek readers, he chose Hagar and Sarah, Abraham's wives-in-conflict, to illustrate the conflict between law and grace. While some have questioned Paul's use of such Jewish material with a largely Gentile audience, the objection fails to recognize the wide use of the Old Testament in the early church. When Paul was with the Galatians, he had spent much of his time explaining God's plan as revealed in the Old Testament. Further, Paul's opponents would have immersed the Galatians in Old Testament studies, attempting to prove that Paul's gospel message was secondary to the truth of the law. By using the Hagar/Sarah relationship to picture the promise of freedom in the gospel, Paul was turning a favorite weapon of the Judaizers against them.

The apostle demonstrated again that people are saved because of their faith in Christ, not because of what they do. He contrasted those who are enslaved to the law (represented by Hagar, the bondwoman, or slave) with those who are free from the law (represented by Sarah, the free woman). Hagar's abuse of Sarah (Genesis 16:4) was similar to the persecution that the Gentile Christians were getting from the Judaizers, who insisted that a person had to keep the law in order to be saved. Eventually,

CONTRAST OF SARAH AND HAGAR

Paul contrasted those who were enslaved to the law (represented by Hagar) with those who are free from the law (represented by Sarah).

	Sarah	Hagar	Significance
Name of child	Isaac	Ishmael	Isaac represented God's intervention. Ishmael was born by the ordinary process.
What the child represented	Covenant of Promise (grace)	Covenant of Mt. Sinai (law)	God's promise to Abraham was prior to the covenant with Moses at Mt. Sinai.
Source	Based on Jerusalem above (Spirit)	Based on present Jerusalem (flesh)	The present Jerusalem represents legalism. The Jerusalem above represents life in the Spirit.
Results in life	Leads to freedom	Leads to slavery	Paul wanted the Galatians to experience Christian freedom, not a return to the law.

Sarah triumphed because God kept his promise to give her a son, just as those who worship Christ in faith will also triumph.

Attempts at a law-centered faith fail because they set up human standards in place of freedom. They substitute effort for grace and fear for mercy. They preserve the sting of failure, rather than holding out the promise of hope in Christ beyond our failures.

4:21 Tell me, you who want to be under the law, are you not aware of what the law says?NIV Under the influence of the false teachers (the Judaizers), the Galatians wanted to submit to the Jewish law. Paul, completely "perplexed" by this (4:20), wanted to turn them back to accepting salvation by grace alone. He confronted them directly by saying, "Do you really know what the law says? You want so badly to submit to it, yet do you even understand it?" The Galatian believers, most of them *not* from a Jewish background and thus with little more than an elementary understanding of the Jewish law, may have answered an indignant yes. Hopefully they would have halted long enough to realize the impossible standards under which they were placing themselves.

4:22 For it is written that Abraham had two sons, one by a slave woman and the other by a free woman.NRSV Paul turned to an argument from the Jewish Scripture and the life of Abraham. The

Law, the Torah, included all the books of the Pentateuch, Genesis through Deuteronomy. While the Judaizers focused on the minute aspects of law keeping described in Leviticus and Deuteronomy, Paul turned to another part of the Law, the historical account of Abraham, father of the Jewish nation (see also 3:6-29), to illustrate his point. The Judaizers, indeed all Jews, took great pride in their descent from godly Abraham. However, as John the Baptist and Jesus pointed out, merely being descended from Abraham was not enough to secure salvation (see Matthew 3:9; John 8:37-44). Paul made the same point in this section, though from a slightly different angle.

The story, originally recorded in Genesis 16 and 21:1-21, was summarized by Paul as a fundamental spiritual lesson demonstrated by Abraham, his *two sons,* and his two wives. Abraham had more than two sons, but Isaac and Ishmael were his first two and are the ones important to this illustration. In ancient times, a mother's status affected the status of her children. Paul reminded his readers that Abraham had two types of sons—one born of a *slave woman* and one born of a *free woman.* Paul wanted the Galatians to consider which type of descendant these Judaizers were more like and then decide which they themselves desired to be like.

4:23 His son by the slave woman was born in the ordinary way; but his son by the free woman was born as the result of a promise.[NIV] Besides the contrast in the status of the mothers, the two boys were different in another important way. Abraham's son by the slave woman *was born in the ordinary way;* that is, Ishmael came as a result of the normal birth process. Abraham was very old (in his eighties), but no particular miracle was involved in Ishmael's birth to Hagar. In fact, Ishmael's birth was engineered by Abraham and Sarah to "make the promise come true" by their own plans and efforts, rather than waiting on God's timing.

However, Abraham's son by the free woman *was born as the result of a promise.* When Abraham was ninety-nine years old and Sarah was ninety years old (Genesis 17:1, 17), God appeared to Abraham and promised, "As for Sarah your wife, . . . I will bless her, and moreover I will give you a son by her. . . . Sarah shall bear you a son, and you shall name him Isaac" (Genesis 17:15-16, 19 NRSV). Not only was Isaac's birth the result of a promise, it was also truly miraculous because of Abraham's and Sarah's advanced ages.

By using this illustration, Paul was setting up the distinction between ordinary, man-made religion and supernatural, miraculous, God-made religion. But he directly challenged the assumptions of the Judaizers that they were representatives of the Abrahamic promise. Paul would explain that what happened to Sarah and Hagar pictures the relationship between God and mankind. Though perhaps difficult for us to follow, this was a common type of argument in Paul's day; the same type of argument had probably been used against him by his opponents. As he so often did so well, Paul returned fire on his opponents with their own weapons.

4:24 Now this is an allegory: these women are two covenants. One woman, in fact, is Hagar, from Mount Sinai, bearing children for slavery.[NRSV] Paul's words that *this is an allegory* do not deny the truth of the Genesis account. He meant that the facts in the original story could be applied in an allegorical way. Paul was pointing to a great spiritual truth illustrated by this story, namely, the superiority of Christianity over Judaism.

The two women, Hagar and Sarah, represent *two covenants.* The two well-known covenants were made with Abraham and with Moses. The one covenant with Moses had begun at *Mount Sinai* with the giving of the law (see Exodus 19:20). Hagar was a slave (Genesis 16:1); thus, her children would be slaves, for a child's status equaled the status of his or her mother.

Paul didn't say it, but the readers could infer that the other woman represented the covenant with Abraham (Genesis 17:15-17), the covenant of promise—children of a free woman are free. This covenant of promise looked toward a new covenant, ushered in by Christ. This had already arrived, but the Jews did not accept it.

But why are the Jews compared to Ishmael the Gentile instead of to Isaac, the fulfillment of the covenant to Abraham? Although both sons had the same father, their mothers were different and their descendants became two different races—Ishmael, the Ishmaelites (Genesis 21:18; Psalm 83:1-6); Isaac, the Jews (Genesis 22:16-18). The Jews proudly considered themselves children of God's covenant. However, Paul refuted the claim, reminding them of the "two covenants" and explaining that because of their behavior, the Jews were actually children of the covenant with Moses, the covenant of the law. Paul had obviously twisted the normal interpretation to make a point. The Judaizers claimed superiority for their point of view by claiming that the blessings of the covenant came to descendants of Abraham through Isaac. Gentile Christians could be "adopted" into Abraham's covenant group by accepting circumcision. Paul contradicted the Judaizers by showing that those who promote the law for salvation or sanctification demonstrate the characteristics of slavery to the law. Paul claimed that they were products of the Sinai covenant, not

Abraham's covenant. Trying to win salvation by obeying the law
leads to slavery, and as the Jews persisted in this pattern, they
showed themselves to be enslaved to their law. Thus, the covenant with Moses on Mount Sinai "bears children who are to be
slaves" (NIV). Although the Jews had descended from Abraham
and Isaac, as they tried to piously obey their laws, they were actually slaves to it. As slaves, they were more like children of the
slave woman, Hagar. Thus, they were more like Ishmael than
Isaac.

**4:25 Now Hagar stands for Mount Sinai in Arabia and corre-
sponds to the present city of Jerusalem, because she is in slavery with her children.**NIV Not only do the women and their
children represent two covenants (4:24), they also represent two
Jerusalems. Hagar represents the old covenant given at Mount
Sinai. She also represents *the present city of Jerusalem,* which
was enslaved to Rome and, as the center of the Jewish religious
and legal system, was filled with people enslaved to the Jewish
law. ("Jerusalem" could be used as a general term referring to the
entire nation of Israel.) As Hagar was *in slavery,* so her children
(the Jews) who remain under the old covenant from Mount Sinai
would also remain forever in slavery. Sarah represents the other
Jerusalem (4:26), the promise of faith and freedom.

Paul's assignment of symbols must have shocked the Judaizers. Paul was really condemning the Judaizers. They tended to
practice historical denial about their national experience. For
example, at one time Jesus claimed that his teaching was the
truth that would set them free. The Jews scorned the idea that
they needed to be freed. "We are Abraham's descendants," they
replied, "and have never been slaves of anyone. How can you say
that we shall be set free?" (John 8:33 NIV). The very ones who
claimed freedom were at that moment under the domination of
Rome. Later, Jesus directly challenged their claim to be Abraham's children (see John 8:31-47): "If you were Abraham's children," said Jesus, "then you would do the things Abraham did"
(John 8:39 NIV). Paul was making the same point to the Galatians
and the Judaizers who tried to influence them. Abraham believed
in and obeyed God (Genesis 12:1-4; 15:6; 22:1-14), and he welcomed God's messengers (Genesis 18:1-8).

**4:26 But the Jerusalem that is above is free, and she is our
mother.**NIV Sarah stands for the *Jerusalem that is above,* was
mother of the promised miracle-child, Isaac, and corresponds to
the covenant of Abraham (inferred in 4:24). This covenant promised a future "new covenant" that would begin at the death of

Jesus Christ on the cross. God promised that through Abraham "all peoples on earth will be blessed" (Genesis 12:3 NIV). Through Abraham's family tree, Jesus Christ was born to save humanity. Jesus instituted this "new covenant" between humans and God. Under this new covenant, Jesus died in the place of sinners. Because Jesus took the penalty of our sin upon himself, we can have a personal relationship with God and be blessed beyond measure. Believers who have accepted Christ's sacrifice on the cross on their behalf receive these blessings.

While Hagar represents the "present city of Jerusalem" in its state of slavery (4:25), Sarah represents "the Jerusalem that is above." Jewish thought contained the idea that there was a heavenly Jerusalem and the earthly Jerusalem was just a copy (see Psalm 87:1-3; Isaiah 54:10-14; Ezekiel 40–48). Paul used the concept *she is our mother* to show that faith, not adherence to the law, is the source of our salvation. Paul was stacking the major persons (Abraham, Isaac, Ishmael, Hagar), events (covenants), and sites (Mount Sinai, Jerusalem) of Old Testament history to portray the two tracks of humanity: one under legal slavery, the other under freedom established through faith. By including himself and the Galatians in the *our,* Paul was offering the Galatians the opportunity to claim that they were descendants of Abraham through faith, and that they possessed citizenship in the spiritual Jerusalem. For Gentiles to be included in this way would be as miraculous as the birth of Isaac.

CITIZENSHIP
Usually citizenship is based on a person's nation of birth. It does not change when the person travels abroad. Someone may spend almost his or her entire life in other countries and still maintain citizenship at home. Our citizenship in the "heavenly Jerusalem" as children in God's family will not be fully realized until the end of time (see Hebrews 11:10, 14-16; 12:22; 13:14; Revelation 3:12; 21:2). Though we may not yet be at home, as believers we carry a passport called the Holy Spirit. We should live each day as true citizens loyal to God.

4:27 For it is written: "Rejoice, O barren, You who do not bear! Break forth and shout, you who are not in labor! For the desolate has many more children than she who has a husband."NKJV Paul quoted from Isaiah's prophecy (Isaiah 54:1). Isaiah's words had comforted the Jewish exiles years later in Babylon, proclaiming that they would not only be restored, but that their future blessings would be greater than any in the past. To be *barren* (childless) in ancient days meant great shame and disgrace for a woman. Families depended on children for survival, especially when the parents became elderly. Israel had been unfruitful, like a childless woman, but God would give great blessings and would change their mourning into rejoicing.

Paul applied the comparison of former-versus-later blessings, prophesied by Isaiah, to his Hagar/Sarah analogy. Sarah, who had been barren, was blessed with Isaac. Her child was a gracious gift, not the result of work. Because God had promised to bless Abraham and his descendants, she ultimately would have *many more children* (the Christian church grew rapidly and is still growing). While the Jews knew (or should have known) from their own Scriptures that Gentiles would turn to God, two changes astounded them: (1) The Gentiles did not have to become Jews first (as the Judaizers preached); and (2) so many Gentiles became believers that they soon outnumbered Jewish believers. Instead of fulfilling their privileged role to bring God's plan into reality, these Jews were insisting on remaining in control. Their inability to recognize God's acceptance of the Gentiles made them equally unable to rejoice!

4:28 Now you, my friends, are children of the promise, like Isaac.^{NRSV} If the Galatians hadn't understood his point yet, Paul spelled it out here. *You, my friends,* the Galatians who had become Christians under Paul's ministry, fit into the analogy as *children of the promise, like Isaac.* Just as Isaac's birth was a miracle of God, so Christianity, offering people the opportunity to be born again, is a miracle of God (John 3:3). Just as Isaac's mother was free. So Isaac was free; so Christianity offers true freedom because it depends not on our actions but on God's unchangeable promises to us. Paul hammered home his point to the Galatian believers: "As children of the promise, you never need to be enslaved to the Jewish laws. You are like Isaac!" This key confirmation ensures that believers are free, possess all the rights as true children, and receive all the love and grace they need.

Paul desired that his Galatian friends would find their spiritual identity in Christ and not in the teachings of the Judaizers. Through Christ, they could rely confidently on their inclusion as "children of the promise." They could claim to be among those God had in mind when he told Abraham, "All peoples on earth will be blessed through you" (Genesis 12:3 NIV).

4:29 At that time the son born in the ordinary way persecuted the son born by the power of the Spirit. It is the same now.^{NIV} If believers are like Isaac, then their experiences will compare to his. Ishmael is *the son born in the ordinary way*; Isaac is *the son born by the power of the Spirit.* Paul reminded his readers of the story in Genesis 21. Abraham had held a feast on the day Isaac was weaned. Isaac was probably about two years old; thus, Ishmael would have been a teenager. Ishmael had teased or mocked his younger half brother—Paul called this persecution. Paul explained that *it is the same now.* That is, the persecution of the older brother on the younger was continuing to play itself out in the later animosity between the nations that had descended from them (Israel and Edom, Psalm 83:1-6), and on into the persecution of those under the law (the Jews) toward those freed from the law (those "born by the power of the Spirit," the Christians).

Paul contrasted the two sons—Ishmael born according to the flesh "in the ordinary way," and Isaac born by the "power of the Spirit." Paul built on the imagery of the work of the Spirit throughout this epistle. In 3:2-5 he referred to receiving the Spirit, and in 3:14, to the promise of the Spirit. In 4:6, Paul explained that it is by the Holy Spirit that we claim our sonship and adoption. So Paul links power, promise, blessing, and faith with the Holy Spirit's work.

Paul constantly had to face persecution from the Jews on his missionary journeys as he preached to both Jews and Gentiles (see, for example, Acts 9:23; 13:45-50; 14:2, 5, 19; 17:5; 18:6; 21:27-31). His most relentless opponents were the Judaizers, who wanted to kill Paul (Acts 23:12-15). Jesus had taught that believers would face persecution (Matthew 5:10-12).

4:30 But what does the Scripture say? "Get rid of the slave woman and her son, for the slave woman's son will never share in the inheritance with the free woman's son."NIV The first question is: What happened when Ishmael persecuted Isaac at this feast? As Scripture says in Genesis 21:9-10, Sarah saw this happen, went to Abraham, and demanded that Hagar and Ishmael be sent away.

> The thrilling fact remains that the gospel of freedom is as old as Abraham.
>
> *Archibald M. Hunter*

The second question refers to the application: So what happens to Ishmael (the Jews) and Isaac (Christians) today? Paul answered forcefully. Judaism and Christianity could not coexist as paths to the same goal any more than Ishmael and Isaac could share Abraham's inheritance. Perhaps most ironic was Paul's bold clarification of this old story. The Jews had long held that this verse described God's rejection of the Gentiles. But Paul turned the tables: "You had it wrong. Jews and Gentiles are included together in God's inheritance when they become believers, or 'Isaacs.' Those who reject grace lose their share in the inheritance, whether unbelieving Jews or unrepentant Gentiles. Those are the 'Ishmaels.'" Those in slavery to the law will never share God's inheritance with those who have experienced freedom in Christ and salvation by faith alone.

At last Paul made the point that he had not made earlier in the letter. The Galatians should obey God and *get rid* of the Judaizers. As Hagar and Ishmael were cast out, so must these false teachers be put out from among them.

INTOLERABLE
We must not equate differences of opinion with false teaching. This is especially true in the context of the Christian church. Yet today, churches sometimes tolerate teaching that clearly twists Scripture or outrightly abandons the Bible as the source for Christian truth. When there is no accountability to truth within a church, whatever spiritual life may exist under that roof will not be there long.

Generally, the committed Christians within a church ought not leave the church immediately. Too often, those caught in the middle (those who do not yet understand the theological issues at stake) become deeply hurt by the sudden exit of fellow members. An effort at clarification, recommitment to truth, and even, if necessary, church discipline should be carried out before believers regretfully depart.

4:31 So then, friends, we are children, not of the slave but of the free woman.NRSV Paul tied up his allegory, and indeed all the points he proved with it, with the simple word *so*. He assumed that his *friends* in Galatia understood, accepted, and would obey his words. With one final point as if to nail the argument without question, he repeated that *we* (that is, Paul and the Galatian believers, and indeed all believers of all time, including we who live today) are children not of slavery but of freedom. That freedom must be treasured because of the price paid for it.

5:1 For freedom Christ has set us free. Stand firm, therefore, and do not submit again to a yoke of slavery.NRSV We have freedom from slavery to our sinful desires or to the well-meaning but unable-to-save Jewish law. But the freedom came at great price. In order for us to enjoy ultimate freedom, someone had to set us free, and that someone was Christ Jesus (John 8:32, 36). Because Christ has freed all believers, we should rest in it. Christ has set us free from legalistic formulas, from God's judgment upon sin, from all man-made rules, and from the subjective experiences of fear and guilt. We are to live it out, practice it, and rejoice in it!

To turn back to the law and try to earn what Christ has already given mocks his sacrifice.

Paul's command to the Galatians who wanted to return to legalism was to keep on standing firm in their God-given, blood-purchased freedom, refusing to *submit again to a yoke of slavery* to the law (see 1 Peter 5:9). The Jews of Paul's day spoke of "taking the yoke of the law upon oneself"; to them this was a noble effort, the essence of their religion. Undoubtedly the Judaizers had used this sort of language to convince the Galatians to follow the Jewish law. So Paul took the very same wording and expressed it in the negative—"Do not submit to the yoke of the law, for it is slavery."

FREE INDEED!
Christ died to set us free from sin and from a long list of laws and regulations. Christ came to set us free—not free to do whatever we want because that would lead us back into slavery to our selfish desires. Rather, thanks to Christ, we are now free and able to do what was impossible before—to live unselfishly. Those who appeal to their freedom so that they can have their own way or indulge their own desires are falling back into sin. But it is also wrong to put a burden of law keeping on Christians. We must graciously but firmly resist those who would enslave us with rules, methods, or special conditions for being saved or growing in Christ. Don't let anyone enslave you.

Galatians 5:2-26

Paul's application of the Genesis account of Sarah and Hagar exposed the real danger facing the Galatians—they were on the brink of losing their freedom in Christ. Early in the letter (2:4), Paul identified those who had stirred up trouble in Jerusalem when he had gone there to explain his message to the Gentiles. He described them as those who had "infiltrated our ranks to spy on the freedom we have in Christ Jesus and to make us slaves" (Galatians 2:4 NIV). What the Judaizers had attempted to do in Jerusalem, they also attempted in Galatia. Paul expressed dismay at the report that though the Galatians had been growing in their faith, they were being influenced by those trying to destroy God's work of grace in them. In this paragraph, Paul had two objectives: (1) exposing what would actually happen if the Galatians returned to the "yoke of slavery," and (2) confronting the Judaizers with the fruitlessness of their system.

HUMILIATION
During a series of meetings conducted by Billy Sunday, a remarkable exchange took place. Billy usually would arrange to have a "mourners' bench" at the front of the huge tent, where those who were repentant could come and kneel in the sawdust to confess their sins. After one meeting a rather brusque woman approached the preacher. Her furs betrayed her social standing. She appeared to be offended and informed Billy that she would never stoop to come forward in a meeting and humiliate herself in front of all those people in order to be converted. She could just as well believe in Christ right where she was sitting, without this embarrassing display. Billy's response demonstrated a profound understanding of the nature of freedom: "Madam, you are quite right. Kneeling here in repentance in front of the crowd is not a requirement for salvation. But in your case, because you have made humiliation a price you are unwilling to consider in exchange for the salvation of your soul, I can assure you that you will not be converted until you have repented of your pride."

Even in the heat of his attack on the Galatians' errors, Paul still managed to communicate the majesty of freedom in Christ. His words convey both frustration and exultation. Paul spoke with the breathlessness of someone running a brilliant race, who strains from his own exertion while joyfully urging on fellow runners who are about to give up. Paul gives us every reason to stay in the race!

5:2 Listen! I, Paul, am telling you that if you let yourselves be circumcised, Christ will be of no benefit to you.NRSV Paul gave a serious warning, and he didn't want any of his hearers to miss it. He said, *Listen!* (Greek *ide*—behold, look—a word used as an intense, attention-getting device). In 5:3 he said, "Once again I testify." With apostolic authority, Paul pointed directly at his audience and sealed his argument (see also 1:11-12). If the Galatian believers were to follow the Judaizers' teaching and let themselves be circumcised (the tense of the verb reveals that the Galatians had not yet taken the step, but were considering it), Christ could do them no good. How could this be? What could be the harm in circumcision?

Obviously, only men could be circumcised, but more than circumcision was at stake (see 5:6). Paul was confronting the Galatians because they were trying to fulfill the Jewish law. Insistence on circumcision had become the most prominent feature of the Judaizers' thinking. Paul had nothing against circumcision. In fact, he had been circumcised, and on another occasion he had one of his traveling companions, Timothy, circumcised (Acts 16:1-3). But Timothy had not been circumcised so that he could be saved, or to make him "fully Jewish" before he could become "fully Christian." Yet that was exactly what the false teachers had been teaching. The Judaizers taught that the gospel needed the Jewish law system to make it perfect. Their goal was to mix Judaism and Christianity to produce a self-serving "improvement." But God's way was different—salvation through Christ by grace alone. We can't mix and match works and grace. God has an exclusive arrangement. The Galatians were about to be circumcised as a requirement to "complete" their salvation. But Paul explained that by that very act they would be making Christ's sacrifice by his death *of no benefit.* A free gift cannot be earned. Following the law would mean that they were discarding Christ's death on the cross. They were not only rejecting Christ's provision for their salvation, but obliterating any basis for Christ's guidance in their life as well.

INCORRECT RELIGION
Martin Luther pointed out two ways that people devalue the cross of Christ and make his atonement of no benefit: (1) trusting in their own works, merit, inherent goodness, or religion; and (2) doubting Christ's power to deal with their sin.

The second occurs when Satan uses memories of our past sins and accuses us. He continually points out our shortcomings until our conscience condemns us. Our response must be a Christ-centered faith. Our trust must be in Christ's faithfulness and perfect life, not in our ability to live up to the law's expectations.

The following behaviors indicate those who have given in to Satan's accusations: legalism, pride in a "correct" religion, self-made religion, and frantic efforts to gain God's favor.

Christ's alternative invites us to freedom. His words encourage us when our conscience condemns us:

- "Cheer up, son! For I have forgiven your sins" (Matthew 9:2 TLB).
- "I have come to urge sinners, not the self-righteous, back to God" (Matthew 9:13 TLB).
- "Come to me and I will give you rest—all of you who work so hard beneath a heavy yoke" (Matthew 11:28 TLB).
- "For the Son of Man came to seek and to save what was lost" (Luke 19:10 NIV).
- "Here on earth you will have many trials and sorrows; but cheer up, for I have overcome the world" (John 16:33 TLB).

Paul's appeal went beyond his apostolic authority. When he said, "I Paul" and "I testify" that circumcision can't make us right with God and secure the blessings of Abraham, he was referring to his firsthand experience. Paul knew the futility of following the law as the way to obtain salvation. He was about as Jewish as anyone could get—"If anyone else thinks he has reasons to put confidence in the flesh, I have more: circumcised on the eighth day, of the people of Israel, of the tribe of Benjamin, a Hebrew of Hebrews; in regard to the law, a Pharisee; as for zeal, persecuting the church; as for legalistic righteousness, faultless" (Philippians 3:4-6 NIV). But Paul knew that circumcision (as well as every other part of his strict Jewish upbringing) could not give him salvation. He appealed to the Galatians to not even try to obey the Jewish laws. If they could not save Paul, they could not save the Galatians. "But whatever was to my profit I now consider loss for the sake of Christ . . . that I may gain Christ and be found in him, not having a righteousness of my own that comes from the law, but that which is through faith in Christ" (Philippians 3:7-9 NIV).

TRUSTWORTHY
Trying to be saved by keeping the law and being saved by grace are two entirely different approaches. Christ's provision would be of no benefit to the Galatians if they would continue to try to save themselves. Obeying the law would not make it easier for God to save them. No one is saved by good works or obedience to the law, and works of service must never be used to try to earn God's love or favor. Salvation must be accepted by faith as God's gracious gift. Trust in Christ, not yourself!

5:3 **Once again I testify to every man who lets himself be circumcised that he is obliged to obey the entire law.**NRSV If the Galatian men were to allow themselves to be circumcised, they would be admitting that Christ's death was not sufficient to save them. Choosing circumcision would cause them to lose the value of the free gift of salvation given through Christ. It also would have another devastating effect. Choosing circumcision would mean choosing law keeping (legalism). To choose law keeping meant that one would be *obliged to obey the entire law.*

LIFEGUARDS
If a man is drowning, he instinctively struggles for life. A lifeguard's greatest danger comes if the drowning person panics, flailing his arms and legs, trying to save himself. If the victim relaxes and lets the lifeguard save him, he will be safe. However, if he continues to panic, trying to save himself, he could drown, no matter how helpful the lifeguard tries to be.
    Spiritually, we persist in trying to save ourselves, even when we have met the only one who can truly save us. In so doing, we are in danger of missing the lifeguard of our souls. Paul's answer was, "If you're trusting Christ to save you, then stop trying to save yourself! Don't continue to struggle against him."

Paul might well have repeated his question from 4:21, "Tell me, you who want to be under the law, are you not aware of what the law says?" (NIV). Did the Galatians have any idea what their choice to obey all the Jewish laws would entail? Chances are, the Judaizers had not spelled that out—yet. They may have told the Galatians about some of the food laws (2:12) and about the festivals and holy days (4:10). But to any Jew, circumcision was the first act of obedience to a law that would, from then on, rule every detail of his life. Did the Galatians understand that "whoever keeps the whole law and yet stumbles at just one point is guilty of breaking all of it" (James 2:10 NIV, see also Deuteronomy 27:26)? By becoming circumcised, the Galatians were submitting themselves to an entire system—one that doomed them to failure.

IN FOR A PENNY, IN FOR A POUND
The law requires perfect performance. Once we start trying to obey the law for salvation, the law highlights the sickness of our sin but offers no cure for it. Here are five ways in which keeping the law obligates us to the entire law and demonstrates our . guilt.

1. Our own conscience constantly points out our imperfections. The more we know and the harder we try, the more we realize our shortcomings.
2. When we try to live up to the law, we discover its main purpose—to show us our need for God's mercy and grace.
3. Satan does not hesitate to use every detail of the law to accuse us.
4. Even if we abstain from the vast majority of sins we might commit, we are guilty of endless sins of omission (things we ought to have done but didn't).
5. Jesus' summary of the law, "Love the Lord your God with all your heart and with all your soul and with all your mind and with all your strength" (Mark 12:30 NIV), demonstrates the impossibility of keeping the law. Just as it is impossible to keep the myriad of detailed laws, it is also impossible to keep the first and greatest commandment.

Circumcision symbolizes having the right background and doing everything required by religion. No amount of work, discipline, or moral behavior can save us. If a person counts on finding favor with God by being circumcised, he will also have to obey the rest of God's law completely. Trying to save ourselves by keeping all God's laws only separates us from God.

But why, someone may ask, doesn't keeping part of the law, or the entire law to a degree, count for something with God? Well, it may in fact count for something with God (for instance, as a conscious expression of thanks for what he has accomplished for us), but not if we are expecting God to see our flawed effort as if it were a perfect performance. The entrance requirement to the kingdom demands a holy life. Only as we are clothed with Christ can we be acceptable. Only by grace can we have this vital union with Christ that renders us complete and righteous (2 Corinthians 5:17, 21).

5:4 **You who are trying to be justified by law have been alienated from Christ; you have fallen away from grace.**NIV Paul dropped the "if" of 5:2 and stated his point as though the Galatians had already been circumcised and had turned to the law for salvation. The present tense probably caused shock waves in his listeners. In

Greek, the order of this verse places the effect at the beginning of the sentence, increasing the emphasis (thus it would read, "You have been alienated from Christ, you who are trying . . ."). Those who try to be justified by the law are *alienated* (separated, estranged) from Christ. God allows no middle ground—it is Christ *or* law, not both. Anyone deciding to *be justified by law* moves outside of Christ's sphere, severing any relationship with him. Christ cannot save those who persist in saving themselves.

Following the path of legalism means leaving the path of grace, for the two paths cannot converge. In fact, they take us in opposite directions. If we insist on taking our own "way," we have stepped off "the Way." The choice can be illustrated in the following verses: "There is a way that seems right to a man, but in the end it leads to death" (Proverbs 14:12 NIV). In contrast, Jesus said, "I am the way, and the truth, and the life. No one comes to the Father except through me" (John 14:6 NRSV).

> Therefore the more I went about to help my weak, wavering and afflicted conscience by men's traditions, the more weak and doubtful and the more afflicted I was. And thus, the more I observed men's traditions, the more I transgressed them, and in seeking after righteousness by mine Order, I could never attain unto it: for it is impossible (as Paul saith) that the conscience should be pacified by the works of the law, and much more by men's traditions, without the promise and glad tidings concerning Christ.
> *Martin Luther*

Thus Paul's words *you have fallen away from grace* should not be taken out of context to mean that salvation can be lost. *Grace* did not mean salvation, but refers to the means of salvation. To decide on legalism as the way of salvation is to set aside grace as the way of salvation—thus, to "fall away" from grace. It's like throwing away the life preserver when lost at sea.

WHERE'S THE GRACE?
How a church emphasizes and demonstrates Christ's grace may well be a key issue in selecting a church. Some churches create their own versions of the Galatian problem: spelling out in great detail exactly how their members are to live and serve, while downplaying God's grace. Such churches can be as damaging to believers and searchers as churches whose faith is completely bankrupt. How can a church practically deny the reality of grace and honestly state that they are part of the body of Christ? Beware of church policies and programs that make nonbiblical standards or anything besides faith essential to salvation.

**5:5 But by faith we eagerly await through the Spirit the righ-
teousness for which we hope.**[NIV] In this short verse Paul gave his
doctrine of justification by faith. It is *by
faith* (in Christ and his faithfulness, and
not in works or even the strength of our
believing) that . . . *we* (meaning himself
and all believers, even the wavering
Galatians) . . . *eagerly await* (We don't
work for righteousness; we wait for
God to grow his righteousness in us.)
. . . *through the Spirit* (not through anything we can do or have done, and not
through the law; the Spirit both creates
righteousness in us and enables us to patiently wait) . . . *the righteousness* (Christian perfection that God helps us reach in our
lives and then grants completely in glory) . . . *for which we hope*
("hope" meaning a certain event that has not yet occurred; we
hope for what we already know will happen).

> I am righteous already by
> that righteousness which
> is begun in me, and also
> that I am raised up in the
> same hope against sin,
> and wait for the full
> consummation of perfect
> righteousness in heaven.
> *Martin Luther*

"The righteousness for which we hope" could also be translated, "the righteousness that we expect." This verse could mean
that believers should eagerly wait every day for more growth in
righteousness, or that believers should eagerly await the day
when their righteousness will be complete—the day Christ
returns (see Romans 8:18-25; Colossians 1:5; 2 Timothy 4:8;
1 Peter 1:3-4). Both meanings are true. All believers have been
saved by the cross of Christ, are being saved by the transforming
work of the Spirit, and will be saved by God when he gives us a
new, glorified body (see Hebrews 9:24-28).

But the words *faith* and *Spirit* provide the keys to this verse,
for these words separate the Judaizers' approach to God from the
Christian approach to God. The Judaizers' emphasis on circumcision showed that they were trying to gain salvation "in the flesh."
But Paul pointed out that Christian faith comes "through the
Spirit." The Judaizers' emphasis on the law contrasted sharply
with Christianity's emphasis on faith. Christianity's basic doctrine showed the Judaizers to be wrong—dead wrong.

**5:6 For in Christ Jesus neither circumcision nor uncircumcision
has any value. The only thing that counts is faith expressing
itself through love.**[NIV] Notice how Paul built his arguments. In
5:2 and here he clearly made the point that circumcision had no
benefit for salvation. In 5:4 he stressed the point that seeking justification by any other way than by having faith in Christ was falling away from grace. Then he added the flip side: Being
uncircumcised was not a barrier to salvation. Paul stressed the

BELIEVERS' TRUE IDENTITY IN CHRIST

Romans 3:24	We are justified (declared "not guilty" of sin).
Romans 8:1	We await no condemnation.
Romans 8:2	We are set free from the law of sin and death.
1 Corinthians 1:2	We are sanctified and made acceptable in Jesus Christ.
1 Corinthians 1:30	We are righteous and holy in Christ.
1 Corinthians 15:22	We will be made alive at the resurrection.
2 Corinthians 5:17	We are new creations.
2 Corinthians 5:21	We receive God's righteousness.
Galatians 3:28	We are one in Christ with all other believers.
Ephesians 1:3	We are blessed with every spiritual blessing in Christ.
Ephesians 1:4	We are holy, blameless, and covered with God's love.
Ephesians 1:5-6	We are adopted as God's children.
Ephesians 1:7	We are forgiven—our sins are taken away.
Ephesians 1:10-11	We will be brought under Christ's headship.
Ephesians 1:13	We are marked as belonging to God by the Holy Spirit.
Ephesians 2:6	We have been raised up to sit with Christ in glory.
Ephesians 2:10	We are God's work of art.
Ephesians 2:13	We have been brought near to God.
Ephesians 3:6	We share in the promise in Christ.
Ephesians 3:12	We can come with freedom and confidence into God's presence.
Ephesians 5:29-30	We are members of Christ's body, the church.
Colossians 2:10	We have been given fullness in Christ.
Colossians 2:11	We are set free from our sinful nature.
2 Timothy 2:10	We will have eternal glory.

serious state of church members who fall away. Today we must be alert to church people who listen to teachers from cults. We must avoid anyone who dilutes or diminishes Christ's work in guaranteeing our salvation.

If Paul clearly told the Gentile Galatian believers *not* to be circumcised, what would he say to the Jews, who were already circumcised? Paul gave advice to them in 1 Corinthians 7:17-20. "Each one should retain the place in life that the Lord assigned to him. . . . Was a man already circumcised when he was called? He should not become uncircumcised. Was a man uncircumcised when he was called? He should not be circumcised. Circumcision is nothing and uncircumcision is nothing" (NIV).

Thus, to both believing Jews and Gentiles (those *in Christ*), Paul made the point that *neither circumcision nor uncircumcision has any value* for salvation (see also 3:28; 6:15; Colossians 3:11). Paul's conviction rested on the importance of all it means to be "in Christ" *(en Christo)*—one of Paul's favorite phrases. The expression "in Christ" not only states and clarifies the focus of

our faith; it also helps us understand that all of God's benefits
come to us in Christ. Each aspect of salvation and every component of the life we live after conversion are rooted in Christ. We
have a personal relationship with him; we are clothed with his
righteousness, filled with his Spirit, and incorporated into the
body of believers "in Christ." The chart on the previous page out-
lines the scope of the riches that we have in Christ.

JUST WAIT!
Those convinced that they must "work" for their salvation have
a very difficult time with the word *wait*. And yet "waiting by faith"
describes much of a Christian's experience in life. The legalists
must live in constant fear and denial, for each day ends with
fresh evidence that they have not met the law's demands.
Christians can live daily with the witness of God's Spirit that we
are children of God (see Romans 8:16). In the meantime:
- We wait to see our hoped-for righteousness fully revealed at
  the time God chooses. When we walk by faith, our hope of
  righteousness in God's grace contrasts with the vain hope of
  the legalist, who tries to do it by works.
- We wait for Christ's return and for his merciful verdict on our
  lives at the final judgment.
- With the Spirit's help, we claim and begin to produce the fruit
  of righteousness. Though it will not be fully revealed in this life
  (except through our union "in Christ"), we go on in hope (see
  Romans 8:18-25). Without him, we would not be able to wait
  patiently. God gives us the ability to wait and to hope through
  his Holy Spirit.

Paul later used a similar argument in handling the problem in
Corinth regarding what foods the believers could or could not
eat: "'Food will not bring us close to God.' We are no worse off if
we do not eat, and no better off if we do" (1 Corinthians 8:8
NRSV). In short, these actions didn't matter one way or the other,
as long as a person was in Christ.

So what *does* matter? Paul didn't hesitate to answer the
implied question: *The only thing that counts is faith expressing
itself through love.* To the faith discussed in chapter 4, Paul added
the clarification that it must be faith expressed in love. We are
saved by faith alone; but for these Galatian believers who seemed
to want so desperately to work, Paul was saying, "OK, work, but
don't try to earn your salvation. Instead, let your salvation by
faith result in loving and kind works done to serve others." Genuine faith in Christ is expressed in love for others.

And love, as Paul wrote elsewhere, "is the fulfillment of the
law" (Romans 13:10 NIV). What obedience to the law cannot pro-

duce, love can. Love is the primary fruit of the Spirit (5:22).
Faith is the root, and love is the fruit; it is poured out in our
hearts by the Holy Spirit (Romans 5:5). What the Judaizers
wanted could not be obtained by their method. Ironically, the
love found in the gospel would actually outperform the Judaizers
in their pointless efforts. They were running with a load of works,
trying to earn their salvation, and they would fail before the finish line. Meanwhile, those in Christ were already enjoying the
victory of their salvation. If the only thing that matters is faith
expressing itself in love, then all who call themselves Christians
must be sure their faith is placed solely and squarely in Jesus
Christ and that their lives show forth his love.

Paul was already countering the arguments and ridicule that
would be heaped against the way of faith in Christ. He immediately blunted the accusation that "true faith" would be difficult to
prove by affirming that faith in Christ reveals itself by genuine
love (see also James 2:8, 14-22). Christianity does have moral
demands, but we can't be saved by measuring up to them. Our
salvation motivates and energizes us to love and to live right.

A FAITH CHECKUP
In disregarding the law as a basis for salvation, we must not disregard its basic requirement of love. We are saved by faith, not
by works. But love for others and for God comes spontaneously
to those whom God has forgiven. God forgives us completely,
and Jesus said that those who are forgiven much, love much
(Luke 7:47). Because faith expresses itself through love, you
can check your love for others as a way to monitor your faith.

**5:7 You were running a good race. Who cut in on you and kept
you from obeying the truth?**^{NIV} Returning to his focus on the
Galatian believers *(you),* Paul pictured their Christian life in
terms of a *race*. The apostle, fond of this metaphor, employed it
several times in his letters (see 2:2; 1 Corinthians 9:24-27; Philippians 3:13-14; 2 Timothy 4:7). Paul compared life for the Christian to a race—to be run well, by the rules, and without stopping
or turning back no matter what the obstacles. But always, the
opportunity to participate in the race required faith in Christ.

The Galatians were *running* well. They had accepted the gospel of salvation. Not only had they believed, but they were living
out their faith, allowing it to shape their lives; they were *obeying
the truth*. They weren't sitting around; they were running. They
had received God's Word and had begun to apply the truth. But
despite their good start, someone had *cut in on* them. Paul pic-

tured a racer illegally cutting ahead of another, thus causing that other racer to stumble, lose his pace, go out of bounds, or even fall. Christianity is a serious race, not merely a fun run. There is serious competition from Satan and his deceivers who would like to keep us off track.

Although Paul asked *who,* he already knew the answer. The word "who" is singular; Paul knew that the problem was the Judaizers, and here he was focusing on their leader, whom he probably did not know (see 5:10). Paul warned the Galatians that the Judaizers, instead of helping them along, were actually hindering their faith. Instead of opening up new truths to the Galatians, they kept the Galatians from obeying the truth. The Judaizers represented the interests of Satan. They wanted to keep the Galatians enslaved to the law and derail the new believers. The Galatians would not complete the race if they tried to do it by their own efforts.

INERTIA AND SYNERGY
We must warn new believers to expect difficulties and road-blocks. Even other Christians may inadvertently hinder their development. New believers are vulnerable to distorted teaching by groups who use the Bible to gain an entrance, but who promote their own wrong ideas. Be sure to check up on new believers and find out who or what is influencing them. We all need to be reminded that life in Christ involves a long-distance race to the finish!

5:8 This persuasion does not come from Him who calls you.[NKJV]
The word translated *persuasion (peismone)* indicates a play on words in the Greek that is difficult to translate into English. Verse 7 could be translated, "Who kept you from being persuaded as to the truth?" and verse 10 would follow with, "I am persuaded that you will think otherwise." Thus verses 7-10 have a cohesiveness in Greek that is missed in English.

This "persuasion" referred to the whole system of salvation by works. Paul did not identify this false teaching as specifically coming from the Judaizers. It was more important that the Galatians would realize that it did *not come from Him who calls you.* It was God who had called the Galatians (1:6), but he had called them to salvation by his grace, not by their works (see also Romans 9:11; 1 Thessalonians 2:12; 5:24).

5:9 "A little yeast works through the whole batch of dough."[NIV]
The Galatians had stumbled in their race and had stopped obeying the truth (5:7-8) because they had listened to false teachers. The Galatians had turned away from Christ and had embraced

the impossible-to-fulfill law (5:3-4). Even worse, this false teaching was spreading. Here Paul changed his analogy. *Yeast* is put into bread to make it rise, and it takes only a little to affect a *whole batch of dough.* Jesus used yeast as an example of how a small amount of evil can affect a large group of people (see Matthew 16:5-12). Even if only a small group of Galatian believers was at risk when Paul wrote this letter, he knew that if he didn't get the Galatians back "on track" with the truth, the entire Galatian church would be in trouble.

Some have interpreted this proverb to mean that if even one small item (say circumcision) were allowed to be a requirement for salvation, then the entire system of salvation by grace would be annulled.

DESTRUCTIVE PERSUASION
In these verses Paul included five "destructive persuasions":
1. People and ideas who "cut in." They seem to be fellow runners, but their purpose is to take us out of the race (5:7).
2. People who, by threat or ridicule, cause us to disregard the Bible's truth (5:7).
3. People whose beliefs actually dishonor Christ who called us (5:8).
4. People who practice "yeast tactics," attempting to infiltrate and then gain credibility and control from the inside (5:9).
5. People whose teaching creates mental and spiritual confusion (5:10).

God also participates in our lives in persuasive ways. But God's way of persuading us varies greatly from Satan's (see Romans 10:4; 1 Corinthians 1:30; Colossians 2:3).

Satan's influence produces guilt, oppression, accusation, bondage to sinful habits, a troubled and terrified conscience, an incorrect view of Christ as an unfair judge, discouragement, destructiveness, depression, even suicidal tendencies. However, God's influence produces guiltless freedom, life affirmation, comfort, forgiveness, positive change, love, joy, peace, a correct view of Christ as our loving and merciful Savior, and the lightening of our burdens.

5:10 I am confident in the Lord that you will take no other view. The one who is throwing you into confusion will pay the penalty, whoever he may be.[NIV] In spite of his obvious concern over the Galatian believers and the dangerous situation they faced, Paul believed that they would come to their senses. His confidence was based *in the Lord,* meaning that it was not based on his own reasoning or understanding but on a certainty given him by God. Or to put it another way, Paul knew that as long as the

Galatians remained in the Lord, he could be confident about the outcome of this difficult situation.

JUST A LITTLE
Replacing Christ, or adding some conditions or options to the way of salvation, has the same effect as adding yeast to dough. A little bit of disruption can damage an entire church. A pinch of legalism, a little bit of doubt, a certain amount of taking sides, and a small quantity of divisive criticism—and soon the church won't look at all like what Christ intended it to be. When other church issues replace faith in Christ and loving service to others, the conflict and disruption spread through the church like yeast penetrating dough. Church leaders need to stay tuned in to Christ's message and the Holy Spirit's leading. Don't add anything to the gospel. To do so can disrupt your church.

What was Paul certain about? *That you will take no other view* could mean that they would not accept this "different gospel" (1:6), that they would not turn away from the grace that had given them salvation in the first place, or that they would agree with what he wrote in this letter. Although the specific meaning is unclear, all three possibilities point out that Paul was *confident* that they would return to their first faith.

In addition, Paul also was confident that those causing all this confusion among the Galatian believers would receive their due punishment. While Paul knew that the troublemakers were a group of Judaizers, he singled out *the one who is throwing you into confusion.* Most likely, Paul was pointing out the leader of this group, whom he probably did not know (see 5:7). Paul suspected that this man carried a certain amount of weight as a leader. *Whoever he may be* does not so much stress Paul's ignorance of this person's identity as the worthlessness in Paul's eyes of any status he might carry. "Whoever he may be, however high in leadership or however revered by the Jews, this man is teaching wrong doctrine," Paul was saying. And by the same token, no matter what this leader's position, he would *pay the penalty* for his wrong teaching.

What penalty? Most likely, Paul was referring to God's judgment, not to any specific penalty exacted by a human court of law. At about the same time Paul was writing this letter to the Galatians, James was writing his letter. James had this to say about teachers: "Not many of you should presume to be teachers, my brothers, because you know that we who teach will be judged more strictly" (James 3:1 NIV). Jesus had even stronger words for false teachers: "But if anyone causes one of these little ones who believe in me to sin, it would be better for him to have a large millstone hung around his neck and to be drowned in the depths of the sea" (Matthew 18:6 NIV). That's a penalty worth heeding! We must always be cautious lest we promote our own ideas, values, and agenda to the exclusion of biblical truth.

NO OFFENSE?

The fact that Paul was being persecuted demonstrated that he was preaching the true gospel. His message challenged Judaism with faith and grace instead of the works of the law. If Paul had taught what the false teachers wanted, no one would be offended. But because he taught the truth, he was persecuted from all sides. Have friends or loved ones rejected you because you have taken a stand for Christ? Paul's experience reminds us that we must expect persecution. Jesus said not to be surprised if the world hates us, because it hated him (John 15:18-19). Just as Paul continued to faithfully proclaim the message about Christ, we should continue doing the ministry God has given us—in spite of the obstacles others may put in our way.

5:11 But my friends, why am I still being persecuted if I am still preaching circumcision?NRSV Paul asked a personal question; apparently he was reminded of an accusation against him as he considered the false teachers and the penalty that awaited them. Perhaps some of these false teachers had accused Paul of being wishy-washy on the issue of circumcision, preaching it sometimes, not preaching it at others, depending on his audience. Or perhaps they referred to his zealous preaching before his Christian conversion. The sense of Paul's question could be paraphrased: "If I am promoting circumcision, which everyone knows I do not . . ." If Paul were preaching that people needed to be circumcised in order to be saved, then why were the Judaizers still persecuting him? He would be preaching the same message they preached!

In that case the offense of the cross has been removed.NRSV If Paul were preaching the need for circumcision (thus the need for complete obedience to the law) in order to receive salvation, then *the offense of the cross* would be removed. The word "offense" in Greek means a trap or a stumbling block.

Paul's message of the cross of Christ was offensive and a constant stumbling block to the Jews. The only way that offense could be removed would be if he stopped preaching that Christ died for our sins. If Paul had been preaching obedience to the law and acceptance of the rite of circumcision, then the stumbling block in his ministry would have been removed. But to remove it would be to lose the entire message; for without the Cross, Christianity has no meaning. The very fact that Paul was being persecuted revealed that he did *not* preach circumcision.

To human nature, and especially to Jews brought up to love and revere their law, the concept of needing someone else's death in order to be saved was "offensive." Paul had already referred to Christ's death as the greatest fulfillment of the Old Testament curse: "Cursed is everyone who is hung on a tree" (3:13 NIV). The very thought of describing the Messiah as an executed convict disgusted them. But the impact of Christ's cross on their pride was the greatest stumbling block. As Paul described to the Corinthians, "But we preach Christ crucified: a stumbling block to Jews and foolishness to Gentiles" (1 Corinthians 1:23 NIV). Paul had witnessed the rejection of the gospel by both Gentiles and Jews, each for different reasons. To the Gentiles, the message often seemed like nonsense; to the Jews, the implications were offensive.

CAUTION
The gospel may offend some, but we should not measure our effectiveness by how many people we have offended. An offensive, insensitive, judgmental messenger can prevent the message from receiving a hearing at all! The thought that we might offend should not be an excuse, however, for failing to share the gospel. Those oblivious to their own brashness or insensitivity are often the ones who create undue resistance to the message. If our hearers take offense at the gospel itself, they have created a problem for themselves; if we cause them offense, we have created a problem for ourselves.

5:12 As for those agitators, I wish they would go the whole way and emasculate themselves!NIV Paul's words here, though very harsh, were not meant in jest. He wanted to make another point regarding circumcision. *Those agitators* referred again to the false teachers, the Judaizers, who were preaching that the believers needed to be circumcised. In effect, Paul said that if the false teachers were so concerned about zeal for the law, maybe they shouldn't stop at circumcision but go the whole way and castrate themselves (see Philippians 3:2). According to their own logic, wouldn't this make them even holier? The comparison to pagan rituals was probably not lost on the Galatians. Pagan priests of the prominent cult of the goddess Cybele in Asia were eunuchs, castrated as a part of a sacred ritual. By making this statement,

Paul placed circumcision as no better than the pagan rituals of cutting parts of the body.

This particular train of thought could also be taken to mean that Paul hoped the resulting "impotence" of these men would make them unable to produce any more "children" (followers). At one time circumcision had been the sign of God's covenant with his people. However, with the advent of Christianity, circumcision became as inconsequential as any pagan ritual.

5:13 **For you were called to freedom, brothers and sisters; only do not use your freedom as an opportunity for self-indulgence, but through love become slaves to one another.**NRSV In 5:1, when Paul spoke of freedom, he included himself: "Christ has set us free." In this verse, he applied his words directly to the Galatians and his ministry to them. The word *you* builds on his confidence that they would return to the faith that had saved them (5:10). When Paul ministered among the Galatians, he did not give his converts a new set of rules to obey (as the Judaizers had done), for that would have made them slaves to the law. Instead, the Galatians *were called to freedom.* Paul was the messenger, but they "were called" by God himself, the author of the gospel. The apostle wanted them to "stand firm," to run their race in that very freedom that only Christ can give.

This verse includes an important shift in emphasis. Paul had expressed his harshest wishes to the Judaizers in 5:12. Then he turned to a practical concern he had for the Galatians. If they overcame the attacks of the Judaizers, they would immediately face a different threat to their freedom. Besides legalism, they must avoid giving in to the

> Obedience is the perfection of the religious life; by it man submits to man for the love of God, as God rendered Himself obedient unto men for their salvation.
>
> *Thomas Aquinas*

"flesh" (Greek, *sarx*—translated as "self-indulgence" in NRSV). All people are subject to this type of slavery, for every human being has a sinful human nature, inherently bent toward sin. The context determines that Paul is not denigrating the human body or our identity as made in the image of God. But this verse also makes clear that freedom in Christ does not mean elimination of the *sarx,* for it continues to urge us to indulge ourselves rather than pursue the true purpose of freedom: the opportunity to practice genuine love in service to others.

Paul has already used the Greek term *sarx* eight times in this letter to describe physical life (see 1:16; 2:16, 20; 3:3; 4:13, 14, 23, 29). But at this point, he used *sarx* with a decided negative flavor. Translating the word as "sinful nature" (NIV) or "self-indulgence" (NRSV) reminds us that "flesh" can be an inherent source impelling us to sin. "Flesh" does not mean just a weakness but an almost insatiable, self-oriented power in human nature. Our fallen nature rebels against God and resists his Spirit, producing what Paul called the "works of the flesh" (5:19 NRSV). The demands of our human nature present a constant threat to our real freedom in Christ. We need his ongoing help to keep our "flesh" under control.

GALLERY OF FALSE MASTERS
Although we may be trusting Christ as our gracious master, we must be aware of the ongoing attacks by previous "masters" to reassert their power in our lives. The master called Legalism continues to appeal to our belief that we can work our way into God's favor without any outside help. The master called Label-ism offers lip service to Christ, while promoting pride of owner-ship in having the right beliefs and right connections. And the master called Sinful Human Nature continues to woo us to sim-ply indulge ourselves in whatever might offer pleasure at the moment. These masters vary in their approach, but they never take very long vacations from their efforts to enslave us.

Some commentators have suggested that after dealing with the Judaizers and their adherents in the previous sections of this let-ter, Paul turned his attention to another faction in the Galatian church—those who wanted to cast aside all restraint. They under-stood Christian freedom as freedom from the law, but they went too far in that direction, casting aside all moral restraint and liv-ing in self-indulgence. This view has some validity, though it underestimates how all believers struggle with their own human nature. Temptation to indulge our flesh provides a greater prob-lem than can be explained by a "faction." In any case, the very lifestyle of pagan cultures would have been a constant temptation to these newly "freed" converts. Opportunities to "indulge the sin-ful nature" have rarely been in short supply!

Some of Paul's critics may have condemned his preaching of Christian freedom, saying that it would lead to people living without restraint or guidelines. Paul had an immediate and forceful answer, explaining that freedom was not to be used as *an opportunity for self-indulgence* (see also 5:16-17, 19, 24). The Greek word *aphorme* lit-erally means "a starting point, a base of operations for a military mission." We might even use the word *springboard*. Christian free-dom is not meant to be the base of operations, the springboard and pretext for indulging in everything one's sinful nature desires. The irony, then, would be that Christian freedom would be used to return to slavery to sin—for to fulfill every desire is to be enslaved to those desires. Satan and the flesh use our freedom from law as an opportunity to enflame our desires. Sinful human desires lead to the problems mentioned in 5:26 (conceit, provoking one another, and envy) and to the lack of mutual help described in 6:1-10. When we indulge the sinful nature, we open the door to these kinds of behaviors and attitudes (see 1 Peter 2:16; 2 Peter 2:8-10; Jude 4). The antidotes for indulging the flesh are living in the Spirit and serving one another.

LIBERTY'S LIMITS
Christian freedom cannot be defined as permission to do anything we want. Rather, it is the opportunity to do what Christ wants, without fear that our performance will be counted against us. We are free from endless ceremonial laws, sin, and fear. But we are not free in the sense of totally governing ourselves or being totally autonomous from Christ. We are under the restraint of the Holy Spirit and the constraint of the higher law, the law of love. Freedom must be used to glorify Christ and serve others, not just to fulfill our personal desires.

Slavery to sin comes with being human (Psalm 51:5; Romans 7:18). Slavery to the law comes as a choice, but a foolish one, for it requires hard labor without any hope of freedom. Paul called the believers to "serve one another in love" (NIV). This was freedom at its deepest level, for it allowed people to submit voluntarily to slavery to one another (the Greek verb *douleuete* translated "serve" actually refers to the service of a slave). Serving in this way gives the believer deep joy.

This teaching forms the very heart of Christianity, but it presents a paradox. We are freed from slavery to sin to become slaves to one another. Worldly people cannot understand this—joy in slavery? They don't realize they are enslaved either to sin or to some religious system. People enslaved to sin are not free to live righteously. The other slavery that Paul described comes with the freedom given in Christ. Love for other believers flows outward from what God has done in each believer's heart. The Greek word for love *(agape)* refers to selfless, self-giving love. Christian freedom does not leave believers wandering through life without laws, rules, restraints, or guidelines. Instead, they freely live according to God's standards and glorify God through loving service to others.

5:14 For the whole law is summed up in a single commandment, "You shall love your neighbor as yourself."NRSV In fact, Christian servanthood ultimately does what slavery to the law cannot do—it fulfills the law! Quoting from Leviticus 19:18 (from the Torah, the book of the Law), Paul explained that *a single com-*

mandment summarizes the entire law. If you *love your neighbor as yourself,* you'll find yourself fulfilling God's law. Jesus made this same point (Matthew 22:35-39; Luke 10:25-28).

The Greek word translated *summed up* could also mean "fulfilled." Thus Paul's sentence has two meanings: (1) This law sums up all the others, and (2) this law is fulfilled. In fact, the entire law is fulfilled as the Christian community acts in love toward one another through the power of the Holy Spirit.

Paul made it clear through this letter (and others) that the law cannot save anyone. But he did not cast aside the law as worthless. Believers must still be concerned with it; otherwise Paul would not have made this statement. No one could ever completely fulfill the law; but if someone could, the Christians (not the Judaizers) would most resemble that person. Amazingly enough, one person *did* completely fulfill the law, and Christians (when they act as they should) do indeed resemble him. Their likeness to Christ depends upon the Spirit working in them, developing "fruit" (5:22-23).

DIRECTION
We cannot love our neighbor without being in Christ. Our flesh (sinful human desires) takes our freedom in Christ and uses it to create insensitivity and disregard for our neighbor. We may show love at times and to a few, but it's very difficult to maintain a loving attitude in our own strength. As Christians, we have two indispensable helps: (1) the Holy Spirit (he empowers us to grow in love for God and our neighbor), and (2) Christ's compassion and forgiveness (when we fail to love and serve as we should, Christ forgives us). Express your gratefulness to God for his merciful salvation, and you will discover that his love for others is growing in you.

5:15 If, however, you bite and devour one another, take care that you are not consumed by one another.^{NRSV} Paul used the present tense in these verbs, indicating that these problems were occurring as he wrote. Such conflict threatened to tear the church apart. The verbs increase in intensity—*daknete* (biting, or striking like a snake), then *katesthiete* (devouring, destroying), leading to the real danger of *analothete* (consuming, annihilating) each other. In direct and horrible contrast to the command to love their neighbors as themselves, the Galatians were becoming adept at destroying one another's reputations. Paul's concern as shown in his figurative description of escalating hostility reminds us of Jesus' words in the Sermon on the Mount (see Matthew 5:21-26): "But I tell you that anyone who is angry with his brother will be subject to judgment" (Matthew 5:22 NIV).

A MATTER OF FOCUS
When we believers lose the motivation of love, we become critical of others. We stop looking for good in them and see only their faults. Soon we lose our unity. Have you talked behind someone's back? Have you focused on others' shortcomings instead of their strengths? Remind yourself of Jesus' command to love others as you love yourself (Matthew 22:39). When you begin to feel critical of someone, make a list of that person's positive qualities. When problems need to be addressed, confront in love rather than gossip.

The source of the conflict went back to the false teachers and the confusion they were causing among the believers (5:10). The presence of the conflict supports the theory that factions were developing in the church—some people going with the law-centered teachers, some staying with Paul and the gospel, and some deciding to pursue their every sinful whim based on the "freedom" they had in Christ. Such continued confusion would ruin their faith, their testimony, and ultimately the church itself. While some differences of opinion would be natural, the Galatians had gone beyond that. They disagreed on foundational issues. Like piranhas, they were destroying one another.

TEETH MARKS
We must guard against using destructive criticism. Paul described a church where people were harming one another rather than helping or healing. Criticism can destroy a person's inner resolve to remain faithful. It can actually weaken physical health, undermine character, and drain personal resources. These unnecessary attacks often occur during times when a person needs strength and support to face real challenges. For example, a family in crisis doesn't need to be criticized about sporadic church attendance; they need the support and care of the church.

When we are critical toward others, we are not demonstrating our freedom; we are showing that we may be slaves to our feelings. We must find nondestructive ways to deal with these thoughts and feelings. We must be willing to admit wrongdoing when we do leave "teeth marks" on others by our treatment of them. Love, respect, and honor for other believers work as strong antidotes to the bites of destructive criticism.

LIVING BY THE HOLY SPIRIT'S POWER / 5:16-26

If Christ's summary of the law—"Love the Lord your God with all your heart, soul, mind and strength" and "Love your neighbor as yourself" (see Matthew 22:34-40)—provides the goal of the Christian life, then what provides the motivation and strength to do it? Paul's answer: Live by the power available through the Holy Spirit.

By his extended argument during much of this letter, Paul had refuted those who insisted on a law-centered life. But in 5:13, following his pattern of reserving the final parts of his letters for practical application, Paul turned to the personal, spiritual lives of the Galatians. He had warned them not to follow the teaching of the Judaizers. Here he warned them about following their own wishes and desires. Slavery was a threat from the outside influence of the false teachers, but it was an equal threat from the inside desires of the flesh. Paul began with the warning in 5:13, "Do not use your freedom to indulge the sinful nature" (NIV), and he immediately contrasted it with the second part of Christ's summary of the law, "Serve one another in love" (NIV). Paul wanted them to replace self-indulgence with loving service to others.

In this section, Paul explained that the secret to loving our neighbor as ourselves is by living in the Spirit and not giving in to our sinful human desires. He contrasted the characteristics of a life motivated by the sinful nature and a life motivated by the Spirit.

5:16 So I say, live by the Spirit, and you will not gratify the desires of the sinful nature.NIV The word *so* ties in with verses 13-15. The strategy for removing the divisiveness that marred the Galatian church was to serve one another in love, but that too was humanly impossible. People cannot, in their own power, show love to all people at all times. But God has provided the means to meet his commands—the Holy Spirit.

SPIRIT LED

If you want the qualities listed in 5:22-23, then you know that the Holy Spirit is leading you. At the same time, be careful not to confuse all of your subjective feelings with the Spirit's leading. Being led by the Holy Spirit involves the desire to hear and the readiness to obey God's Word so that you can discern between your feelings and God's promptings. Live each day controlled and guided by the Holy Spirit. Then the words of Christ will be in your mind, the love of Christ will be behind your actions, and the power of Christ will help you control your selfish desires.

God sent the Holy Spirit to be with and within his followers after Christ had returned to heaven. The Spirit would comfort them, guide them to know his truth, remind them of Jesus' words, point out when they did not obey, give them the right words to say, and fill them with power to do good (see John 14–16).

At Pentecost (Acts 2:1-4), God made the Holy Spirit available to all who believed in Jesus. We receive the Holy Spirit (are baptized with him) when we believe in Jesus Christ as Savior. We must understand the baptism of the Holy Spirit in the light of his total work in Christians:

- The Spirit marks the beginning of the Christian experience (Ephesians 1:13-14). We cannot belong to Christ without his Spirit (Romans 8:9); we cannot be united to Christ without his Spirit (1 Corinthians 6:17); we cannot be adopted as his children without his Spirit (Romans 8:14-17; Galatians 4:6-7); and we cannot be in the body of Christ except by baptism in the Spirit (1 Corinthians 12:13).
- The Spirit provides power for our new lives. He begins a life-long process to make us more like Christ (2 Corinthians 3:17-18). When we receive Christ by faith, we begin an immediate personal relationship with God. The Holy Spirit works in us to help us become like Christ.
- The Spirit unites the Christian community in Christ (Ephesians 2:19-22). The Holy Spirit can be experienced by all, and he works through all (1 Corinthians 12:11; Ephesians 4:4).

The phrase *live by the Spirit (pneumati peripateite)* conveys the meaning of the literal translation "by the Spirit keep on walking." Walking means "living" in this context, and it emphasizes the moment-by-moment contact with and guidance by the Holy Spirit for daily decisions and activities. Living "by the Spirit" should be a daily, continuous action by Christians. He is always present, but we must be in touch with him and stay open to his guidance and correction.

We live the Christian life "by the Spirit"—meaning that he gives us the power we need to follow God when his will goes against our nature or desires. Expressed negatively, we cannot live the Christian life without the Holy Spirit. Expressed positively, we experience the truth that "it is God who works in you to will and to act according to his good purpose" (Philippians 2:13 NIV). The tense of the verb is present continuous action, so it conveys "keep on living" or "keep on walking" by the Spirit, portraying the Christian life as a process. We do not obtain salvation by works; neither can we obtain sanctification (growing in the Christian life) by works.

The result? *You will not gratify the desires of the sinful nature.* When we become believers, our sinful nature still exists. But God asks us to place our sinful nature under the control of the Holy Spirit so that he can transform it. This is a supernatural process. We must never underestimate the power of our sinful nature, and we must never attempt to fight it in our own strength. Satan is a crafty tempter, and we have a limitless ability to make excuses. Instead of trying to overcome sin by our own willpower, we must take advantage of the tremendous power of Christ. God provides for victory over our sinful nature—he sends the Holy Spirit to live in us and give us power. But our ability to restrain the desires of the sinful nature depends on how much we're willing to "live by" the Holy Spirit. For each believer, this daily process requires moment-by-moment decisions.

GET WET!
Paul described living by the Holy Spirit as more of a choice than a complex process. Some believe that this part of the Christian life is a mystery. While the actual nature of Christ's saving work may in fact border on the mysterious (see Colossians 1:27), our role is very clear—we must simply trust in him. Living "by the Holy Spirit" means that we submit to his authority, welcome his guidance, accept his correction, live under his restraint, rely on his power, and allow him to unify us with other believers.

Living by the Spirit does not mean a casual part-time relationship. We must treat his control like a shower. If we stand back and stick a hand or foot into the stream of water, we may guess the temperature of the water, but we will never get clean. We must be immersed in the Holy Spirit as if stepping fully into the shower's cleansing and invigorating stream, letting it cover us.

5:17 For the sinful nature desires what is contrary to the Spirit, and the Spirit what is contrary to the sinful nature. They are in conflict with each other, so that you do not do what you want.[NIV] While believers live in this world, they face constant tension between their sinful human desires and their new spiritual life. These two are *in conflict with each other.* We must not infer from Paul's words that our personality has two selves, nor that we have two equal and opposite forces struggling to gain control. In Christ and in the Holy Spirit, we have a victorious new resurrection life. The Holy Spirit in us guarantees our future total redemption and change. *Sarx,* translated as "sinful nature," gives that impression. However, it is better to understand it as "sinful human desires." Though we have new life in Christ, we still have a mind and body prone to rebel and enticed by sinful desires. We must resist those desires.

Paul expands upon this conflict in other letters; for example:

> The greatest of all evils is *not* to be tempted, because there are then grounds for believing that the devil looks upon us as his property.
> *John Vianney*

- *For those who live according to the flesh set their minds on the things of the flesh, but those who live according to the Spirit set their minds on the things of the Spirit. . . . But you are not in the flesh; you are in the Spirit, since the Spirit of God dwells in you. Anyone who does not have the Spirit of Christ does not belong to him. (Romans 8:5, 9* NRSV*)*

(Read all of Romans 8:5-9, 12-17; Ephesians 4:21-24; and Colossians 3:3-15.) The conflict described in Romans 8 and in Galatians 5 differs from the conflict described in Romans 7:7-25. In Romans 7, Paul described how the power of indwelling sin keeps the person under the law from doing what the law requires. He did not mention the Spirit until later in the letter.

We shouldn't be surprised that *the sinful nature desires what is contrary to the Spirit.* We often experience resistance when we follow the Spirit's leading. Satan serves as a persistent teacher of rebellion, and humanity has had centuries of practice. Whatever path we choose, we will hear the whispers of opposition. Whenever we set out to do what the Holy Spirit instructs, we can expect

---

HOW TO DEAL WITH THE SINFUL NATURE

- *Admit that you do have a selfish, sinful human nature.* Jeremiah put it well, "The heart is deceitful above all things and beyond cure. Who can understand it?" (Jeremiah 17:9 NIV). Don't be shocked by your tendency to selfishness.
- *Surrender your selfish nature, with all its tendencies, to Christ* (see also notes on 5:24). Ask God to do whatever it takes in your life to bring you to say, with Paul, "I have been crucified with Christ" (2:20).
- *Commit your actions, thoughts, passions, and capabilities to Christ.* Jesus described this ongoing, daily action as "denying self" (see Luke 9:23-25). Knowing that your sinful nature desires to hinder the Spirit, ask the Spirit to help you deny those desires.
- *Make service to others a top priority for your life.* The Bible even speaks of this process as training in holiness (see 1 Timothy 4:7). Loving and serving others helps restrain our selfish desires.

---

the flesh to flare up in opposition. When we decide to share the gospel, our sinful human nature will make us feel foolish. When we decide to commit ourselves to some service, the flesh hinders us with evil desires. The flesh relentlessly tries to thwart the leading of the Spirit.

Conversely, each time we follow our sinful human nature, we will receive (through our consciences, God's Word, or even other believers) reminders not to follow those sinful desires.

RESIST!
Our resource for resisting "the desires of the sinful nature" is the Holy Spirit. We can ask God to expose and help us contradict our sinful desires. Remember, these desires include more than sexual desires. In fact, in Galatians, Paul was responding to debates about the law, not sexual immorality. Christians were enflamed with anger against those on the other side.

Because of who we are, depending on the Spirit's help becomes essential. He can be the warning signal that alerts us that we have gone against or are about to violate the Father's will. The world will encourage us to "listen to our hearts" or will try to drown out the Spirit's guidance with other sounds—but we will receive dependable guidance by listening carefully to him.

True believers realize the deadly power of sin. No longer their master, sin now attacks like a powerful enemy. Sinful desires still pop up, like guerrilla forces, attacking us when we least expect it. And when we attempt to follow the Spirit's desires, we find the attacks growing in intensity, indeed they "war against [the] soul" (1 Peter 2:11 NIV). In other words, having wrong desires doesn't always mean we have sin in our life. If we are in tune with the Holy Spirit, sinful human desires will attempt to block his leading.

Because of this conflict, believers *do not do what [they] want.* This phrase has one of three possible meanings: (1) The sinful nature keeps believers from doing the good that the Spirit desires; (2) the Spirit keeps believers from doing the evil that their sinful nature desires; or (3) the sinful nature and the Spirit work against each other, hindering each's desires. The third explanation seems likely. If we function normally, our desires and the Spirit will counter each other's moves. So we must realize this warfare, claim the Spirit's victory, focus on Christ's help, and rely on the guidance of the Holy Spirit.

What does our sinful nature desire? And what does the Holy Spirit desire? Paul will answer these questions in the following verses.

ONLY THROUGH HIM
Paul describes the two forces conflicting within us—the Holy
Spirit and the sinful nature (our evil desires or inclinations that
stem from our bodies; see also 5:16, 19, 24). Paul is not saying
that these forces are equal—the Holy Spirit is infinitely
stronger. But having a superior ally doesn't help us if we refuse
to depend on him. If we rely on our own wisdom and strength,
we will make wrong choices and take the wrong actions. If we
try to follow the Spirit by our own human effort, we will fail. Our
only way to freedom from our evil desires is through the
empowering of the Holy Spirit (see Romans 8:9; Ephesians
4:23-24; Colossians 3:3-8).

5:18 But if you are led by the Spirit, you are not under the law.^{NKJV}
Some might have wondered if Paul was moving into a form of legal-
ism all his own. So he reiterated that believers *are not under the law.*
Yet freedom from the law does not imply freedom to do whatever
one pleases (5:13). Neither do we live in the Spirit in some sort of
"middle ground." Instead, we live on another plane altogether—we
have truth as opposed to falsehood; we have grace as opposed to
works; we act out of love as opposed to keeping laws; we are supervised by the Spirit as opposed to being supervised by the law.

So what does a Christian do? How does a Christian live? The
"works" of Christianity come from the Spirit indwelling the
believer. The Christian is *led by the Spirit.* But the Christian must
make up his or her mind to follow where the Spirit leads, especially when the sinful nature constantly rebels, in order to do the
acts described in the next three verses. For more on the Holy Spirit's leading, see 5:16 and 5:25.

HOUSE RULES
When Paul says that those under control of the Spirit are not
under control of the law, he's talking about accountability for
Christians. Paul does not invalidate the law; he only states that
the law is no longer in charge—the Holy Spirit takes control.
    Most parents establish certain house rules when raising their
children. These "laws" cover such things as who gets in the
house when Mom and Dad are away, where kids can and can't
go without having specific permission, additional responsibilities when a parent is not present. But when parents are there,
the "laws" take on a secondary function. Mom and Dad still
have the rules, but they supervise personally. The Holy Spirit's
presence means that we are free from having to worry about
measuring up to the law; now we have the freedom to even go
well beyond the law because we have a direct link with the Holy
Spirit himself.

:19-21 **The acts of the sinful nature are obvious.**^{NIV} Paul contrasted the
works of our sinful human desires and the works of the Spirit-
filled life in 5:19-21 and 5:22-23. Paul's use of the word *obvious*
(*phanera*—self-evident, manifest) probably did not mean readily
visible, for some of the sins listed are private (although may well
manifest themselves at some point—as with hatred or jealousy).
Instead, the word means that these sins obviously come directly
from sinful human desires. In other words, once the behavior has
been identified, we know its source.

DENIAL
We use the term *denial* to describe the all-too-frequent habit
people have of overlooking problems in their lives, refusing to
accept responsibility, and neglecting to take required action.
Denial fits well with Paul's warning that acts of the flesh are
clearly identifiable. Denial does not mean the *inability* to see
something wrong; rather, it means the *unwillingness* to see
what is wrong. Denial must be overcome before we can repent.
The psalmist's prayer can help us be honest in our relationship
with God: "Who can discern his errors? Forgive my hidden
faults. Keep your servant also from willful sins; may they not
rule over me. Then will I be blameless, innocent of great transgression" (Psalm 19:12-13 NIV).

Paul's list of sins falls into four categories. These particular
sins were especially prevalent in the pagan world, and the Galatians would have readily understood them. With few exceptions,
we recognize these sins as present in our own time as well. (The
following word list is quoted from NIV.)

In the first category three sexual sins are mentioned:

Sexual immorality (*porneia*—fornication)—Any form of illicit
sexual relationship. The term serves to spotlight forbidden sexual behavior between people or indirect participation as an
audience. We derive our term *pornography* from this Greek
word.

Impurity (*akatharsia*)—Moral uncleanness. Perhaps no sexual
act has taken place, but the person exhibits a crudeness or
insensitivity in sexual matters that offends others and leads
them to false conclusions about the other person's character.
An example today would be the excessive use of sexual humor
(or what is supposed to be humor), where people make statements with a sexual double meaning.

Debauchery (*aselgeia*—licentiousness)—Open and excessive
indulgence in sexual sins. The person has no sense of shame or

restraint. Debauchery is the outwork-
ing of sexual immorality and impurity.

The next two sins are religious sins
particular to pagan culture:

> The true Christian's
> nostril is to be
> continually attentive to
> the inner cesspool.
>
> *C. S. Lewis*

Idolatry *(eidololatria)*—Worship of
pagan idols. A person creates substi-
tutes for God and then treats them as if they were God. This
person is giving in to sinful human desires.

Witchcraft *(pharmakeia)*—Involvement with the powers of evil,
at times using potions and poisons. With idolatry, a person acts
in a submissive role in relation to evil; with witchcraft, the person is an active agent who manipulates the powers of evil.

The next eight sins pertain to conduct toward people (inter-
personal relations) that has been motivated by sinful desires:

Hatred *(echthrai)*—A condition of fixed enmity between groups.
This may be real, unresolved conflict whose cause has been
forgotten but which has yielded a harvest of bitterness toward
one another.

Discord *(eris)*—Competition, rivalry, bitter conflict—the seeds
and the natural fruit of hatred.

Jealousy *(zelos)*—A feeling of resentment that someone else has
what another feels he or she deserves. The negative aspect of jealousy depends on its context. This word has also become the
English word *zeal*. Earlier, Paul used the verb forms three times,
referring to two forms of zeal—one negative, one positive (4:17-
18). Zeal, then, intensifies any of the other characteristics in this
list.

Fits of rage *(thumoi)*—Outbursts of anger for selfish reasons.
The plural form conveys the meaning of continual and uncon-
trolled behavior.

Selfish ambition *(eritheiai)*—The approach to life and work that
tries to get ahead at other people's expense. Not only might this
refer to what we call "workaholism," it also implies a mercenary,
aggressive attitude toward others in the pursuit of one's goals.

Dissensions *(dichostasiai)*—Strong disagreements or quarrels.
The attitude that can quickly develop between people when a
disagreeable attitude prevails. Whatever the topic or issue, as
soon as one side states its opinion, the other party immediately
champions the opposing view, as a matter of "principle."

Factions *(haireseis)*—Divisions created among people because of
dissensions. This describes the tendency to look for allies in conflict, to form power blocks. The almost spontaneous generation of
cliques demonstrates this characteristic of sinful human desires.

VICES AND VIRTUES

The Bible mentions many specific actions and attitudes that are either right or wrong. Look at the list included here. Are there a number of characteristics from the wrong column that are influencing you?

VICES	VIRTUES
Neglecting God and others	*The by-products of living for God*
Sexual Immorality *(Galatians 5:19)*	Love *(Galatians 5:22)*
Impurity *(Galatians 5:19)*	Joy *(Galatians 5:22)*
Lust *(Colossians 3:5)*	Peace *(Galatians 5:22)*
Hatred *(Galatians 5:20)*	Patience *(Galatians 5:22)*
Discord *(Galatians 5:20)*	Kindness *(Galatians 5:22)*
Jealousy *(Galatians 5:20)*	Goodness *(Galatians 5:22)*
Anger *(Galatians 5:20)*	Faithfulness *(Galatians 5:22)*
Selfish Ambition *(Galatians 5:20)*	Gentleness *(Galatians 5:23)*
Dissension *(Galatians 5:20)*	Self-control *(Galatians 5:23)*
Arrogance *(2 Corinthians 12:20)*	
Envy *(Galatians 5:21)*	
Murder *(Revelation 22:12-16)*	
Idolatry *(Galatians 5:20; Ephesians 5:5)*	
Witchcraft *(Galatians 5:20)*	
Drunkenness *(Galatians 5:21)*	
Wild Living *(Luke 15:13; Galatians 5:21)*	
Cheating *(1 Corinthians 6:8)*	
Adultery *(1 Corinthians 6:9-10)*	
Homosexuality *(1 Corinthians 6:9-10)*	
Greed *(1 Corinthians 6:9-10; Ephesians 5:5)*	
Stealing *(1 Corinthians 6:9-10)*	
Lying *(Revelation 22:12-16)*	

Envy *(phthonoi)*—A desire to possess something awarded to or achieved by another. Or even the twisted logic that cries "Unfair!" about another's circumstances and expresses the wish, *If I can't have that, they shouldn't get it either!* It's sad to note, but many of these social sins are often seen in our churches today.

Finally Paul lists two sins, common to pagan cultures, that are often connected with the rituals of idol worship:

Drunkenness *(methai)*—Excessive use of wine and strong drink. Later Paul used this tendency to highlight the contrast between living by the flesh and living by the Spirit: "Do not get drunk on wine, which leads to debauchery. Instead, be filled with the Spirit" (Ephesians 5:18 NIV).

Orgies *(komoi)*—Drunken, carousing "parties," often filled with sexual promiscuity, were associated with festivals of some pagan gods. The feasts in honor of Bacchus were particularly infamous for their immorality.

And the like—Paul added an "etc." to show that the list was by no means complete.

FAMILY FEUDS
In the life of almost any local church one will find evidence of how sinful desires have affected relationships. Lasting feuds go on between certain families or groups. The hostility exists under a thin cover of civility, but from time to time it erupts. Often those directly involved may have inherited the feud from others (grandparents, family friends, former members, etc.). They no longer even understand why they feel the way they do toward that group or family, but the feelings run deep.

Because sinful human desires work so powerfully, we need the Holy Spirit's help. The conflict exists because it continues to be fed by both sides. If repentance and the laying down of weapons happens on both sides, they can agree to peace. Such healing may open the way for a remarkable new receptivity to the gospel in that community.

I warn you, as I did before, that those who live like this will not inherit the kingdom of God.^{NIV} Paul repeated his warning. The phrase *as I did before* enlightens us, for it reveals that while Paul was spreading the gospel to Gentile congregations across the Roman Empire, he was applying the gospel to morality. He gave his listeners certain guidelines to follow as "standard Christian behavior." The freedom he preached was not a moral wilderness of "easy believism" but a guided tour of life under the influence of God's Spirit.

Those who live like this will not inherit refers to the lifestyle of people who habitually exhibit these characteristics. This does not mean that believers who lapse into any of these sins will lose their salvation. People who habitually exhibit these characteristics reveal themselves to be enslaved to sinful human desires. They are not children of God; thus, they cannot have any part in the inheritance. The priceless gift had been offered, but they had refused to receive it. The gift had not been withheld from them; they simply had withheld themselves from the gift (see also 1 Corinthians 6:9-10; Ephesians 5:5). People who have accepted Christ and have the Holy Spirit within them will manifest that new life by making a clean break with such sins as listed above.

The kingdom of God has two aspects: (1) its presence in

human hearts at conversion, and (2) its future coming at the
end of the age. Paul was most likely thinking of the future
kingdom promised to all believers. However, as long as a
person insists on the habits of the flesh, he or she will not
experience even those aspects of the kingdom of God that
are possible in this life.

MAKE A BREAK
We all have evil desires, and we can't ignore them. In order for
us to follow the Holy Spirit's guidance, we must deal with them
decisively (see 5:24). These desires include obvious sins such
as sexual immorality and witchcraft. They also include less obvious sins such as selfish ambition, hatred, and jealousy. Those
who ignore such sins or refuse to deal with them reveal that
they have not received the gift of the Spirit that leads to a transformed life.

5:22-23 But the fruit of the Spirit is . . .^{NKJV} Paul's introduction of the
word *fruit* is filled with meaning. While we might have expected
him to say, "The works of the Spirit are," Paul needed to use a
fresh term. He had used "works" enough throughout this letter.
Besides, "works" indicates lots of activities that people must do.
"Fruit," however, is singular, indicating that all the fruits exist as
a unit (like a bunch of grapes rather than many different pieces of
fruit) and that all are important to all believers (unlike "gifts" that
are dispensed differently to different people). So Paul conveyed
the meaning of a full harvest of virtues. Also, "fruit" is a by-prod-
uct; it takes time to grow and requires care and cultivation. The
Spirit produces the fruit; our job is to get in tune with the Spirit.
Believers exhibit the fruit of the Spirit, not because they work at
it, but simply because they are filled with the Holy Spirit. The
fruit of the Spirit separates Christians from a godless, evil world,
reveals a power within them, and helps them become more
Christlike in their daily lives. In contrast to the list it follows,
Paul did not describe these characteristics as obvious. The pre-
vious ones reside in us; the following ones come as a result of the
Spirit's presence.

Again, the characteristics fall into categories. The first three
are inward and can come from God alone:

Love *(agape)*—Love as shown by Jesus, whose love is self-sacri-
ficing and unchanging, and as demonstrated by God who sent
his Son for sinners (Romans 5:5). Love forms the foundation
for all the other fruit listed. Elsewhere, Paul breaks love itself
down into various components (see 1 Corinthians 13), so that

"love" turns out to bear little resemblance to the emotional meaning so often given to the word.

Joy *(chara)*—An inner rejoicing that abides despite outer circumstances. This characteristic has little to do with happiness and can exist in times of unhappiness. It is a deep and nourishing satisfaction that continues even when a life situation seems empty and unsatisfying. The relationship with God through Christ remains even in the deserts and valleys of living.

> *Egkrateia* [self-control] is that great quality which comes to a man when Christ is in his heart, that quality which makes him able to live and to walk in the world, and yet to keep his garments unspotted from the world.
>
> *Barclay*

Peace *(eirene)*—An inner quietness and trust in God's sovereignty and justice, even in the face of adverse circumstances. This is a profound agreement with the truth that God, not we, remains in charge of the universe.

The next three concern each believer's relationships with others:

Longsuffering *(makrothumia)*—Patiently putting up with people who continually irritate us. The Holy Spirit's work in us increases our endurance.

Kindness *(chrestotes)*—Acting charitably, benevolently toward others, as God did toward us. Kindness takes the initiative in responding to other people's needs.

Goodness *(agathosune)*—Reaching out to do good to others, even if they don't deserve it. Goodness does not react to evil but absorbs the offense and responds with positive action.

FRUITFULNESS
The fruit of the Spirit is the spontaneous work of the Holy Spirit in us. The Spirit produces these character traits that are found in the nature of Christ. They are the by-products of Christ's control; we can't obtain them by *trying* to get them without his help. If we want the fruit of the Spirit to grow in us, we must join our lives to his (see John 15:4-5). We must know him, love him, remember him, and imitate him. As a result, we will fulfill the intended purpose of the law: to love God and our neighbors. Which of these qualities do you want the Spirit to produce in you?

The last three fruit present more general character traits that ought to guide a believer's life:

Faithfulness *(pistis)*—Reliable, trustworthy.

Gentleness *(prautes)*—Humble, considerate of others, submissive to God and his Word. Even when anger is the appropriate response, as when Jesus cleared the temple, gentleness keeps the expression of anger headed in the right direction. Gentleness applies even force in the correct way.

Self-control *(egkrateia)*—Mastery over sinful human desires and their lack of restraint. Ironically, our sinful desires, which promise self-fulfillment and power, inevitably lead us to slavery. When we surrender to the Holy Spirit, initially we feel as though we have lost control, but he leads us to the exercise of self-control that would be impossible in our own strength.

Against such there is no law.NKJV God gave the law to make people aware of their sin and to restrain evil. But no one would make a law against these fruit (virtues), for they are neither sinful nor evil. Indeed, a society where all people acted thus would need very few laws at all. Because God who sent the law also sent the Spirit, the by-products of the Spirit-filled life harmonize perfectly with the intent of God's law. A person who exhibits the fruit of the Spirit fulfills the law far better than a person who observes the rituals but has little love in his or her heart.

GARDEN
To understand the fruit of the Spirit, we must see ourselves, not as individual trees, but as an entire garden under the cultivation of God's Spirit. His purpose involves not simply the production of a single kind of fruit but all the fruit, each becoming ripe as it is needed. No one person can perfectly exemplify all the fruit all the time. We are all needed to produce God's harvest of virtue. We must not be discouraged if our love or patience is not perfect. It is the constant flow of the Spirit in all of us that produces all the fruit. Don't let your lack of fruitfulness in some areas destroy what the Holy Spirit is trying to do in you today.

5:24 Those who belong to Christ Jesus have crucified the sinful nature with its passions and desires.NIV Paul made it clear in this letter that sinful human desires *(sarx*—the flesh) and the Holy Spirit oppose each other. Believers, while receiving the Holy Spirit, also have sinful desires within. So how do believers gain the victory? The answers lie in these last three verses. (See also the chart on page 190, The Old Self Is Dead, But Sinful Human Desires Live On.)

Those who belong to Christ Jesus (believers) have victory over the sinful desires to the degree that they have *crucified* "the flesh" *(sarx)*—Paul's term for the principle of sin and

THE OLD SELF IS DEAD BUT
SINFUL HUMAN DESIRES LIVE ON

In Scripture, the *old self* (old man) represents the corrupt sinful state we inherited from Adam. The *sinful human desires* (flesh) represent our tendency to sin. In Christ, our old self was crucified but our sinful human desires live on.

The Old Self → *Dead when we became believers*

Romans 6:6	"We know that our old self [old man, *palaios anthropos*] was crucified with him so that the body of sin might be done away with." (NIV)
Romans 6:11	"Count yourselves dead to sin." (NIV)
Romans 6:22	"You have been set free from sin and have become slaves to God." (NIV)
2 Corinthians 5:17	"So if anyone is in Christ, there is a new creation [*kaine ktisis*]: everything old has passed away; see, everything has become new." (NRSV)
Galatians 2:20	"I have been crucified with Christ." (NIV)
Ephesians 4:22-24	"You were taught, with regard to your former way of life, to put off your old self [*palaion anthropon*], which is being corrupted by its deceitful desires; to be made new in the attitude of your minds; and to put on the new self [*kainon anthropon*], created to be like God in true righteousness and holiness." (NIV)
Colossians 3:3	"For you died, and your life is now hidden with Christ in God." (NIV)
Colossians 3:9-10	"You have stripped off the old self [*palaion anthropon*] with its practices and have clothed yourselves with the new self [*ton neon*], which is being renewed in knowledge according to the image of its creator." (NRSV)

Sinful Human Desires → *Active as long as believers live*

Romans 8:5	"Those who live according to the sinful nature [*kata sarka*] have their minds set on what that nature [*sarkos*] desires; but those who live in accordance with the Spirit have their minds set on what the Spirit desires." (NIV)
Romans 8:7	"For this reason the mind that is set on the flesh [*sarkos*] is hostile to God." (NRSV)
Galatians 5:16	"Live by the Spirit, I say, and do not gratify the desires of the flesh [*epithunian sarkos*]." (NRSV)
Galatians 5:24	"And those who belong to Christ Jesus have crucified the flesh [*sarka*] with its passions and desires." (NRSV)
Colossians 3:5	"Put to death, therefore, whatever in you is earthly [*ta mele ta epi tes gen*—your members on the earth]." (NRSV)

rebellion still at work in us (see 5:16-17). Believers know that
this does not mean we actually die, for our sinful human
desires don't really die—life would be so much easier if they
did! Instead, our sinful human desires continue to persuade
and seduce us. Many Christians are confused because the "old
self" (or "old man," *palaios anthropos*) has been crucified
(Romans 6:6; Colossians 3:9-10; Ephesians 4:22-24) and has
died; but the "flesh" still attacks us and hinders the Spirit
(even though its power over us is broken).

THE ACT OF CRUCIFIXION
How do we crucify our sinful human desires?
1. *Belong to Christ.* The process begins when we recognize
   our old self as crucified with Christ in the historical sacrifice
   at Calvary. We personalize Christ's death: If he died for sinners, then he died for me. He is Lord of my life. I belong to
   him.
2. *Crucify our sinful desires.* We treat our self-centered ego as
   dead and unresponsive to sin, while at the same time we
   foster our new life of fellowship with Christ (see Colossians
   3:3). We have exchanged a self-centered life for a Christ-
   centered life. We restrain our sinful desires by relying on the
   words of Christ, example of Christ, and love of Christ.
3. *Live by the Spirit.* As we have been joined with Christ in his
   death, we have risen with him to a new life (2:20-21). We
   have the Holy Spirit's power to live each day as he produces
   his fruit in us.
4. *Keep in step with the Spirit.* We don't have to keep recrucify-
   ing the old self. That was done once for all when we trusted
   Christ (Romans 6:3-6). But we must restrain our sinful
   desires. We must continuously harmonize our life with the
   Spirit's guidance and actively pursue his interests.

Like a real crucifixion, the death of our sinful human desires is
slow and painful . . . and lifelong. In many ways, our sinful
human desires may need to be "recrucified" daily. But the picture
conveyed by this "crucifixion of the flesh" shows us that God has
broken the power of sin at work in our body. That remains a fact
even when it may not feel that way to us. We need no longer live
under sin's power or control. God does not take us out of the
world or make us robots; we will still experience the temptation
to sin, and sometimes we will sin. Before we were saved, we
were slaves to our sinful desires, but now we can freely choose to
live for Christ (see also Colossians 2:11; 3:9).

But what happens when we sin? Christ's death made forgiveness available to us. As believers continue to repent of sin, they
will always receive God's forgiveness—all because of Christ's

death on the cross on our behalf. We can experience victory over our sinful human desires because we are united with Christ in his death, having "crucified" that sinful nature. Our evil desires, our bondage to sin, and our love of sin have been nailed to his cross. Now, united by faith with him, we have unbroken fellowship with God and freedom from sin's hold on us. Our conduct and attitudes change, and the fruit of the Spirit grows within us because of what Christ did for us.

NAIL IT!
In order to accept Christ as Savior, we need to turn from our sins and willingly nail our sinful human desires to the cross. This doesn't mean, however, that we will never see traces of these evil desires again. As Christians we still have the capacity to sin, but we have been set free from sin's power over us and no longer have to give in to it. We must daily commit our sinful tendencies to God's control, daily crucify them, and moment by moment depend on the Spirit's power to overcome them (see 2:20; 6:14).

Passions and desires (pathemasin, epithumiais) can be positive traits in other contexts. When they are used to summarize the character of the sinful nature, they are obviously negative (sinful), for the sinful nature can desire nothing else. The two nouns could be taken together to mean "passionate desires" and refer to wrong sexual longings.

5:25 If we live in the Spirit, let us also walk in the Spirit.^{NKJV} The word *if* could also be translated "since," for Paul was not expressing doubt as to the presence of the Holy Spirit in his life or in the Galatians. God gives new life; therefore, all believers *live in* (are alive because of) *the Spirit.*

Because it is the Holy Spirit who gives new life, believers ought to *also walk in the Spirit.* Apart from the working of the Holy Spirit, a person cannot please God. The verb translated "walk" means literally "follow in the steps of [or] stay right in line with." When the Holy Spirit leads, believers must follow. We "follow the Leader" and should have no doubt about who is in charge. To the Colossian Christians Paul wrote, "So then, just as you received Christ Jesus as Lord, continue to live in him" (Colossians 2:6 NIV). Since believers have been made alive by the Holy Spirit, he ought to direct the course of their lives. Unless we actively pursue contact with the Holy Spirit and obey his leading, we will be unable to resist the passions and desires of our flesh.

Paul used three key phrases for the Holy Spirit's work in our
lives:

1. Live by the Spirit (walk by the Spirit) (5:16, 25).
   - Recognize that the Holy Spirit is a gift to us, not given
     because of our own merit (Acts 1:4, 8).
   - Receive the Holy Spirit by believing in God's promise in his
     Word (Galatians 3:2, 14).
   - Be strengthened by the Holy Spirit (Romans 8:11; Ephesians
     3:16).
   - Acknowledge the Holy Spirit as the source of the gifts for
     ministry (Ephesians 4:7-12; 2 Timothy 1:6).
2. Be led by the Spirit (5:18; Romans 8:14).
   - Set your mind on what the Spirit desires (Romans 8:5).
   - Show his love (Romans 5:5).
   - Receive his joy (Romans 14:17; 1 Thessalonians 1:6).
   - Demonstrate hope (Romans 15:17).
3. Be guarded by the Spirit (in step with the Spirit) (5:25; John
   14:26; 16:13).
   - He aids in prayer (Romans 8:26-27; Ephesians 2:18; 6:18).
   - He inspires us to worship (Ephesians 5:18; Philippians 3:3).
   - He shapes our character (Galatians 5:22-23).

**5:26 Let us not become conceited, provoking one another, envying
one another.**NKJV This verse seems like a last-minute addition to a
section that could have easily ended with verse 25. Paul probably
focused on particular problems in Galatia. He explained that if
they would "walk in the Spirit," step-by-step, they could solve
any attitude problems in the church. Perhaps even living by the
Spirit might be used by some as an occasion for pride.

The apostle mentioned three particular problems. They are the
opposite of serving, and they remain three prevalent sins in the
church today. (1) Some were being *conceited;* they had an exces-
sively favorable opinion of their own ability or importance. It

could be that those who had not fallen prey to the Judaizers were acting this way, or those who had followed the Judaizers were act-

---

FRUIT OF THE MONTH
Cultivating fruit takes time and effort. Developing an awareness of the Spirit requires some thinking and studying about the fruit. The following outline may help you dedicate each month to a fruit of the Spirit:

1. Look up all the biblical references to that particular fruit.
2. Pray throughout that month that God will produce that fruit in you.
3. Consider ways to make that fruit visible in your life. Be sure to imagine that fruit being present in various settings— school, work, home, etc.
4. Note when others express that fruit in some way.
5. Make that fruit a theme in your home. Ask other family members to take these steps with you.
6. Affirm in some way (by phone call, conversation, or letter) a person who exemplifies the fruit you want to display in your own life. Thank him or her for being your model.
7. Ask family or trusted friends to give you feedback on the presence of that particular manifestation in your life. Perhaps even ask them for suggestions about when that fruit is particularly lacking.
8. Conclude the year with a party around a huge fruit salad and share with your family what you have discovered about the fruit of the Spirit!

---

ing conceited because they believed they were "more spiritual." In any case, conceit causes problems where it flourishes. Don't let pride over having the right point of view affect your church (see Philippians 2:3). (2) Everyone seemed to have taken part in *provoking one another;* they were causing annoyance and anger, the opposites of the virtues the Holy Spirit desired. Some people can't resist starting verbal fights in church. Don't bait others to get embroiled in conflict. Don't be an irritant in your church. (3) Finally, they were *envying one another;* they wanted to have what others had earned or achieved, whether recognition, status, money, or even spirituality. This also could do nothing more than divide the believers and ruin the church's unity in Christ. Don't give in to envy.

Pride makes us perpetually vulnerable to temptation. When Satan can't stop our spiritual growth, his tactic immediately changes to using pride. As soon as we notice progress, we should expect pride to set in. This will especially be true if we measure our growth against the progress others are making. Growth should be cause not for pride but for humility and thanksgiving because it comes from God.

POPULARITY CONTEST
Everyone needs a certain amount of approval from others. But those who go out of their way to secure honors or to win popularity become conceited and show they are not following the Holy Spirit's leading. Those who look to God for approval won't need to envy others. Because we are God's sons and daughters, we have his Holy Spirit as the loving guarantee of his approval. Seek to please God, and the approval of others won't seem so important.

OUR WRONG DESIRES VERSUS THE FRUIT OF THE SPIRIT

The will of the Holy Spirit is in constant opposition to our sinful desires. The two are on opposite sides of the spiritual battle.

Our wrong desires are:	The fruit of the Spirit is:
Evil	Good
Destructive	Productive
Easy to ignite	Difficult to ignite
Difficult to stifle	Easy to stifle
Self-centered	Self-giving
Oppressive and possessive	Liberating and nurturing
Decadent	Uplifting
Sinful	Holy
Deadly	Abundant life

Galatians 6

The flow of thought from chapter 5 to chapter 6 reminds us that the original letter that Paul wrote had no breaks. In the last verses assigned to chapter 5, Paul had already begun to urge the Galatians to express the "fruit of the Spirit" in their relationships. In 5:25-26, Paul offered practical counsel for living "by the Spirit": keeping in step with the Spirit on the one hand, while avoiding pride and envy on the other. In this section, Paul spelled out in practical terms what a "life in the Spirit" should be like.

Paul immediately pointed to a problem in the church that can be made worse when believers have inadequate spiritual maturity. What happens in a group of Christians when one of them commits a sin that attracts the church's attention? When thinly veiled pride and envy are present, some believers may actually experience smug satisfaction in seeing the failure of a fellow Christian. Paul wanted to prevent any possibility that the Galatians would become a group prone to "shoot their wounded." He told the leaders to restore someone who may have sinned. Leaders must examine themselves, show humility, and be accountable.

Paul outlined the importance of believers balancing their responsibility for their own spiritual growth alongside their responsibility to help others. They are not only to "keep in step with the Spirit" (5:25 NIV) but also to encourage others to keep the same pace. Whatever a Christian's progress or frustration in any day, he or she is to keep going and growing in Christ: "We do not give up!" (6:9 NIV). The results, Paul assured us, will be well worth the effort.

6:1 **Brothers, if someone is caught in a sin, you who are spiritual should restore him gently.**NIV Paul concluded his letter to the Galatians by affirming the confidence that he had already expressed to them in 5:10. He believed that the Galatians would return to their original faith, get rid of the Judaizers, and get on with the business of walking in the Spirit (5:25). Thus he again addressed them as *adelphoi* (brothers, friends). Paul was modeling the same gentle approach that he wanted them to practice with each other. Paul both demonstrated and taught how believers should walk in the Spirit.

Paul addressed the problem of individual sin by explaining corporate (group) responsibility. A Christian may sin alone, but because he or she participates in the body of Christ, his or her sin affects the whole. In 1 Corinthians 12:12-27, Paul explained in detail the "body" aspects of the Christian experience. "If one part suffers," he wrote, "every part suffers with it" (1 Corinthians 12:26 NIV). Our reaction to other Christians' sins ought not to be how we can rid the church of these sinners. Rather, we should help our brothers and sisters who are fellow members of the body of Christ.

> The correct attitude to other people is not "I'm better than you and I'll prove it" or "You're better than I and I resent it," but "You are a person of importance in your own right (because God made you in his own image and Christ died for you) and it is my joy and privilege to serve you."
>
> *John Stott*

The phrase *if someone is caught in a sin* can also be translated "if anyone is detected in a transgression" (NRSV) or "if a man is overtaken in any trespass" (NKJV). The original expression presents a vivid picture. "Caught" in a sin could mean either that a believer catches another believer sinning, or that the sinning believer has been trapped or caught by sin. "Entrapped by sin" seems most likely because the verb occurs in the passive voice. "Overtaken" also conveys that the sinning believer was caught and overwhelmed. This could refer to an impulsive sin. In either case, "caught" expresses a strong sense of surprise, as the person was "caught red-handed" in a sin. "Detected" pictures a believer unexpectedly discovering that another believer is trapped in some sin.

EXPOSURE

The media perversely delights in exposing the sins of those who claim to be believers. It is sad but true that often others knew about the wrongdoing but did nothing. Silence or inaction regarding sin in the church tends to be read by outsiders as complicity or fear. In reality, people have disobeyed God's instructions and should be confronted with their sin.

By failing to deal with sin among ourselves in a biblical way, we invite the ridicule of the world. We don't help ourselves or our brothers and sisters by hiding their problems or by instantly expelling them. Appropriate confrontation, confession, restoration, restitution, and forgiveness would give the world two difficult pills to swallow: (1) It could no longer excuse its own sin by pointing to believers' failings, and (2) we would weaken the sensational quality of exposing a cover-up in the church.

It is uncertain whether "sin" refers specifically to following the Judaizers or to any sin (such as the works of the flesh described in 5:19-21). But we can assume that Paul's concern for the Galatians certainly extended far beyond the immediate challenges they were facing from the false teachers. No church, indeed no believer, is completely free of sin, for sinful human desires still exist in believers (as Paul explained in 5:16-18). We must not report every sin or point out each person's failings. While Paul didn't explain the word *sin,* he focused on the type of sin that entraps a person, refusing to let him or her go and causing damage to his or her faith. If Paul meant the sin of following the Judaizers, he certainly wanted the church to help the person out of that sin and restore him or her to the fellowship.

RESTORATION
The word translated "restore" has a number of meanings, all of which help us understand how to restore someone who has been caught in sin:
- *setting a broken bone.* We should be helping to reduce pain and promote healing and rehabilitation.
- *mending a fishnet.* We should repair torn relationships in order that they might be returned to useful service.
- *refitting a ship after a difficult voyage.* We should fix the damage, restock the supplies, and prepare the vessel for its next voyage.

Restoration doesn't happen easily or simply. Sometimes those stung with self-discovery reject our efforts to help. We must persevere in the process because God views the restored person as very valuable.

The believers may have wondered how the church should deal with members who have fallen into sin. Should the sin be overlooked in the name of love? Should the sin be exposed to everyone? If not, who needs to know, and what should they do about it?

Paul did not recommend ignoring unrepented sin because, no matter how well hidden, sin will eventually cause problems in the church. Neither did Paul recommend a public humiliation of the sinner, for that would not achieve the objective of restoring the person to the fellowship. Paul recommended action, but he gave advice as to who should act and how the action should be taken.

Action should be taken only by those *who are spiritual.* Who are these people? Paul was referring to men and women who walk in the Spirit in the sense that Paul had explained at the end of chapter 5. Only those mature in the faith (see also Hebrews 5:13-14) and mature enough to handle this situation properly should deal with it.

In other words, the new, immature believers should not deal with the delicate subject of sin (and sinners) in the church. In addition, mature believers should discern when to confront sin (see Matthew 18:15-20). As explained earlier, sin exists in every church, but those less mature in the faith might categorize some personality traits or strong opinions as "sin." Every person's fault need not be dragged into the light for all to see, but persistent sin that destroys the person and hurts the fellowship must be resolved.

LEGALISTS AND RESTORATION

A person can win a race by running faster than everyone else or by having everyone else quit before the finish line. Legalists aren't sure that they will be good enough to gain God's acceptance, and sometimes they take comfort from someone else's failure. The law provides little room for restoration, so legalists tend to gloat on the failures of others.

Legalists often choose an unbending standard to measure themselves and others. Depending on their own degree of success, legalists exhibit a number of judgmental ways to react to others: false pride, "holier-than-thou" attitudes, and a noticeable lack of love and forgiveness. If you find yourself gloating on someone else's failure, you may be slipping into legalism.

Next Paul clarified what the spiritually mature should do for the one caught in sin by using one word: *restore (katartizete)*. When leaders confront a person caught in sin, they should avoid humiliating, punishing, or using the person as a public example. Instead, the leaders' purpose should be to restore the person to the fellowship of believers (see 2 Timothy 2:24-26). The Greek word came from a medical term for setting a broken bone. In the New Testament, the word meant "mending nets" (see Matthew 4:21). In both cases, the picture helps demonstrate that a fallen Christian should be neither neglected nor rejected as if he or she were lost. Instead, mature believers should help get the person on the right track, encourage repentance and accountability, offer assistance if needed, and warmly accept the repentant person back into the church. All church discipline aims at this goal.

Finally Paul explained how to restore in one word: *gently.* He used the same word form in 5:23, translated "gentleness." Those walking in the Spirit and exhibiting the fruit of the Spirit will be gentle. They should apply that quality in dealing with sin in the church. They should be humble and patient, realizing that no one is immune to sin—even the "entrapping" kind. They must speak the truth while being considerate of the other person's feelings. They must always act in submission to God and his Word. Then leaders can help without resentment or a judgmental spirit (see also 2 Timothy 2:24-26; James 2:13).

> Christians must have strong shoulders and mighty bones.
>
> *Martin Luther*

Take care that you yourselves are not tempted.NRSV The Greek verb *skopon* means "keep an eye on" or "look out for" and is here translated *take care* (or "watch yourself," NIV). Paul changed from plural to singular, perhaps indicating the individual's responsibility to keep an eye on himself or herself and to look out for temptation so as not to be tempted to fall into sin as well. The church has a duty to help erring believers, but each individual believer must take responsibility for dealing with sin and temptation. In situations such as the apostle was describing, those who restore a fallen one could face two temptations: (1) They might be tempted to have spiritual pride, or (2) they might be tripped up by the same temptation faced by the one they are trying to correct. Paul wrote the same advice to the Corinthians, "So, if you think you are standing firm, be careful that you don't fall!" (1 Corinthians 10:12 NIV).

SHARE THE LOAD
The church can foster a help-one-another attitude among its members. When we find ourselves under a burden too heavy, we should know that others will help carry our packs. When another believer is overwhelmed by his or her own sin and failings, all believers should be there to encourage, support, and pray. While mature believers must do the work of restoring, even the young and immature believers can help bear burdens, and thereby strengthen their own faith. When another believer faces pain and sorrow, all believers should be ready to offer a word of encouragement, assistance, and persistent prayer on the other person's behalf.

6:2 Bear one another's burdens, and so fulfill the law of Christ.NKJV Paul used the Greek word *bastazete,* translated *bear,* in three different forms at other times in this letter. In 5:10, Paul said that any false teacher among them would "pay [bear] the penalty" for spreading error and confusion among the Christians. This would be a heavy burden indeed, for it referred to God's judgment. In 6:5, he called each believer to "carry [bear] his own load." He pictured a traveling load, like a shoulder pack, that each person carries on his or her back. Finally, in 6:17, Paul explained, "I bear in my body the marks of the Lord Jesus." Paul's use of this particular verb may pic-

WHAT GOD WANTS US TO DO FOR OTHERS

Besides the command to "carry each other's burdens" (6:2), the New Testament tells us many other attitudes we should have toward others, and actions we should do for others. Below is a sampling:

Love one another	John 13:34-35; 15:12, 17 Romans 12:10; 13:8 1 Thessalonians 3:12; 4:9 1 Peter 1:22; 4:8 1 John 3:11, 23; 4:7, 11-12 2 John 5
Encourage one another	Ephesians 5:19 1 Thessalonians 4:18; 5:11 Hebrews 3:13; 10:24-25
Be at peace with one another	Mark 9:50 Romans 12:16 1 Peter 3:8
Humbly serve and submit to one another	John 13:14 Galatians 5:13 Ephesians 5:21 Philippians 2:3 1 Peter 4:9-10; 5:5
Show kindness and honor to one another	Romans 12:10; 15:7 1 Corinthians 11:33; 12:25 Ephesians 4:2, 32 Colossians 3:13 James 4:11; 5:9
Instruct one another	Romans 15:14 Colossians 3:16
Forgive one another	Colossians 3:13
Stop judging one another	Romans 14:13
Pray for one another	James 5:16

ture Jesus shouldering (bearing) his cross on the way to Golgotha (John 19:17). As used in this verse, *burdens* refers to the heavy or oppressive burden that a believer cannot carry alone. It could be financial burdens; it could be burdens of temptation. We must help "bear" the loads that others find too heavy to carry alone. However, we must not regard this load as a burden, but a joy. Like people hiking a trail, we not only shoulder our own backpacks, but we help out with other people's loads when the trail gets too steep, they get too tired, or their feet get blistered—whenever they need assistance.

To bear one another's burdens brings joy; for not only can the believers help one another in tangible ways, but at the same time they also *fulfill the law of Christ.* How so? As Paul had explained

in 5:14, "For the whole law is summed up in a single commandment, 'You shall love your neighbor as yourself'" (NRSV). Jesus
told his disciples on the night before his crucifixion, "A new commandment I give to you, that you love one another" (John 13:34
NKJV, see also John 15:12). The "law of Christ" is his "new commandment" summed up when we show love for others. In a sense
Paul was saying, "If you insist on carrying burdens, don't carry
the burden of the law; instead, in love, carry one another's burdens. Then you not only help one another out and build unity
among yourselves, you also fulfill the law of Christ!" Or, in other
words, when we help others with their burdens, we do Christ's
work (see Romans 15:1-3; 1 Peter 5:7).

MAY I HELP YOU?
No Christian should ever think that he or she is totally independent and doesn't need help from others. And no one should
feel excused from the task of helping others. The body of
Christ, the church, functions only when the members work
together for the common good. Do you know someone who
needs help? Is there a Christian brother or sister who needs
correction or encouragement? Humbly and gently reach out to
that person, offering to lift his or her load (John 13:34-35).

**6:3 For if those who are nothing think they are something, they
deceive themselves.**NRSV However, some believers either would
refuse to follow Paul's command to help bear one another's burdens or would do so in order to be noticed and receive praise.
Both motives come from conceit. Those people may have
regarded themselves as too spiritual to dirty themselves with
others' problems and failings. They may not have wanted to
make the effort to care about others in need, or they may have
been motivated by attention getting, not helping others.

The Greek words in this sentence make strong contrasts. What
these people "think" *(dokei)* about themselves contrasts sharply
with what they really "are" *(on)*. A person's inflated self-image as
"something" (or "somebody," *tis*) noteworthy has little value if
the facts demonstrate that he or she is actually "nothing" (or
"nobody," *meden*) of any consequence. Paul was anxious to warn
the Galatians not to tolerate any form of spiritual superiority, no
matter how cleverly disguised.

Paul explained that these people's lack of love for others
revealed both their worthlessness to the body of Christ and also
their bankrupt spiritual state. They *think they are something* or
"somebody important." But such people were really *nothing* or

"nobody." Paul was deliberately negative and used exaggeration (hyperbole) to correct arrogance in those acting self-important. When we humbly come to God, we are "something" loved and valuable; when we are blinded by sinful pride, we are "nothing" to him.

INTOLERANCE
Reading Paul's words in our times may raise questions about the apostle's intolerance. Did he really have a right to invalidate the claims of those other teachers? Or should he have been more open-minded and inclusive about the variety of opinions and beliefs present in the Galatian church?

Paul was dealing with revealed truth. He was confronting teachers who themselves were very intolerant. In addition, he was doing them a favor by confronting them with their error because if they believed him, they would be in a position to respond to the gospel. If you believe the truth of God's Word, sooner or later you will find yourself in disagreement with those who do not believe.

Those who persist in this attitude *deceive themselves.* These conceited people were the only people who thought they were "too good" or "too spiritual" to help, or "so good" and "so spiritual" that everyone should have noticed their help. They were deceiving no one but themselves. Measured against God's standards, no one amounts to anything. Only by Christ's righteousness imparted to us and by God's Spirit within us do we become acceptable to God. And, as Paul already had explained in chapter 5, that Spirit will produce results in believers' lives. The true "somebodies" in the church yield the Holy Spirit's fruit in their lives, and these people won't even be concerned about their status. They will be busy helping others.

6:4 Each one should test his own actions. Then he can take pride in himself, without comparing himself to somebody else.NIV While some people may be conceited regarding their burden bearing, others may feel as though they can't "bear burdens" as well as others. Some might be afraid of grief or pain; some others might get tongue-tied in trying to offer encouragement; others may be so shy as to be unable to approach needy people. Conversely, some may have experienced others who, under the pretense of helping, exploit the vulnerability of a person in trouble or violate a trust that was placed in them regarding very personal matters. Both our abilities and motives need healthy, ongoing examination.

REMEDIES
Failing eyesight often happens so gradually that a person makes small adjustments (squints, holds reading material at arm's length, etc.) along the way. But an eye examination reveals the truth—the person's eyesight may have deteriorated significantly. Our ability to detect pride works the same way. The Scripture offers three remedies for our self-deception:
1. *Watch yourself (6:1).* Remind yourself that you are nothing apart from the value that God gives you. Beyond that, imitate Christ, doing what he did while disregarding your own desires for position and respect.
2. *Test your own actions (6:4).* Be sure you are doing your best; examine yourself under the guidance of the Spirit and God's Word. Don't compare yourself with others; instead, focus on the character of Christ.
3. *Carry your own load (6:5).* Be accountable and trustworthy. Answer to other believers, and serve them by your holding them accountable.

Here Paul offered the solution. *Each one should test his own actions.* The Greek word *dokimazo,* translated "test," could also mean "scrutinize" or "prove." The word often described God's scrutiny of the work of an evangelist or teacher. Each of us should examine our own conduct, asking whether we have accomplished what God has required. We know what God has prompted us to do in the case of bearing others' burdens; thus, we must ask if we did it. Each individual must answer to God. So we should compare ourselves to God's standard, not *to somebody else.* Good pride is being able to say, "I have lived up to the potential God gave me." We will not be judged on the basis of how we have matched up to others, but on how we have met God's expectations. The danger of comparing ourselves with others is that we either come out ahead (a cause for false pride) or behind (leading to lowered self-esteem and the danger of not doing any more for others at all). Christians have different gifts and abilities, but God does not excuse us from bearing others' burdens. We are not responsible to do everything or to make the same contributions as others; we are responsible to accomplish what God has called us to do.

Then, says Paul, *he can take pride in himself.* This "pride" is very different from the conceit explained in 6:3. In Greek, *kauchema* literally means "boast, report." This pride focuses, not on a person's own accomplishments, but rather on what God has done through his or her life. This pride glorifies God, not oneself. This pride says, "We are unworthy servants; we have only done our duty" (Luke 17:10 NIV). The context determines that Paul gave the same advice that he urged the Romans to practice: "For by the grace given to me I say to everyone among you not to think of yourself more highly than you ought to think, but to think with sober judgment, each according to the measure of faith that God has assigned" (Romans 12:3 NRSV).

GREAT EXPECTATIONS
When you do your very best, you feel good about the results. There is no need to compare yourself with others. People make comparisons for many reasons. Some point out others' flaws in order to feel better about themselves. Others simply want reassurance that they are doing well. When you are tempted to compare, look at Jesus Christ. His example will inspire you to do your very best, and his loving acceptance will comfort you when you fall short of your expectations.

6:5 For each one should carry his own load.NIV In 6:2, Paul encouraged the believers to bear one another's burdens. Here, he says that each believer should carry his or her own load. This is not contradictory, but complementary. We should bear one another's burdens while shouldering our own. Each person's *own load (to idion phortion)* refers to each believer's responsibilities and duties. Jesus spoke of this burden in Matthew 11:30 when he promised, "My burden is light." Each person carries this light load like a shoulder pack. While we each bear our own load, we also must help those with their overwhelming loads. Then everyone will be able to make it to the end of the trail together.

Throughout this paragraph Paul maintained a balance between conscious personal responsibility for one's own life and looking out for the needs of others. He gave the Philippians similar counsel when he wrote: "Do nothing out of selfish ambition or vain conceit, but in humility consider others better than yourselves. Each of you should look not only to your own interests, but also to the interests of others" (Philippians 2:3-4 NIV). By laying aside our attitudes of superiority, we can be ready to help others.

> Your checkbook reveals all that you really believe about stewardship.
> *Ron Blue*

6:6 Those who are taught the word must share in all good things with their teacher.NRSV After describing how the Holy Spirit helps believers in their relationships with others, Paul explained how the Holy Spirit would affect their use of money. (See 1 Timothy 5:17-18 as a parallel passage.)

Some commentators hesitate to apply 6:7-9 to the use of money. While these verses also have a broader application, Paul

primarily focused on the thought that he had begun in this verse—
believers' responsible use of money. Bearing each other's burdens as well as following through on our commitments requires
faithfulness in our financial decisions.

SELF-ESTEEM
Much of today's educational emphasis promotes self-esteem.
The idea is to have pride in yourself whether you accomplish
anything or not. Having removed references to God or the Bible
from the classroom, education bases self-esteem on positive
thinking. A person attempting to affirm his or her own worth will
drift from pride to worthlessness and back.
    The Bible provides the basis for the worth of each individual
in relation to God—being part of his creation and bearing his
image. Thus, each of us has worth because God thinks enough
of us to have sent Christ as the supreme sacrifice. But the biblical view of self-image (or self-confidence) differs markedly from
the world's. The Bible promotes a humble self-confidence that
recognizes that every talent and accomplishment has been
given by God. We do not create our own self-worth. It comes
from God. Because we do not dream it up, no one can take it
from us. No negative performance or objective analysis can
render us worthless. Neither is our self-worth hollow, for it
comes from the heavenly Father who loves us.

Paul's first admonition prescribed support of each Christian
teacher (the true teachers as opposed to the false teachers) in the
Galatian churches. These teachers were serving full-time in
preaching and teaching. The congregations *(those who are taught
the word)* should voluntarily and generously provide for the
teachers' needs. This included financial support and sharing material items and services, as well as personal encouragement *(all
good things)*. While the radical giving and sharing of the early
church in Jerusalem (recorded in Acts 2:44-45) was a model, all
churches were not required to follow it. Instead, Paul recommended a spirit of giving among the believers in the churches
that he had founded, especially regarding their care for those who
were devoting their time to ministry. Most likely Paul had mentioned this, for he usually set up leaders in the churches before he
moved on. He must have explained how they were to be cared for
by the church members. But the Galatians apparently needed a
reminder.

As opposed to the fees and taxes that paid for teachers in the
Jewish and Greek religions, Paul's wording emphasized that this
giving and sharing with the Christian teachers was really a part-
nership. As the teachers taught the "good things" of the gospel,

the believers reciprocated with sharing "good things" to provide for the teachers. Jesus gave the same advice in Luke 10:7. In the context of the principle Paul was about to state, the teachers were sowing the good seed of God's Word and had a right to expect a harvest of goodness from their students.

HONOR THY TEACHERS
Paul instructed students to take care of the material needs of their teachers (1 Corinthians 9:3-14). It is easy to receive the benefit of good Bible teaching and then to take our spiritual leaders for granted, ignoring their financial and physical needs. We should care for our teachers, not grudgingly or reluctantly, but with a generous spirit, showing honor and appreciation for all they have done (2 Corinthians 11:7-9; Philippians 4:10-19; 2 Thessalonians 3:7-9; 1 Timothy 5:17-18).

6:7 **Do not be deceived, God is not mocked; for whatever a man sows, that he will also reap.**^{NKJV} This sentence, inserted within Paul's flow of thought regarding money, gives a general principle about the attitudes of kindness, giving, and sharing. Those doing the mocking were the self-righteous, pious Christians who were boasting about their spiritual superiority (5:26; 6:3). While people can deceive one another, and even themselves, about their motives and attitudes for giving, they cannot deceive God. Paul said that these believers themselves must *not be deceived* or "led astray." This phrase is a formula that precedes a severe warning of a prophetic nature (see also 1 Corinthians 6:9; James 1:16). The passive tense indicates that some of the Galatians had already been deceived in this matter of financial responsibility. The phrase *God is not mocked* reveals the immutability of this natural law of God. The Greek word literally means "turn up the nose at." This could also be translated "God is not fooled" or "You cannot mock [or fool] God." What they sowed, they would reap. *Sow* means "spread, utilize, invest." Whatever we use as key values determines the course of our life. Jesus taught the importance of investing our time and utilizing our resources wisely for the kingdom. He said, "Do not lay up for yourselves treasures on earth, . . . but lay up for yourselves treasures in heaven. . . . For where your treasure is, there your heart will be also" (Matthew 6:19-21 NKJV). Paul's concept parallels what Jesus taught.

While believers have received God's special blessings and promises, God does not change the positive and negative of the natural law that *whatever a man sows, that he will also reap.*

From farming to finances, this saying holds true (Proverbs 22:8). A farmer plants corn and grows corn; he should not expect nor desire anything else. Believers must decide what crop they want and plant accordingly, for what they get back will be directly related to what they put in, as Paul explains in the next verse.

REAPING OR WEEPING?
It would certainly be a surprise if you planted corn and pumpkins came up. It's a natural law that we reap what we sow. The principle holds true in other areas as well. If you gossip about your friends, you will lose their friendship. Every action leads to results or consequences. If you plant to please your own desires, you'll reap a crop of sorrow and evil. If you plant to please God, you'll reap joy and everlasting life. What kind of seeds are you sowing?

6:8 The one who sows to please his sinful nature, from that nature will reap destruction.[NIV] Believers who use their lives and *sow* their resources in wasteful indulgence in order to do no more than *please [the] sinful nature (sarx,* flesh, see note on 5:13) will earn a harvest of *destruction.* The Greek word *sarx* refers to the unregenerate, uncrucified self. Those who invest their lives in fulfilling sinful human desires are practicing the works of the flesh that Paul listed in 5:19-21. Paul was most concerned about the libertine tendencies of the Galatians who were practicing sins particularly harmful to the church: quarrelsomeness (5:16, 21), conceit (5:26), envy (5:26), indifference to needs (6:1-2), and pride. Those who live like this will not inherit the kingdom of God (5:21). When we sow to the flesh, we bring these seeds of destruction into our life.

The one who sows to please the Spirit, from the Spirit will reap eternal life.[NIV] Believers who *sow* their resources and invest their lives *to please the Spirit* have a far different harvest. Their harvest *will reap eternal life* (see Romans 6:20-23).

> To "sow to the flesh" is to pander to it, to cosset, cuddle and stroke it, instead of crucifying it.
> *John Stott*

How do we sow "to please the Spirit"? When we use our resources to grow spiritually and to support the Lord's work so that others can enter the kingdom and grow spiritually, we are sowing to please the Spirit. Why? Because our harvest results in spiritual growth and souls reached for the kingdom; thus, our harvest lasts forever. This kind of stewardship of our resources can only be done through the power of the Holy Spirit. When the Holy Spirit controls a believer's life, the results are amazing. As

5:22-23 pointed out, the fruit borne in a believer is life changing. That change will affect the believer's handling of money, use of talent, and investment of time.

Because of our sinful human desires, we will always resist the initiatives of the Holy Spirit. Because actions that "please the Spirit" often involve eternal matters, the harvest may not actually come until eternity. Christian efforts, such as character building or caring for others, have long-range results. But, as Paul will write, just because the harvest is not immediate does not in any way lessen its reality!

6:9 Let us not become weary in doing good, for at the proper time we will reap a harvest if we do not give up.^{NIV} While good works will never earn salvation, Paul did encourage believers to persist in *doing good* (see comments on 6:10). Paul included himself in his admonishment, saying that while we do good, we should *not become weary* and *give up* or lose heart. By repeating this admonition twice, Paul placed great emphasis upon perseverance. Faithful Christians will find innumerable ways to do good. Using the fruit of the Spirit and sharing the burdens of others, we will persevere in our works of service.

FULL CIRCLE
As Paul brought this letter to a close, he was inspired by the Spirit to provide us with a well-rounded picture of healthy, spiritual living. Living by the Spirit is not an individualistic achievement, nor does individual participation get lost by making every action a "shared responsibility." Life in the Spirit involves a continual ebb and flow of receiving and giving. Those who practice the ministry of restoration today may themselves require restoration tomorrow. Those who have their burdens lifted today may be called to lift another's burdens in the days to come. Christians, in obedient and growing relationship with God, discover wonderful support from one another along the way. The biblical picture proves true: Christians are parts of the body of Christ; each one is charged with a function so that together all bring glory to God.

Paul may have been feeling very weary as he considered his hard work and suffering on behalf of the churches in Galatia. It is discouraging to continue to do good and serve God while receiving no word of thanks and seeing no tangible results. But results take time. Jesus pointed out to the disciples that months elapse between planting and harvesting (John 4:35). To continue the analogy of sowing and reaping, a farmer will have no harvest to reap if he becomes too weary to labor in the fields or if he gives up

altogether. The harvest will not reap itself. Every aspect of farming, planting, maintaining, and finally the harvesting takes hard
work. So, too, believers must not become weary and give up
when they follow the Holy Spirit's guidance, grow spiritually,
and do good for God's kingdom. While it may seem at times like
a losing battle, we are assured that *at the proper time we will reap
a harvest.*

What kind of harvest did the apostle have in mind? His original statement of the parable "A man reaps what he sows" (6:7
NIV) was a warning. But in the space of three verses, the principle
has been used to encourage believers to serve faithfully even
when facing weariness. A Christian will reap a harvest of present
blessings: the fruit of the Spirit, well-instructed believers,
restored sinners, and mutual support. But ultimately he or she
will reap the harvest of eternal life in the Holy Spirit (6:8).
Though the proper time is the time of God's own choosing, Paul
was most likely referring to the time of the fulfillment of God's
promises at Christ's second coming (1 Timothy 6:15).

FROM FURROW TO SICKLE
Paul challenged the Galatians and he challenges us to keep on
doing good and to trust God for the results. Our weariness can
be eased by the strength we find in the Spirit and by the relief
we find when other Christians help us bear our burdens. We
must not fall back into a self-serving, self-centered life, for that
denies our claim to be Christ-centered persons.

As Christians, we must persevere. A farmer, for all the work
done, doesn't "make" the crops grow. The principles of nature
mirror spiritual principles. We are to persist in sowing goodness. In due time, we will reap a harvest of goodness. Whether
that "due time" is in this life or the next (or maybe both) is not
for us to decide. But as the farmer knows his crops will grow, so
we know that our harvest is sure. For more on persevering, see
1 Corinthians 15:58; 16:13; Philippians 1:27; Hebrews 12:3.

6:10 **Therefore, as we have opportunity, let us do good to all
people, especially to those who belong to the family of believers.**NIV The wordplay on "time" *(kairos)* in 6:9 and 6:10 does not
come through in English. The word is translated "season," or
"time" in 6:9, referring to God's proper timing—the harvest will
not be reaped before God says so. In this verse, the word is translated *opportunity,* meaning that every time we can do good, we
must do so—the timing for doing good is always right. The
opportunity is not optional. We are to treat it as strategically
placed by God in our path. Our settings may continually change,

but each one will bring a fresh opportunity for helping and serving. In concluding his letter to the Colossians, Paul issued a similar challenge: "Be wise in the way you act toward outsiders; make the most of every opportunity" (Colossians 4:5 NIV).

This word for "time" in Greek conveys the meaning that once missed, we cannot regain the opportunity. We cannot miss the "time" of the harvest; we dare not miss the "time" of doing good. In both cases, when the time is past, it will never return. How often have we looked back and regretted missing a chance to say a word of encouragement or to do a kind deed?

God calls believers to *do good to all people,* believers and nonbelievers alike. The fruit of the Holy Spirit must be shared with both the Christian and the non-Christian world. Jesus made it quite clear that doing good would not always be easy: "But I tell you: Love your enemies and pray for those who persecute you" (Matthew 5:44 NIV). Some fields may be very difficult to "work," but our purpose should be to sow goodness anyway!

GOOD DEEDS
Does Paul's emphasis on good works contradict his teaching that salvation is by faith and not by works? No, because the Pastoral Epistles encourage good works for all the believers (Titus 2:4; 3:8, 14), for leaders (Titus 2:7), for the wealthy (1 Timothy 6:18), and for widows (1 Timothy 5:9-10). Jesus himself stressed good works based on love. Paul does not teach that those good works were needed for salvation, but he does stress the practical side of the Christian faith, expressed by good works (see, for example, Ephesians 2:10; Colossians 1:10; 1 Thessalonians 5:12; see also 1 Peter 2:12). Does your church encourage everyone's involvement and service? What can your chruch do to help every member identify the good works they should be doing?

If Paul still had in mind our financial responsibility, we should be willing to help others financially whenever we are able. But we should focus particularly on the needs of *those who belong to the family of believers.* This "family" (*oikeios,* household) refers to all who have become God's children by believing in Christ; thus, all God's children are related (Ephesians 2:19). The Christian family extends far beyond the walls of a particular church or the limits of a particular denomination to include all true believers. Paul's directive parallels Jesus' words: "By this all men will know that you are my disciples, if you love one another" (John 13:35 NIV).

When Paul told individual believers to "do good," he spoke to their responsibility in the community as well as in the church. The church is not meant to become merely a social agency, but individual believers can work together in meeting social needs, giving time and resources as God calls and enables them. Sowing seeds of kindness to those in need expresses Christ's love and prepares hearts to receive the gospel.

PAUL'S FINAL WARNING / 6:11-18

We can hardly imagine how Paul felt as he dictated this letter. Perhaps he took up the parchment and reread his arguments and instructions. Some time may have passed since the original dictation. The letter was complete, but Paul decided to add some final thoughts, shaping the words in large and forceful movements of the pen and praying that this letter would be used by God to get his Galatian brothers and sisters back in the race.

He left the Galatians with a strong word-picture of the cross of Jesus Christ. The decision that faced his readers was not really between two competing voices of authority; rather, the choice was between denying the Cross or finding through it the only true way of life.

6:11 See what large letters I make when I am writing in my own hand!NRSV Up to this point, Paul had probably dictated the letter to a scribe. Then he took the pen into his *own hand* to write his final, personal greetings. Paul did this in other letters as well, to add emphasis to his words and to validate that the letter was genuine (see 1 Corinthians 16:21; Colossians 4:18; 2 Thessalonians 3:17). Paul pointed this out, perhaps because the contrast in the original letter was obvious. Paul's scribe, if trained in writing, would have written in well-formed Greek characters. Paul, a preacher and not a scribe, had a less precise writing style. Another theory is that Paul wrote in large letters due to poor eyesight (see 4:13-15). Most likely, however, Paul wrote in *large letters* for emphasis, as these last verses reiterate the main points of this epistle. They were his signature. If these "large letters" were printed in our Bibles in all capital or boldface letters, we would understand the effect of Paul's style and why he mentioned it.

6:12 Those who want to make a good impression outwardly are trying to compel you to be circumcised.NIV As Paul concluded the key points of his letter, he referred again to the Judaizers, the false teachers who were causing all the trouble and confusion in Galatia. Paul referred to them as *those who want to make a good impression outwardly.* The Greek word for "to make a good impression" *(euprosopesai)* carries the sense of being insincere. The false teachers had insincere motives in *trying to compel [the Galatian believers] to be circumcised* because their goal was to win the Galatians to Judaism, not to see them fulfill the law. The word *compel* means to force or drive someone to a particular course of action.

PRIDE BY ANY NAME
With thinly veiled pride, a church or spiritual leader may attempt to validate a ministry as blessed by God by pointing to numbers of decisions, new members, or baptisms. Then a smugness often emerges that alienates other believers, causes divisions within the body of Christ, and presents to the world a picture of Christians in competition for the greatest numbers of conquests. Such boasting does not honor Christ.

The only reason they do this is to avoid being persecuted for the cross of Christ.^{NIV} Circumcision provided an easy way out. The Judaizers taught circumcision for salvation in order to avoid *being persecuted.* If the Judaizers could persuade the Galatian Gentile Christians to be circumcised, they could protect their status as a sect of Judaism. By making the Galatians proselytes of Judaism (with a messianic twist), they could avoid the backlash from Jewish nationalists in Palestine who were trying to wipe out Gentile sympathizers. That was their form of genetic purification. These zealous Jews hated the Gentile intrusion. The Cross of Christ offended the Jews; even worse were Gentiles who had no loyalty to the Jewish legal system. The Judaizers wanted the best of both worlds. By insisting on circumcision, they felt they were protecting the Jerusalem and Judean churches from persecution.

The Judaizers had brought legalistic issues to the surface, but their rejection of the death of Christ ran deeper. To accept the Cross includes accepting certain beliefs: that people are sinners under God's curse, that a personal sacrifice was required, that only the death of Christ on the cross could secure people's salvation, and that people can do nothing to obtain that salvation except to accept Christ's sacrifice on their behalf. People don't want to be told they are sinners who can do nothing but accept someone else's help. Human nature would much prefer to earn salvation, if only to be able to have pride along with the accomplishment. To preach anything else would incur persecution, as Paul would learn over and over again. The Judaizers could avoid persecution by giving people a way to "earn God's favor." But as Paul clarified earlier in this letter, what they offered was slavery to the law, and no salvation at all.

6:13 Not even those who are circumcised obey the law, yet they want you to be circumcised that they may boast about your flesh.^{NIV} In addition to attacking the Judaizers' motives to make a good impression and escape persecution, Paul attacked them because all they wanted to do was *boast about your flesh.* In other words, they wanted to report the number of circumcisions back to their superiors. For the Judaizers to "sell" Judaism to the Christians meant selling them a worthless product. The Judaizers compelled the believers to be circumcised, as they had been, thereby bringing them under the law with them. Yet the Judaizers themselves (and indeed all Jews, *those who are circumcised*) did not and could not obey all the law. If the Jews themselves couldn't keep the law, how futile it was to compel new Christians to accept circumcision that would bind them to that same law. Worse yet, the Judaizers did this for the sake of pride—personal pride, religious pride, national pride—yet pride all the same. Not a very strong base for dealing with someone's eternal destiny!

> Humans are very seldom either totally sincere or totally hypocritical. Their moods change, their motives are mixed, and they are often themselves quite mistaken as to what their motives are.
>
> *C. S. Lewis*

PICK A LAW, ANY LAW
Some of the Judaizers were emphasizing circumcision as proof of holiness, but were ignoring the other Jewish laws. People often choose a certain principle or prohibition and make it the measure of faith. Some may condemn drunkenness but ignore gluttony. Others may despise promiscuity but tolerate prejudice. Some who are adamant against homosexuality ignore child abuse. The Bible in its entirety is our rule of faith and practice. We cannot pick and choose the mandates we will follow.

6:14 May I never boast of anything except the cross of our Lord Jesus Christ, by which the world has been crucified to me, and I to the world.^{NRSV} To *boast* with puffed-up pride would be sinful arrogance. While the Judaizers sought to please people, escape persecution, and boast in statistics, Paul had an entirely different perspective (see 2:20-21). We already know he did not seek to please people and that he regularly faced persecution— but he did boast. However, his boasting was never of anything *except the cross of our Lord Jesus Christ.* Paul could boast about the Cross because of what the Cross had accomplished in his life. At one time, Paul had been like the legalists—worried only about

SYMBOLS
The Cross of Paul's day differed markedly from the Cross of ours. The very fact that we use crosses as jewelry speaks pointedly to the change in the image of the crucifix. Greeks, Romans, and Jews agreed about very few things, but the nature of a cross was one of them. It was a symbol causing revulsion, shame, and terror. Death on a cross was the epitome of humiliation.

The cross became dear to Christians because of its connection with Christ's work of salvation. Sadly, in places where the church has been long established, the cross can become a symbol that hides false pride and even tyranny. The cross of Jesus Christ was a rough, rugged, blood-soaked instrument of excruciating death. On it the Son of God allowed himself to be nailed so that he might take upon himself the sins of the world—your sins. Little of that shocking message is brought to mind by silver, gold, and jewel-encrusted symbols of power and accommodation that abound in the church today. Those lovely, sanitized crosses may motivate expressions of appreciation for beauty; rarely do they confront an arrogant mind with the need for repentance. Remember the real cross and the real sacrifice there for you.

pleasing people and counting heads. But now everything was different—so different, in fact, that it was as though the world had been crucified to him and that he had been crucified to the world. Paul had no need of the earthly and selfish motives and ambitions. He had let go of the worldly, outward standards and symbols of honor and success *(the world has been crucified to me).* He treated them as enemies of God. For Paul to say *I [have been crucified] to the world* meant to be crucified with Christ (see 2:20). He accepted no God but the Lord God; no motive or power could rival the power of God living in him by the Spirit. Paul's only motive was to serve his Lord. His only boast was "the cross" (the only way of salvation) of "our" (that is, salvation belongs to every believer personally) "Lord Jesus Christ" (the only God, Savior, and Messiah).

CRUCIFY THEM
The world is full of enticements. Daily we are confronted with subtle cultural pressures and overt propaganda. We may escape these destructive influences by asking God to crucify our interest in them, just as Paul did. How much do the interests of this world matter to you? (See 2:20 and 5:24 for more on this concept.)

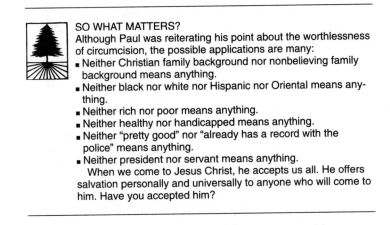

SO WHAT MATTERS?
Although Paul was reiterating his point about the worthlessness
of circumcision, the possible applications are many:

- Neither Christian family background nor nonbelieving family background means anything.
- Neither black nor white nor Hispanic nor Oriental means anything.
- Neither rich nor poor means anything.
- Neither healthy nor handicapped means anything.
- Neither "pretty good" nor "already has a record with the police" means anything.
- Neither president nor servant means anything.

When we come to Jesus Christ, he accepts us all. He offers salvation personally and universally to anyone who will come to him. Have you accepted him?

6:15 Neither circumcision nor uncircumcision means anything; what counts is a new creation.NIV Paul, a circumcised Jew, knew that his circumcision counted for nothing as a means to salvation. Neither was uncircumcision a detriment to salvation (as the Judaizers were teaching). Neither of these outward markings makes any difference to God regarding salvation. The cross of Christ made such distinctions valueless and put all people on equal ground. As Paul had already stated bluntly, "In Christ Jesus neither circumcision nor uncircumcision has any value" (5:6 NIV). When a Jew becomes a believer, he or she becomes *a new creation* (more literally, a new "creature")—likewise when a Gentile becomes a believer. That is *what counts;* the only thing that matters is being born again. "Therefore, if anyone is in Christ, he is a new creation; the old has gone, the new has come!" (2 Corinthians 5:17 NIV; see also Romans 12:2; 1 Corinthians 7:19; 2 Corinthians 3:18).

How does one become a new creation? By believing on the Lord Jesus Christ and what he accomplished on the cross. What is a new creation? Men and women born again by the power of the Holy Spirit, living by his transforming power.

6:16 As for those who will follow this rule—peace be upon them, and mercy, and upon the Israel of God.NRSV This sentence underlined Paul's entire argument. Paul had the final say. He halted any further debate with the Judaizers, for he captured the very ground they thought they could stand upon. He knew that he had knocked down every pillar of their argument. Then he turned to his listeners before leaving and gave them both a blessing and a warning.

This rule (kanoni) refers to the gospel message Paul had defended throughout this letter—that we receive salvation by grace through faith alone. Paul might have said, "To those who believe this rule"; however, he chose the word *follow* to emphasize the Galatians' problem. They had initially believed, but they hadn't "followed" or "walked" or "grown" in that belief and thus had fallen prey to false teachers.

INSIDE OUT
It is easy to get caught up with the externals. Beware of those who emphasize actions that we should or shouldn't do, with no concern for the inward condition of the heart. Actions are an expression of, not a substitute for, a living trust in Christ. They may have cultural significance, but they are not spiritual requirements. Exhibiting a good life without an inward change leads to a shallow or empty spiritual walk. What matters to God is that we are completely changed from the inside out (2 Corinthians 5:17).

But to those who did follow (and he hoped this would include all the Galatian believers), Paul wished *peace* and *mercy*. "Peace" was a common greeting and benediction (see, for example, Psalm 125:5 and 128:6). At the beginning of this letter, Paul had greeted the Galatians with "grace and peace" (1:3). Here he chose "peace and mercy." These two characteristics would return in great force if the Galatians would follow through on their original commitment to Christ. The exit of the Judaizers and the renewed commitment to bear each other's burdens would yield a harvest of peace and mercy. He saved "grace" for his final phrase in the letter.

Commentators differ on the meaning of the last phrase of this verse, depending on how each interprets the Greek word *kai*. Some translate it "and" (as above in NRSV) or "in addition to." Others translate it "even" or "that is to say." The translation determines how Paul meant the phrase *the Israel of God*.

The phrase itself invites notice because it is unusual and therefore has given rise to at least three streams of interpretation:

1. "The Israel of God" refers to the Christian church made up of Jewish and Gentile believers. Against this argument, the point is made that Paul did not use this specific concept in the extended discussion of the relationship of Gentiles to Israel in Romans 9–11. In favor of this interpretation, the claim is made that both the Old Testament and the New Testament include examples of Jews as well as non-Jews being accepted by God apart from racial considerations.

2. "The Israel of God" applies exclusively to Jewish Christians. The intent of Paul's phrase, then, is read: "Grace and mercy on the Gentile Christians (and also) on the Jewish Christians."

Supporters of this view envision Paul wanting to express specific encouragement to both groups. Detractors of this interpretation point out that Paul has been at pains throughout this letter to teach that there can be no significant distinction between Christians of Jewish or Gentile background.

3. "The Israel of God" represents the Jewish people as a whole, as in the "all Israel" of Romans 11:26-27. This interpretation seeks to reemphasize the special purpose of God through the nation of Israel. The phrase is said to mean "the Lord's Israel" and to apply to the true remnant who really follow the Lord as he intended from the first. The weakness of this interpretation would be that it goes against everything Paul had been saying about the necessity of faith.

The first interpretation works best. The immediate context of Galatians, with Paul's analysis of the significance of Sarah and Hagar and God's eternal purposes having included the Gentiles all along, points to the first interpretation. In other words, by the phrase "Israel of God," Paul meant that the church is made up of all true believers, whatever their social or ethnic backgrounds.

6:17 **From now on let no one trouble me, for I bear in my body the marks of the Lord Jesus.**^{NKJV} Paul ended his letter with a request that this trouble stop. His words *from now on let no one trouble me* did not mean that if the legalizers continued to harass the churches that he would not want to hear about it. Nor was he addressing the legalizers and asking them to stop making trouble—their goal was to make as much trouble as possible for Paul and the Christians. Instead, Paul did not want the Galatian churches to trouble him any longer by turning away from the faith to legalism. Paul had aptly argued against the Judaizers' teaching in this letter, ending the need for more to be said about them. He expected the Galatian Christians to return to the faith and stand up for themselves against the false teachers. He had provided the ammunition; they should use it.

Paul did not want to hear of any more heresy creeping into the Galatian churches. The suffering he had endured for the faith should be enough to encourage these believers to remain steadfast against false teaching. Paul bore on his body *the marks of the Lord Jesus.* This was not circumcision; instead, the marks were the scars Paul received when he was persecuted for the sake of the gospel. Some of these he received while he was in Galatia (recorded in Acts 13–14; see also Philippians 3:10; Colossians 1:24). The word *bear* reveals that these marks were not a burden carried lightly. Paul had earned the right to be heard by his track record. The word *marks (stigmata)* was used for the brands put on animals or slaves to signify who owned them. To Paul, these "marks" revealed who "owned" him—"the Lord Jesus." (Paul referred to some of these persecutions in other letters; see 1 Corinthians 4:11; 2 Corinthians 4:8-12; 6:5, 8-10; 11:23-33.)

What marks of the Lord Jesus do we have? For many of us, our skin is baby smooth. We have no scars of conflict or persecution because we keep ourselves so well insulated from pain and suffering. Yet the gospel will not reach the ends of the earth unless Christians lay aside fear of physical and emotional discomfort to reach out to others.

6:18 May the grace of our Lord Jesus Christ be with your spirit, brothers and sisters. Amen.[NRSV] Unlike many of Paul's other letters, Paul included no personal greetings or remarks as he concluded this letter. Perhaps he did not want to lighten the solemnity of the letter's contents, but wanted to close the letter in a way that would cause the Galatians to think of nothing but acting upon Paul's words. Instead, he closed as he had begun in 1:3, wishing *the grace of our Lord Jesus Christ* on these believers, whom he again lovingly called *brothers and sisters.* Grace was exactly what Paul hoped would be the result of his entire urgent letter to them—that they would return to the gospel of salvation by grace.

NO TURNING BACK
Paul's letter to the Galatians boldly declares the freedom of the Christian. Doubtless these early Christians in Galatia wanted to grow in the Christian life, but they were being misled by those who said this could be done only by keeping certain Jewish laws.

How strange it would be for a prisoner who had been set free to walk back into his or her cell and refuse to leave! How strange it would be for an animal, released from a trap, to go back inside it! How sad it would be for a believer to be freed from the bondage of sin, only to return to rigid conformity to a set of rules and regulations!

If you believe in Jesus Christ, you have been set free. Instead of going back into some form of slavery, whether to legalism or to sin, use your freedom to live for Christ and serve him as he desires.

BIBLIOGRAPHY

Bauer, Walter, William F. Arndt, Wilbur F. Gingrich, and Frederick Danker. *A Greek-English Lexicon of the New Testament and Other Early Christian Literature.* Chicago: University of Chicago Press, 1979.

Boice, James Montgomery. "Galatians." In *The Expositor's Bible Commentary,* edited by Frank E. Gaebelein. Vol. 10. Grand Rapids: Zondervan, 1976.

Bruce, F. F. *Commentary on Galatians.* Grand Rapids: Eerdmans, 1982.

Burton, Ernest DeWitt. "A Critical and Exegetical Commentary on the Epistle to the Galatians." In *The International Critical Commentary.* Edinburgh, Scotland: T. & T. Clark, 1921.

Cole, R. Alan. *Galatians.* Tyndale New Testament Commentaries. Grand Rapids: Eerdmans, 1988.

Hunter, Archibald M. *The Layman's Bible Commentary: Galatians, Ephesians, Philippians, Colossians.* Atlanta: John Knox Press, 1982.

Lightfoot, J. B. *The Epistle of St. Paul to the Galatians.* Grand Rapids: Zondervan Publishing House, 1980.

Longenecker, Richard N. *Galatians.* Word Biblical Commentary Series. Dallas: Word Books, 1990.

Luther, Martin. *A Commentary on St. Paul's Epistle to the Galatians.* London: James Clarke & Co. Ltd., 1953.

Stott, John R. W. *Only One Way: The Message of Galatians.* Downers Grove, Illinois: InterVarsity Press, 1968.

Tenney, Merrill C. *Galatians: The Charter of Christian Liberty.* Grand Rapids: Eerdmans, 1957.

Walvoord, John F., and Roy B. Zuck. *Bible Knowledge Commentary: New Testament Edition.* Wheaton, Illinois: Victor Books, 1983.

INDEX